FORCED OPTIONS

FORCED OPTIONS

Social Decisions for the 21st Century

ROGER LINCOLN SHINN

THIRD EDITION
With "Reconsiderations"

The Pilgrim Press
Cleveland

To friends around the world—especially in

Japan, Korea, Hong Kong, the Philippines, Thailand,
    Singapore, and Indonesia;
China;
India;
Egypt, Kenya, Nigeria, and South Africa;
Turkey, Lebanon, Iran, and Israel;
Puerto Rico and Jamaica;
the Soviet Union, Czechoslovakia, Romania, and East
    Germany;
Denmark, Sweden, and Finland;
the United Kingdom, France, West Germany, the
    Netherlands, Switzerland, Italy, and Greece—

who have welcomed me to their own soil, troubled my conscience, and helped me begin to glimpse this wonderful and
fearful world as they experience it.

Copyright © 1982, 1985, 1991 Roger Lincoln Shinn
All rights reserved

No part of this publication may be reproduced, stored in a retrieval system,
or transmitted in any form or by any means, electronic, mechanical,
photocopying, recording, or otherwise (brief quotations used in magazine
or newspaper reviews excepted), without the prior permission of the
publisher.

Library of Congress Cataloging-in-Publication Data
Shinn, Roger Lincoln.
  Forced options : social decisions for the 21st century : with
"Reconsiderations" / Roger Lincoln Shinn.—3rd ed.
      p.   cm.
  Includes index.
  ISBN 0-8298-0934-1 :
  1. Social ethics. 2. Christian ethics. 3. Distributive justice.
4. Decision-making—Social aspects. 5. Technology—Social aspects.
I. Title.
HM216.S463   1991
303.3'72—dc20   91-38012
                                                     CIP

Third Edition
10 9 8 7 6 5 4 3 2 1
The Pilgrim Press, Cleveland, Ohio

Contents

93001

Preface

The writer of a controversial book likes to keep the discussion going. And the writer of a tract for the times likes to keep abreast of the times. For these two reasons I welcome the opportunity for a third edition of this book.

The first edition (Harper & Row, 1982) appeared in the series Religious Perspectives, edited by Ruth Nanda Anshen. The second edition (Pilgrim Press, 1985) added an Epilogue, updating the original text. Now, almost a decade after the initial publication, I can reexamine my position in the light of new events and continuing public arguments. The twelve chapters of the original book are unchanged; but this Preface is revised, the "Reconsiderations" are new, and the index takes account of these changes. A reader might want to begin by skimming the "Reconsiderations" in order to gain a perspective on the entire text.

The reason for the book is a belief that we (the human race) are making social decisions loaded with portentous consequences for ourselves and our descendants. Human power, magnified by science and technology, forces us to make ethical choices that have no precedents. Often the choices are unconscious, or they become conscious only in retrospect. I am trying to call attention to them in the hope that we may choose more wisely and generously.

That general purpose leads to three more particular aims. First, I want to relate ecological sensitivity, so heightened in our own time, to the age-old issues of social justice within societies and on an international scale. Too often the interests of justice and of ecology have been set in competition, as though the champions of justice wanted to serve human needs at the cost of ecological damage and the ecologists wanted to protect the ecosphere at the

cost of perpetuating poverty and injustice. I believe that ecology
and justice, rightly understood, intensify the importance of each
other and call for radical changes in human societies. I am glad
that I now find far more agreement on this insight than when I
first wrote this book.

Second, I explore the religious and theological meanings of the
present situation, because I think those meanings are an essential
part of the problem and of possible solutions—even for resolute
secularists who think they have no religious beliefs. The theology
of this book is more often implicit than explicit, because I think
implicit theology is the more fundamental and the more powerful.
But at some points, especially in Chapter 10, the theological
concerns become explicit.

Third, I examine methods by which persons and communities
make ethical decisions. Here I look especially at the contribu-
tions of faith and of science to social decisions. I examine the
method that I find actually at work in individuals and society, in
the hope of clarifying it. This is the subject of the final chapter,
which some friendly critics have called the most important chapter of the book.

By pursuing these three aims in their intricate interactions, I
hope that this book will fit a niche in the present literature and
will make some contribution to public discussion.

Obviously I am exploring many areas to which specialists give
a lifetime. If my forays into so many fields seem brash, I can
answer that people today, whether leaders of nations or ordinary
citizens, have to make decisions on subjects on which they are
amateurs. That is the nature of life. And that is one of the
problems I take up in my final chapter.

Beyond this I can add that I have relied on many friends of
diverse abilities to teach, advise, and correct me. Every chapter
of the book has been tried out in lectures or discussions in various
forums in North America, Europe, Asia, and Africa, where critics
have sharpened and disturbed my thinking. Most chapters are
based on earlier published articles and responses to them. But
nothing here is simply reprinted or reedited. The rethinking of
the various issues in the context of a sustained argument has led
to new ideas not anticipated in the earlier essays.

Morningside Heights in New York City is a marvelous place to grapple with the world. My teaching opportunities at Columbia University, New York University, the Jewish Theological Seminary, and Union Theological Seminary, along with many seminars and action groups that bring together people of varied skills and experiences, have provided a continuous opportunity for learning.

Participation in the World Council of Churches for many years, especially its program on Church and Society, has helped me see human problems through the eyes of people in many societies. While writing this book, I also edited *Faith and Science in an Unjust World: Report of the World Council of Churches' Conference on Faith, Science and the Future*, Volume 1, Plenary Presentations (Geneva: World Council of Churches, and Philadelphia: Fortress Press, 1980); and this present book owes much to that one. The mixture of professional perspectives, ideologies, and national experiences in that celebrated conference at the Massachusetts Institute of Technology was emblematic of the situation of our world.

I have been impressed with the ethical passion of many eminent scientists, who have generously educated me on issues I here discuss. Most of the ideas and information in this book first came to me in conversations. In supporting my arguments, however, I have generally used published sources, in order to facilitate public debate.

My opinions are sprinkled throughout this book, but I do not present any total program for action, because that will be the work of many people throughout the world for decades to come. What I want to do most of all is raise to visibility problems now hidden in our social processes and usually resolved, if at all, by inertia or silent manipulations. I hope I have done this without hysteria but with enough abrasiveness to stir people to their own thinking and activity.

ROGER L. SHINN

Union Theological Seminary, 1991

PART I

OPENING THE SUBJECT

1. Social Decisions

Forced options are as old as human life, but it was that scintillating American psychologist-philosopher William James who in this century gave the term currency. A *forced option,* says James, is a decision that allows no escape. Any efforts to delay it for long, to sit it out, to compromise indefinitely are themselves decisions—as surely as is the deliberate choice of one of the alternatives.

James defines forced options in his famous essay, "The Will to Believe." His specific concern there is belief in God. That issue has its own immense importance. But in this book I am using James's theme to get at a set of social issues for our time.

THE LOGIC OF THE FORCED OPTION

The forced option is a simple point of logic. Some options are avoidable and some are forced. That is, some decisions can be put off indefinitely or evaded forever; others cannot. To recognize a forced option is not to say that any single course of action is forced. On the contrary, James emphasizes human freedom, not fatalism. What is forced is a decision.

Many of life's options can be avoided. James gives as an example the challenge, "Either love me or hate me."[1] You may do neither. Most of the people in the world you do not know and do not love or hate in any intense personal way. This option is not forced.

On many scientific theories you probably are wiser not to take a stand. If asked whether you believe in the Big Bang, in black holes, or in quarks, you can reply that you don't know. It is easy enough for most of us to live and die without making such decisions and without being any the worse off for not making them.

But some options are forced. Many a person has faced the decision: "Have surgery, or don't." Air fighter pilots, when planes go out of control, must decide—in a hurry—to bail out or stay with the plane. To put off a decision about marriage is sometimes to lose the chance of marriage—at least of a particular marriage. In such cases a refusal to decide, a failure to decide, is itself a decision. Even to delay a decision is itself a decision, often a portentous one.

Suppose that instead of saying, "Love me or hate me," I cry out to you, "Pay attention to me." I have confronted you with a forced option. Granted, there are compromises: you can give me reluctant, divided, half-hearted attention. But either you give the kind of attention I ask, or you don't, and in either case there are consequences. It may be that I have presented you a tragic dilemma. You cannot possibly respond to all the people clamoring for your attention, some of them magnifying their clamors with millions of dollars worth of advertising, public relations, and media arts. To a few of them, probably not rich ones, it is important that you pay attention. It may be terribly important—terribly, in the most literal sense—for their sake and for yours. That's the kind of world we live in.

The point of this book is that societies today face forced options of momentous importance. Of course, societies, knowingly or not, have always faced forced options. The difference today is that human beings have acquired technological powers that increase the pace of events and the scope of actions, so that decisions come faster and more hangs on these decisions than in past ages. Weapons, inventions that liberate us from drudgery and open new possibilities for human achievement, techniques that chew up irreplaceable resources—these are transforming the conditions of life for us and generations to come.

In such a world even apathy is a kind of decision. If a society is apathetic about starvation in its midst or across an ocean, it is deciding to let people starve. Subjectively such apathy is different from a hatred that wills the starvation of people; objectively the two attitudes have about the same consequences.

So part of my argument in this book is that indecision and delay can be as criminal as resolutely evil acts. But I must quickly note also that premature decisions can be harmful as well. There are times for delay. My guess—an uninformed guess—is that when the Vatican was deciding whether or not to silence Galileo, somebody proposed waiting for a while to see what would come of Galileo's teachings. And somebody else—I'm still guessing—replied: "But to delay a decision is itself a decision to let this dangerous movement continue." So the premature decision was made, and the regret and ridicule of it have persisted for centuries.

There are risks in both decisiveness and indecisiveness. To say that is simply to say that responsible human living is not easy. And there is no escaping the responsibility of being human.

Jean-Paul Sartre, in an insight akin to that of William James but in a different ethos, says that human beings are "condemned to be free."[2] It is the social dimensions of this compulsory freedom that are the subject of this book. That those social dimensions have profound personal meanings will, I hope, become clear.

HOW SOCIETIES "DECIDE"

Social decisions are more complicated than individual decisions. Even the decision of a single person may be so intricate that a whole corps of friends and relatives, psychoanalysts, the CIA, lawyers, and juries could never give an adequate account of it. Social decisions multiply the complications.

In some cases there are social mechanisms for decision making. Society acts through designated authorities: legislative, executive, and judicial. At other times decisions made by controllers of economic institutions reverberate through the world. At still other times the issue is settled by a complex of many individual decisions, the influence of mass media, the workings of the market, the political process, and some combination of purposes and accidents.

When people vote for government officials, they participate in a crudely democratic process of decision making. I say crudely not out of disrespect for a process that I greatly value, but out of an acknowledgment of what happens. People vote for a candidate's program (or selected parts of it) or for the candidate's sincerity, glamor, pledges, or skillfully contrived image—not for everything the candidate will do with an electoral "mandate." Most voters sooner or later complain about decisions of officials they helped elect.

Similarly, when people buy products in the market, they vote with their money. These votes are real: they elect some corporations to riches and consign others to failure. But the same people usually do not know that they are voting, with their cash and credit, for pollution, traffic jams, highway casualties, patterns of racial and sexual discrimination in industry, the transformation of vast landscapes, the consumption of irreplaceable resources, changes in the international balance of trade, and hundreds of other consequences of their votes.

To take a single important example: nobody decided, in any precise sense, that the United States in the 1970s and 1980s would be so utterly dependent on imported petroleum. As late as 1945, this country was the world's greatest exporter, and until 1948 we were a net exporter, of petroleum. No president, no Congress, no Supreme Court on any given date voted to change the flow of petroleum so drastically that this nation would tremble at political upheavals on the other side of the globe. Yet this social decision "happened." A set of events and processes brought a result that caught the nation by surprise.

The suddenness of the surprise is incredible. In 1974, Secretary of State Henry Kissinger said to James Reston:

In 1969, when I came to Washington, I remember a study on the energy problem which proceeded from the assumption that there would always be an energy surplus. It wasn't conceivable that there would be a shortage of energy.[3]

Obviously Kissinger should have known better. There were a few people who had long been trying to tell our society what was happening. We might wonder how so huge a problem could slip up on Kissinger and on a nation unawares. It is not as though Kissinger— and a whole host of public figures in seats of power—had low IQ's or were high school dropouts. These disastrous misjudgments of our recent national history were made by those whom David Halberstam called "the best and brightest." The problem was that they were not paying attention to important facts and voices. Nobody, as I have already said, can pay attention to everything.

In retrospect it is easier to see how some social decisions happen. In the case of petroleum millions of individuals made decisions about their patterns of life and consumption. Some legislative and executive acts operated, half intentionally and half unintentionally, to shift traffic from railroads to automobiles. Tax structures did the same. Wars consumed energy and altered uses of energy. Corporations and small family businesses maneuvered for survival, efficiency, and convenience. City planning (and lack of planning) separated people from their jobs and from the old-fashioned corner grocery. Merchandising techniques affected buying patterns. A "revolution of rising expectations" hitched itself to rising consumption of energy. A few warnings about extravagance were unpersuasive, partly because for a long time the annual new discoveries of oil fields outpaced the annual consumption of oil. Then came the day when, in retrospect, the society could see that it had "decided" on a binge of energy consumption that left it dangerously vulnerable.

Thus people and societies, living in confusion, decide some things and later wake up to see that they have decided other things also. It is as though some occult power—the Providence of religious tradition or Hegel's "cunning of history"—were overruling human decisions, whether in grace or in judgment.

Yet I would insist that there is *some* freedom and rationality in the historical process. Persons and societies can look at evidence, pay attention to people and things that matter, and exercise some control over their own futures. I would not exaggerate this freedom and rationality. To assume total responsibility for the course of history is to ask such foolish questions as "Who lost China?"—as though China (or Vietnam or Iran or the lives of our own children) were ours to lose. But people do have an intelligence and a moral capacity to face up to some issues and make responsible decisions.

I am here arguing against the fatalism that is popular today, whether in the popular vogue of astrology or in the more intellectual formulations of some brilliant thinkers. Herman Muller, geneticist and Nobel laureate in biology, began what was perhaps the last major public address of his life: "Of course we—that is, humanity—will take our biological evolution into our own hands and try to steer its direction, provided that we, humanity, survive our present crises. Have we not eventually utilized, for better or worse, all materials, processes, and powers over which we could gain some mastery?"[4] It is that *of course* that I reject. I assume that people are capable of rejecting some options.[5] We even might—I do not know whether we will—reject the large-scale nuclear war that threatens all civilization. If we inflict that war on ourselves, it will be out of a combination of fear and anger and pride, not out of a simple determination to do whatever we can do.

Muller, despite some dark premonitions about the way this human race might use its new powers, is basically hopeful. Jacques Ellul in *The Technological Society* is more pessimistic. He reifies "technique" and sees it as an enslaving power, to the extent that "in the present social situation there is not even a beginning of a solution, no breach in the system of technical necessity."[6]

Against these voices with all their eloquence, I insist that people, not things or techniques, make decisions. But I quickly grant that actions have unexpected consequences, and it is easy to construe those consequences as a fate. When Henry Ford started making automobiles, he had little inkling of the changes cars would trigger in American life: the transformations in the shape of cities and countrysides, the obsolescence of old skills and the emergence of new ones, innovative styles of labor organization, the change in sexual practices, the growth of credit and installment buying, the energy crisis, the accidental deaths of fifty thousand people a year in this one nation. The list could go on indefinitely. Ford did not approve of all that happened. This industrialist, who said, "I'll give them cars in any color they want, so long as it's black," disdained at least some of the status systems and advertising devices that followed his break-through. We can speculate as to how Henry Ford—or the various presidents of the United States, or our parents and ourselves—might have acted differently if people had foreseen all that was to happen.

The new art of "technology assessment" is the beginning of a way of coping with such changes. But if the most sophisticated form of technology assessment had been in operation at the time of the first assembly line, it still would not have assessed all that was to come from that experiment. Even so, in every stage of the intricate process, it was people, not cars and assembly lines, who made the decisions.

Today, far more than when Emerson uttered the words, people have the sense that "Things are in the saddle, riding man." My argument is that, although options are forced, the recognition of options opens the way to responsible ethical decisions. To succumb to fate is to dehumanize ourselves. We—the human race—have the possibility of affirming and enhancing our humanity. Whether we shall do so or not, I am not sure.

THE AGE OF "HYPOTHETICALITY"

The German physicist Wolf Häfele has developed the idea that the human race is moving into a new stage of history that might be called the age of "hypotheticality." By that he means that human beings are making momentous decisions on the basis of knowledge that is inconclusive and that will "necessarily and ultimately remain inconclusive."

Some critics have replied that human actions have always had a hypothetical quality. But that reply misses the point.

In the past, Häfele says, technical progress has proceeded by trial and error. Innovators get a bright idea and try it out. If it works, they develop it further. If it fails, they correct it or try an alternative idea. The method has a long record of success. It is a good method, provided the failures are not catastrophic.

Think of air travel as an example. After centuries of human dreaming about it, a few people in the twentieth century experimented with airplanes. They had some successes and some failures. Some pilots crashed and died, but they did not take whole cities or nations with them. Gradually—though quickly, when we realize what has happened in less than a century—thousands of experiments proceeding by the method of trial and error resulted in a huge system of worldwide air transportation.

Today, if you plan an air trip, you know that you take some risk of a crash that could kill you. In that sense, the outcome is hypothetical—for you, but hardly for the world. On the basis of a vast body of evidence you know that the risk is small, so small that you probably don't think about it. Or if you do, you may recall that the risk of traveling by automobile is higher. Or you may figure that there is risk in staying home and taking a bath. Although any prediction about *your* safety on the trip is inconclusive, the world (i.e., government agencies, insurance companies, airlines, and individuals who bother to dig out the data) has a vast body of statistical evidence on the safety of the whole process. The world has "decided," in that vague process by which social decisions happen, to use air travel on a big scale. It has decided that the risks are, in the current jarring jargon, "acceptable."

Meanwhile, the method of trial and error continues. After every major error—every big air crash—there is an investigation and an attempt to prevent similar future errors. The system is not perfect, but the world lives with it and likes its benefits.

The new situation is that the world is engaged in some huge experiments for which there is no body of experience furnishing actuarial evidence about the safety of the outcomes. The method of trial and error is discomforting, because the results of error could be catastrophic. Experimenters and whole societies proceed on the basis of hypotheticality.

Think of several examples. Treaties for arms limitation depend on methods of inspection which, though highly effective, cannot guarantee the absolute certainty that critics of the treaties want; meanwhile, the arms race itself is still further from guaranteeing security. Fluorocarbons used in aerosol spray cans—part of the innocent gadgetry that entrances affluent societies—appear to be reducing the ozone layer that surrounds the earth and protects it from ultraviolet rays; ozone depletion, which may also be caused by supersonic airplanes, may lead to an increase in cancer, harm to vegetation, and quite unpredictable changes in climate. Genetic experimentation, which brings healing or prevention of excruciatingly painful diseases, may accidentally produce new lethal microbes for which plants, animals, and people have no immunity defenses; the probability is low but not as low as zero. Any greatly expanded use of fossil fuels or solar energy may change the climate of regions or even the whole earth irreversibly, and nuclear energy has its obvious risks. In all these cases the human race is entering unexplored territory—a "continent" of hypotheticality.

Scientists and technologists, to be sure, have a long history of experience in dealing with the unknown. Much of their work is expansion of the known into the unknown. The new factor is the immensity of the consequences of errors and accidents. There is also the problem of the unknown-unknown (the "unk-unk" as engineers sometimes call it). Not only do we not know what the effects of some actions will be; sometimes we don't even know what it is that we don't know.

I return to Häfele's thesis. (I have been illustrating and expanding it, perhaps beyond his intentions.) He writes:

It is probable that "hypotheticality" will characterize the next stage of human enterprise. The magnitude of technological enterprises will be so great that it will not be possible to proceed with the absolute certainty that there will be no negative consequences. The magnitude of the undertaking and the intellectual impossibility of eradicating all contingency make the prospect for "hypotheticality" even more certain.[7]

One might make some conjectures about past ages of hypotheticality. Three or four hundred million years ago some biological creatures left the sea and risked life on dry land. From the little we know about them, we assume that they did not weigh the probability of success and decide to do some pioneering. They just did it. They took a total risk with a total lack of information. I suppose most of us are now glad for their risk taking. Our decisions can hardly be more momentous than that—except for the new scale of possible destruction. But the total risk of those distant ancestors of ours was to themselves; they did not risk the whole biological enterprise. Most forms of life stayed in the sea, totally unaffected by the new experiment on land—except in the remote sense that millions of years later land-based creatures would jeopardize sea-based creatures.

Today the risks are more global in scale and more immediate in consequences. That fact changes the nature of ethical responsibility.

THE ETHICAL AND THE TECHNICAL

All the issues I have been mentioning require decisions that combine ethical and technical judgments. To meet them requires both moral responsibility and specialized knowledge.

Such ethical decisions are an old story in human experience. It is unethical for a physician to prescribe quack nostrums or poisons instead of healing medicines. But what are quack nostrums and what are poisons and what are healing medicines? Sometimes doctors know, but sometimes the angry controversies on such questions hit the Food and Drug Administration and the press. A "good doctor" is both ethically responsible and competent.

But medical practice is something of a special case. Throughout human history most people most of the time have known—or have believed that they knew—what is good and right. The moral problem was the will to do the right.

In our time there has been an increase in the number of issues on which people are genuinely perplexed about the right answer. New knowledge and skills mean new possibilities for action, and some of the possibilities are loaded with both promise and peril.

There are no ethical traditions that tell us precisely what to do about ozone depletion, DNA experimentation, or the various forms of energy that attract the world. Helpful though the traditions may be, they are silent on many of the "forced options" of our epoch.

One of our needs is a theory of ethics and decision making for use in previously unexplored areas. Without a theory, we are left to *ad hoc* and impulsive decisions. But theories, I believe, are not first elaborated, then "applied" to practice. Ethical theories arise out of practice and perplexity and struggle. Therefore the sequence of this book moves through a series of major issues of our day, touching occasionally on the wider theoretical issue they raise. Then in Chapter 12 I draw out some conclusions about a theory of ethical decision making.

2. Some Scenarios and Preliminary Reflections

As the saying goes, we have to be interested in the future because that's where we're going to spend the rest of our lives. The wisdom of decisions that look beyond the immediate present depends on some expectations about the future. But that future is always uncertain.

We know a few things about the future. In the twenty-first century neither Leif Ericson nor Christopher Columbus will "discover" America. Nobody will invent the wheel or the Latin language. Astronauts will not find that the moon is made of green cheese or that it provides inexhaustible resources of petroleum. The two-car, one-helicopter family will not become normative around the world. There will still be death and taxes.

We can be fairly sure about some other things. The civilizations of the world will not center around a few desert oases. Armies will not fight wars with the crossbow. The white race will not extend its power over the world. Conceivably such statements may be mistaken, but that is not likely.

About many other traits of the future we have very little knowledge. The weapons of the next century may be as unexpected to us as Eisenhower's weapons were to Julius Caesar. Communication may be as far beyond our present practices as the telegraph was beyond the ken of the first societies to invent smoke signals. The structure of cities may be as different from ours as our megalopolises are from the centers of early agricultural societies. Cancer may kill more and more people, or it may become as rare as polio. We do not know. The only certainty is that nobody has a certain picture of the future.

The effort to think responsibly about the future requires a combination of a rigorous respect for fact and a lively imagination. With some yearning for both of these qualities of mind, I am going to sketch four possible scenarios of the future. The four are so different that they cannot possibly all take place. I expect none of them, because I expect surprises. But each of them selects *some* present tendencies of history and projects them into the future. And each points to some decisions, some forced options, in our lives today.

I am dating these scenarios in the year 2100—as good or bad a year as any. It is distant enough to show the consequences of some things people are now doing. It is close enough that some of today's children can expect their children still to be living, and many of today's youths can expect their grandchildren to be living. Another advantage of the year 2100 is that a few more or less scientific projections are available for that time, and I can weave some of them into stories that, in other ways, do not pretend to be soberly scientific.

TECHNOTOPIA

By the year 2100 the world has recovered from the near breakdown at the end of the twentieth century. At that time the population of the globe had reached 6.5 billion, and about 20 million people starved in one year. Energy shortages disrupted the economies of several societies. Sporadic revolutions disturbed many areas of the world. Many nations had nuclear weapons. Once in a while a few got lost or stolen. Small countries and even terrorist gangs discovered that, even if they could not come close to winning a war, they could frighten major powers. The seizing of hostages, both internationally and domestically, became epidemic around the world. Fear—everywhere endemic, often intense—haunted most societies.

In a sudden show of strength the United States, the Soviet Union, and China collaborated to impose a world dictatorship. In 2005 they organized a combined military and scientific elite, which seized power and imposed a stern rule. One society after another accepted the simple choice of food and obedience rather than starvation and chaos. The few resisting societies were, within three years, brought into submission by a strict embargo of food, energy, and raw materials for industry.

The world dictatorship announced its endorsement of individual and regional autonomy in many activities of life. Rather than eliminate the structure of nations with their symbolic auras and their traditions, whether democratic or oligarchical, it encouraged their perpetuation but greatly reduced their power. Officials imposed absolute control on international commerce, beginning with food and petroleum, then going on to all other commodities. The dictatorship dismantled all national armies, setting up its own world police force and intelligence agency. It established a monopoly of nuclear weapons. Its arsenal by now is small, compared with those of a century ago, but sophisticated and diversified. It learned to defeat terrorists, first, by refusing ever to submit to their demands and, second, by making certain that there were no sanctuaries to which terrorists could flee.

In the first twenty-five years of the dictatorship there was some rivalry for power between the scientific and the military blocs within the oligarchy. Gradually the scientists came to dominate. It became obvious that, although each bloc needed the other, the generals needed the scientists more than the scientists needed the generals— and the whole world needed scientific advances in order to survive. The world government used military power decisively to maintain order, but increasingly the scientists issued the orders.

Now, within slightly less than a century of the new era, the world population has stabilized at ten billion people. Reductions are under way, but the authorities have decided to move slowly because there is already such a preponderance of older people, in stark contrast to the situation a century ago. The change in procreative habits was hard to work out, but not so hard as some had expected. The great symbolic change came in 2012, when the Vatican issued a solemn encyclical on the moral duty of persons to limit reproduction. Some of the older bishops complained, but the pope resolutely stuck to her position and made a worldwide tour advocating it.

Governmental regulation of population is now strict but fairly simple. Since 2030 every youth has been inoculated at puberty with a longterm contraceptive. Parenthood requires a specific decision on the part of the persons, a governmental license, and a medical act; there are no "accidents" of conception. At first there was some conniving to disobey, with an underground market in illegal contra-contraceptives. Government met this by compulsory abortion of nonlicensed fetuses. Only a few such acts were necessary to end the civil disobedience.

The dictatorship set the goal of gradually moderating the great disparities between rich and poor regions. It organized the world into regional economies. Its control of international commerce meant, among other things, that no region could export petroleum to North America and that North America could not export food to any except the poorest regions. But apart from such controls, regions were allowed many choices. For example, a region could choose to have low population with relatively high consumption or a higher population and lower consumption. As it turned out, the regions have been tending toward nearly uniform practices.

Activities destructive of the environment are rigorously prohibited. Governmental officials closely monitor all inventions and industrial processes.

Historians now refer to everything prior to the nineteenth century as prehistory. The nineteenth and twentieth centuries are called primitive civilization, and they are divided into the coal age, the petroleum age, and the age of nuclear fission. In the late twentieth century the oil reserves of the Western Hemisphere and the Middle East dwindled. China's vast resources brought a major shift in the world's economies, which the Western nations tried to counter by nuclear reactors. Then, by the end of the century, the mass production of electrical power from photovoltaic cells, first used practically in twentieth century spaceships, relieved the worst shortages of energy. Soon after, the nuclear fusion process proved successful, though expensive. One of the first acts of the world dictatorship was to decree a phasing out, over a ten-year period, of the burning of all oil and the diversion of the remaining oil resources to the petrochemical industry.

Large reflectors, launched into geostatic orbits in space, beam solar energy to receptors on the ground. Their use is precisely planned, not only to provide energy, but also to stave off the encroaching ice age that, according to climatologists, began almost imperceptibly as long ago as 1940. Scientists are already worrying about what to do in a future era when the climate changes and the earth overheats, but political leaders see no point in planning for anything so distant.

Historians recall the early part of the century with its exhaustion of some raw materials, particularly mercury, tin, lead, and zinc. But industry has compensated with new techniques of recycling and substitution. Scientists have invented a series of atom transformers, modern equivalents of the medieval philosopher's stone, which they use not to turn base metals to gold, but to turn the earth's crust into almost (although not quite) everything they want.

Machines do a large part of the work. North American scientists advocated expanded use of their own technologies, which would enable five percent of the world's people to produce food enough for all. However, in order to avoid unemployment and the extravant American consumption of energy, the world dictatorship settled for a worldwide average of twenty-five percent. Industry is largely robot-operated. For a time it seemed that there would be some problems of too much leisure, but the world government met that by a moderate return from capital-intensive to labor-intensive production. The Chinese example provided a helpful model that was considerably relaxed in its worldwide usage. In addition, many jobs became available through a multiplication of police forces and psychiatric counselors.

Public transportation is highly developed, but there are throughout the world a few million automobiles—fewer than there were in the United States alone in the twentieth century. Progress in development of compact and lightweight batteries has made electrical cars useful for urban transportation. For long-range travel hydrogen-powered cars finally proved to be practical and, with occasional exceptions, safe.

Housing for the reduced population of the earth is practical, if monotonous. Homes are built according to styles originated long ago by Buckminster Fuller and a host of his successors, and new materials enable builders to make housing available, now that the world's population is finally beginning to diminish. The world still tolerates a few remnants of the giant metropolitan centers of the past, but none of the ancient sprawling suburbs with their economic inefficiencies.

Homes are elaborate communication centers. Most families now have two-way television sets, computer terminals, microprocessors of information. Consumers in the home can tune in to pictures and detailed descriptions of foods and industrial products, then can order them by punching a keyboard in the living room. Instead of old-fashioned postal processes, with the physical movement of messages on paper, people receive news and personal or business correspondence by facsimile processes.

Every individual carries an I.D. card with photograph and fingerprints. It serves as a driver's license (for qualified drivers), a social security card, and a credit card in the virtually cashless economy. No one can get a job or buy food without it. Because there is so little cash, old-fashioned muggings and robberies have become futile; and elaborate systems for detection of criminals have eliminated most other crimes.

Although the mass media of communication are operated by world and regional governments, uncensored small-scale publication is possible, although expensive. A few journals in scattered parts of the world have recently estimated that the average age of the top officials of the government, though never publicly announced, is now 123 years. It is surmised that biological scientists have discovered medical antidotes to aging. It appears that, despite the reduction of infant mortality to almost zero, human longevity has not increased except among the highest governmental officials. The rumor is that government will not make public the new discoveries, since the birth of infants and the death of old people is essential to the social system, but that governmental leaders are themselves adopting the new techniques. Physicians also seem to live long lives. The recent death of the world's financial officer at an age not announced but estimated at 137 is taken as evidence that the new medical methods are not totally effective.

The strict regulation of life, once accepted in a spirit of resignation by people frightened of starvation and chaos, causes some resentment. But most people think that the absence of war, crime, and hunger makes the system a good bargain. Even so, a world governmental commission is secretly investigating methods of encouraging personal freedoms and initiatives without disturbing the social equilibrium. The commission, after concluding that sexual expression has about reached its limits of variety and fascination, is investigating the possibilities of new programs in the arts, elaborate forms of entertainment, and religious revivals.

AFTER THE NUCLEAR HOLOCAUST

Just how it started nobody knows. The evidence was destroyed in the war. It happened in the year 2015. Lingering rumors say that the United States and the Soviet Union both claimed that they were only retaliating. One theory is that U.S. intelligence was not certain whether nuclear weapons landing on American cities originated in the Soviet Union or in Latin America, and that the Pentagon judiciously sent counterweapons in both directions. In any case the warfare swiftly escalated and soon the world was involved.

Somehow, due to a freak of atmospheric activity, subequatorial Africa escaped the worst of the radioactive clouds that enveloped much of the world. The Americas and Europe were desolate and remain so. Their cities are deserted, even after eighty-five years. It is reported that a few people survived and still live in rural areas there, but not much news reaches the rest of the world. China, it is said, was not as utterly destroyed as North America and Europe, but its urban centers were devastated and a greatly reduced population manages subsistence farming.

Mediterranean Africa was hit as badly as Europe, but people in the rest of Africa learned to live without any imports or intercontinental commerce. The petroleum of Nigeria and Angola was exhausted long ago. A few other discoveries of petroleum have been locally useful, but there is no massive exploitation of them. People say that it takes petroleum to run an industry but it takes an industrial system to drill deep petroleum wells. No one knows how to break the vicious circle. There are no airplanes, automobiles, or trucks on the continent. The great cities—Nairobi, Dakar, Johannesburg—could not survive without petroleum imports, and they were quickly evacuated.

The drought that hastened the expansion of the Sahara desert southward caused great suffering. Nobody knows whether it was due to natural causes or atmospheric changes brought about by the nuclear holocaust. For a time there was serious starvation. The tribes that had never become dependent on industrial development survived. Much of the rest of African society learned to re-adapt to rural tribal life. Many urban Africans were astonished to learn that the Nuba Tribe, for example, had long maintained a high health rate with a low technology.

A few African intellectuals are confident that they understand the antiquarian technological skills of the late twentieth century. They have annual meetings and read papers to each other. They even talk about possibilities of a technological revolution that will produce inexhaustible supplies of energy through nuclear fission or fusion. But all their conversation is academic and theoretical. There is no adequate economic infrastructure to build the systems they talk about. Fires, for example, are mainly of wood. There is no steel industry.

Now and then somebody proposes the colonizing of Europe and North America. There are said to be great deposits of coal and iron ores there. It is conjectured that technologists could use raw materials from these underdeveloped countries as the basis for an industrial revolution. But rumors tell of lingering radioactivity that makes these areas still too dangerous for conquest and colonization.

The general assumption is that the future of the human race will be agrarian and that social units will be small and self-sufficient. People expect little change during their lifetimes or those of their children.

Occasionally people speculate about the ruins of the abandoned African cities. There are legends and folk songs about the life that once prevailed in those cities, and a few traditional rituals are traced to their origins in urban life. Some people look on those cities with regret and envy: they appear to be a wonderful achievement, now denied to the present generation. Others look at them with revulsion: they represent a frantic way of life, combining privilege and oppression. The older members of the tribe tell of traditional lore about city folk who scarcely knew their neighbors, who were dependent on large institutions for jobs, who were afraid to walk on the streets alone at night, who became alcoholics and drug addicts as they tried to overcome their frustrations. Contemporary life looks better. Now people share their wealth and their poverty. Song and dance are for everyone —not activities that some people pay others to do, as tradition has it was once the case. All people join in common rituals and celebrations.

Yet, say some, it would be nice if we could have just a little of the luxury that the bygone urban societies produced and used so badly.

THE AGE OF PLUTONIUM

Looking backward, the choice now seems inevitable. Threatened with an energy shortage, the world had to go all-out with the nuclear option. A few still disagree, saying that their ancestors should have opted for a simpler, less intricate technology and social order. But most people dismiss them as romantic neo-primitives.

Nuclear energy has been, in a way, a great success. But everybody also sees its problems.

Looking ahead, technological optimists and pessimists argue ceaselessly. The problems facing the human race are immense, but some say that continued research will bring new solutions. Others say that the "technological fix" has already shown its limitations and cannot be counted on for rescue.

The world has become accustomed to a mix of productivity and austerity. Historians smile cynically when they report that people in the twentieth century sometimes held up the United States and Western Europe as economic models for what they called the "developing countries." How, they wonder, could anybody, even in those intoxicating days, really think that India could ever have the number of cars per capita that the United States did? Or how did aeronautical enthusiasts ever assume that half the human race would use air transportation—as was the case for a short while in some societies?

Some of the energy shortages of the past have, indeed, been overcome. Energy now comes primarily from "nuclear parks." The world has three thousand of these. The average one includes eight fast-breeder reactors, producing forty million kilowatts of electricity. To achieve this, the world started in the twentieth century to build four new reactors per week. Now it is continuing that pace of expansion, but is also building two per day to replace worn out ones.[1]

A large part of the world's economic activity is used to prepare and transport the nuclear materials, to dispose of the wastes, and to seal off the worn-out reactors. Fifteen million kilograms of hazardous plutonium-239 are processed and transported each year.

A worldwide surveillance system operates to prevent accidents, sabotage, and robbery. The system was accepted reluctantly, but after a few accidents and acts of terrorism the world decided it was necessary. There is constant monitoring of the nuclear parks, the waste disposal apparatus, and the materials in transit. The guards are themselves monitored according to a complicated system.

A central world authority enforces safety standards and supervises disposal of wastes. It prescribes means for the disposal of the radioactive wastes with a half-life of 24,400 years. Caverns in deep granite strata of the United States, the Soviet Union, and China have proved useful for waste disposal. It is expected that these geological formations will be stable for many millennia. Initially the nations involved refused to accept wastes from outside their borders, but eventually under pressure they agreed.

There is an increasing feeling that the system may be getting unmanageable. A vigorous debate is under way about the practicality of economic growth. Some say such growth is the only way to maintain employment and raise the standard of living of the world's poor people. Others say consumption has come close to its limits. Great hopes center on the development of a successful fusion reactor and of economical ways of transforming solar energy into liquid fuels. Every decade of this century has heard predictions of an early achievement, but thus far the necessary technology has proved elusive.

AFTER THE REFREV

In the peaceable world of 2100 historians are still trying to understand how the human race made the transition from the insecurities of 1990. Some emphasize the counterculture within the industrialized societies of those days: the movement of people satiated with competitive industrialism to the point where they fled the cities and took up subsistence homesteading, either in family units or in communes. Others point to the example of China, which established a nearly self-sufficient economy by deliberately exalting human labor over advanced machine labor and by requiring all citizens to spend some time in common labor. Still others accent the contribution of the Club of Home, an organization of technological and intellectual elites, which adopted the slogan, "Earth Is Our Home," and predicted disaster unless industrialized societies adopted lifestyles less destructive of the environment. A different group of historians say that the world, haunted by fear of war and economic failure, was ready for any social system that promised security. Finally, there are those who say that a movement of prophetic mysticism, arising simultaneously in scattered parts of the world, led to the Refrev—that combination of reformation and revolution that modified human values and aspirations on such an amazing scale at the turn of the century.

Somehow the human race did what almost everybody had said would be impossible. It engaged in a large-scale effort at social planning combined with radical decentralization. There were, to be sure, disgruntled resisters. Millions of dollars went into advertising campaigns to persuade people to cling to the hallowed values of individual initiative and competition as the means toward increasing production, consumption, and self-fulfillment. But a majority of people found attraction in the new heresies and persuaded or pressured the rest into going along.

What was most amazing was the combination of groups not used to working together—mystics and technologists, capitalists and socialists, to some extent even rich and poor. Some were lured by the vision of a new style of life, others moved by the looming disaster accompanying old styles. The slowest to change were the political and economic leaders of the wealthy societies, who did not want to give up what they had. But they finally had little choice when a series of international cartels, formed on the pattern of OPEC (the still remembered twentieth-century Organization of Petroleum Exporting Countries), withheld exports, and when several threats from nuclear-armed terrorists in starving countries scared them out of their wits.

When E. F. Schumacher won the Nobel Prize in economics—the first posthumous Nobel award ever made—the fraternity of economists first gasped, then took a look at his ideas. A poll of economists in professional societies around the world showed that only twenty-one percent had studied his work. But ten years later a comparable poll showed that sixty-seven percent took him seriously—the largest agreement among economists ever recorded by this poll. The United Nations sponsored an international conference—the seventy-seventh in a series of ineffective ones, according to one press tabulation—and this time found wide agreement on charting a new pathway for the world.

Soon the world organized itself into a large number of economic units, relatively self-sufficient. International trade was drastically reduced, partly because it was becoming intolerably expensive in the face of petroleum shortages and price rises, partly because an ethos of self-reliance spread through most societies.

Use of nuclear energy was phased out, by international agreement, by the year 2005. All nations contributed through the United Nations to a research fund for development of alternative forms of energy, especially in rural societies. The biggest single gain came in appropriation of solar energy. Windmills made a spectacular return to popularity. Organic energy farms produced great quantities of methane and alcohol. Sewage treatment processes produced methanol. Simultaneously there was a concerted effort to reduce waste of energy and to moderate consumption. High prices were already having that effect; a combination of rationing and tax policies tended to move the process along and also to equalize wealth. Travel and transportation, both international and domestic, have been dropping throughout the century and now, by 2100, are minimal compared with fifty or a hundred years ago. People cannot afford to travel much, and highly ingenious communications systems make decentralized organizations more efficient than the old centralized ones. No longer do people begin work already exhausted by the commuter's ordeal. About half the world's people live in three-dimensional cities of a style first planned by Paolo Soleri way back in the twentieth century. These cities, rarely exceeding half a million inhabitants, are designed to bring together opportunities for living, employment, and recreation. The thrust of planning is toward a high-technology, low-energy economy. Public transportation is efficient. Private ownership of automobiles is forbidden, but people may rent cars (powered by methanol) for special occasions.

There is some grumbling about a culture that constantly emphasizes economy, moderation in consumption, and meticulous recycling of materials. Some people say that creative enterprise is stifled, but others point to the resources that are put into technological research, for example, in organic farming, energy production, home designing, and utilization of substitutes for scarce resources.

Two years ago television networks in Europe and North America began showing ancient films of the 1970s. Public authorities moved to suppress the films, charging that their portrayals of extravagant consumption were a pornographic titillation of desires that could not be satisfied. The exhibitors protested in the name of freedom of speech. Suddenly the public authorities changed their policy. Instead of forbidding the films, they bought them and ran them repeatedly on the air. Their rationale was that the films, showing the intense unhappiness in antiquated affluent societies, especially when alternated with wartime documentary films from those days, were a sound education for people, who compared the miserable past with the better present.

REFLECTION NO. I: URGENCY AND IGNORANCE

My four more or less playful scenarios have their foolish aspects. Anybody looking at them twenty-five years from now will ask why I explored some possibilities and ignored other more important ones. In fact, anybody can ask that question now. The point is that these or any other scenarios lead to some reflections on the human situation and the forced options that face the human race. I shall here state three of these reflections in a preliminary way.

The first is that this present generation is acting in ways that open up some possibilities for the future and foreclose others. And we are doing it with very little awareness of what we are doing. We act in a frightening ambience of mingled urgency and ignorance.

The urgency has to do with the momentous and hurried decisions that we are making for future generations who have no voice in our decisions. The ignorance is that we know so little—and sometimes care so little—about how our actions affect others, both now and in times to come.

This generation is consuming irreplaceable resources, and it is consuming replaceable resources at rates faster than they can be replaced. It is populating the earth far beyond the numbers that traditional technologies can support. It is meddling with the atmosphere in ways that may be irrevocable and may heighten the hazards of cancer and genetic damage for a long, long future. It is tampering with climate by acts that may flood the coastal plains of all the continents and destroy civilizations. It is playing an intercontinental game of "chicken" with armaments of disastrous power.

Yet it is possible that this generation is creating a scientific technology that can enable future generations to cope with some of these problems better than we do now. We simply do not know. We live with the "unk-unk" that I mentioned in Chapter 1: we know neither the destination of this civilization nor the hazards of getting there. In that sense we are like the Abraham of old: "he was called to go out to a place which he was to receive as an inheritance; and he went out, not knowing where he was to go" (Heb. 11:8).

In the present perplexities of technological civilization there is a deepening suspicion, which I share, that a self-destruct device is built into the system. It is not the self-destruct mechanism that engineers design for space rockets, in order that ground controllers can deliberately destroy the rockets if something goes wrong. It is an unintended self-destruct apparatus put into the system by eager, groping, blundering people who are doing things for the first time and don't know entirely what they are doing. With a kind of wistful, pathetic effrontery this generation is making portentous decisions. It will not live to see the consequences of all of them.

REFLECTION NO. 2: THE ETHICAL AND THE TECHNICAL (VARIATIONS ON A THEME FROM CHAPTER I)

Technology is a way of solving problems. Its modern successes have been so great that people often fail to notice that technical decisions usually involve decisions about values and commitments. The sudden emergence of ethical issues in what seem to be technical decisions often takes the world by surprise.

The surprise interrupts a social habit: the habit, created by the amazing successes of technology, of looking to technology to solve most human problems. Civilized peoples no longer feel the dependence, so common in past ages, upon capricious demons or gods. They feel dependent instead upon wizards whom they expect to seize nuclear and solar energy or bring off another round in the Green Revolution. Oswald Spengler early in this century coined the prescient phrase, "the priest of the machine."[2] Not the old miracle of transubstantiation but the new miracles of technology awe this modern world.

Technology has answered—or removed from human concern— even stubborn ethical problems. If that seems an implausible proposition, the record makes it persuasive. Think of one of the most elemental of all ethical problems. What do people do when there is not enough food for everybody? Do some starve and some survive? Are there extra rations for warriors and pregnant women? Does brute force, political authority, or the market arbitrate decisions? What are justice and mercy? How does coercion impinge on freedom? Countless societies have struggled with such ethical questions.

But if a technical miracle of irrigation or hybridization increases food supplies, the problems are solved. There may still be conflicts about who eats steaks and who eats beans, and such conflicts may be more than a society knows how to handle. But the issue of starvation has been overcome. A technical solution has removed an ethical problem.

A world accustomed to look for technical solutions to human problems is jolted when that formula fails. The failures are likely to produce a sense of betrayal. The trusted savior has let us down. That, I think, accounts for the undercurrent of revulsion against technology in our culture and some of its subcultures and countercultures. The response of many young people to the polemics against technology in Jacques Ellul or Theodore Roszak—or the response to their own experience of disappointed expectation—is a case in point. The purported savior turned out to be a fake, maybe even a demon.

Now the announcement is coming, often from the centers of scientific research, that some problems have no technical solutions. Jerome Wiesner and Herbert F. York, eminent scientific leaders, argued in 1964 that there was no technical solution to the dilemma of increasing nuclear armaments and decreasing national security.[3] Every round of escalation, aiming at neutralizing another nation's weapons, is matched by that other nation, thus increasing the possibility and power of destruction. Garrett Hardin in "The Tragedy of the Commons," an essay of 1968 that quickly became famous, picked up the theme of Wiesner and York, then went on to define a class of problems that he called "no technical solution problems."[4] The first book in the series of reports to the Club of Rome, *The Limits to Growth,* quoted Hardin with agreement.[5]

Hardin's theme is that, whatever help may come from scientific techniques (and he is a scientist who advocates many such techniques), major contemporary problems require changes in human values and morality. There is no adequate "technical fix." Although I have major disagreements with Hardin on specific moral changes that he urges, I want for the moment to underline his main argument. When he says, "It is time we turn our attention from the things of mankind to man himself," he puts the action on the terrain familiar to prophets, saints, and poets. It is the turf that religious communities and sometimes universities have claimed as their concern.

But are religious communities and universities capable of clear thinking about the contemporary human crises? Or are they so compromised in existing patterns of life that they cannot find freedom for fresh thoughts and acts? And are they able to bring together the ethical and the technical aspects of life in ways adequate to the coming age?

For if there is no "technical fix" for most human problems, there is also no "religious fix" or "ethical fix." That is, there is no religious or ethical guidance for concrete policy decisions unless it has worked its way through the meaning of the scientific-technical revolutions of our time. Whatever churches may do as communities that sustain and strengthen people, they cannot give moral advice on today's urgent social issues *unless* they do a more adequate technical job than they usually want to do. And whatever universities may do for the advance of various intellectual disciplines, they will not prepare students to cope with this world if they isolate their schools of humanities and of sciences from each other.

The great social decisions before this and the next generation are in arenas where the ethical and the technical interact. The two are distinguishable—and it is often important to distinguish them—but not separable. So the big issues cannot be left to technologists who are ethically illiterate or to moralists who are technically ignorant. In most technological arguments, there are ethical issues, obvious or hidden. In most ethical arguments, there are technical issues that need clarification. Most of the chapters of this book deal with the meeting of the technical and the ethical.

To complicate issues further, the technical and ethical never meet in a vacuum. They meet in a political and ideological context, and the context often determines the outcome. Technology is a form of power. If the problem of a society or a world is that some people have too much power over others, there is no technological fix. A technological leap will usually mean increased power for the powerful, so it may heighten the intensity of the problem.

A UNESCO report[6] gives these figures:

	Developing Nations	Developed Nations
Number of scientists	6%	94%
Expenditures	3%	97%
Number of scientists per million population	98	2,579

As long as such a situation prevails, most of the world will have reason to distrust scientific-technological answers to their pain.

REFLECTION NO. 3: WHAT IS AT STAKE

Civilizations have always been vulnerable. We need no Gibbon, Spengler, or Toynbee to tell us that civilizations do not last forever. They weaken and die, whether by exhaustion or catastrophe. Human life persists, but the complex of arts and sciences, of ethos and political organization that define civilizations does not endure. I am not persuaded that the monotonous cycles of Spengler or Toynbee really fit the variety of civilizational experiences. But surely it is obvious that civilizations come and go, leaving some heritage, great or small, to the human future.

This is not only a melancholy thought; it is something more frightening than that. In the past the downfall of a civilization was a local affair. Pristine civilizations could arise elsewhere on this fertile planet. The decline of Babylonian and Egyptian empires did no harm to the Athenians and Romans who built their civilizations much later. And the end of "the glory that was Greece and the grandeur that was Rome" was not fateful for nascent Arabian or North European civilizations.

The new and frightening fact is that, in some real though not very clear ways, the human race now shares in a worldwide civilization. The emergence of "one world" is in its way an impressive achievement, but it means that the vulnerability of a particular civilization becomes the vulnerability of all civilization. It is quite possible that a crash of contemporary civilization, whether in nuclear apocalypse or ecological exhaustion, would mean the end of industrial eras like our own familiar one.

There is deep irony in this situation. In 1916 John Dewey (a thinker from whom I have learned much) declared: "Wholesale permanent decays of civilization are impossible."[7] Why? Because of scientific method. Any particular civilizational achievement might fail. But scientific method, unknown to the Babylonians and Egyptians but now securely achieved, could always repair the damage or initiate fresh starts. However, it is the destructive uses of scientific method that today threaten the world. If once the Chinese did not know or care about imperial conflicts between Egyptians or Babylonians, today all the world will know and care if the United States and the Soviet Union destroy each other, along with a lot of spectators.

Ecological failure is less spectacular, but it may also be irremediable. Traditional failures were local or regional; a change in the world's climate is global. If solar satellites and nuclear fusion eventually replace exhausted fossil fuels, that will be a spectacular scientific achievement; but any major breakdown in the system will be a monstrous threat, because the human race cannot then revert to fossil fuels while it gradually rebuilds an intricate system to replace them.

From some religious perspectives even a crash of world civilization is not a disaster. If all values are located in eternity, no temporal events have final significance. The faithful seek a security immune to the anxieties and conflicts of a perilous history.

But for any faith that looks for divine judgment and grace in history, what happens to our civilization is important. Granted that no civilization and no planetary history will last forever, responsible human beings have some stake in the life that they know. They will seek to prevent needless suffering and to exercise human creativity as they negotiate the changes that are part of historical existence, always and especially in this epoch.

What is at stake in the forced options of our time? Perhaps human survival. Perhaps maintenance of the kind of life that is worth living. The perils to both are real. But there are possibilities of enacting better scenarios than any I have written for this book.

Part II

THE BIG PROBLEMS

3. The Worldwide Energy Emergency

At the basis of everything is energy. All objects are organizations of energy. All living creatures require energy; human creatures know it. Energy creates and destroys. Although it is everywhere—in the farthest reaches of the galaxies and in the nucleus of the atom, in the air and the land and the sea—some forms of it can be packaged and delivered, bought and sold, stolen by stealth or plunder. Our modern world is adept in all these processes. The idiosyncratic distribution of energy can, within a few years, make impoverished nations incredibly wealthy, make powerful nations feeble, and send frightening tremors around the globe.

This world, which used to take energy pretty much for granted, has suddenly become an energy-conscious world. It is discovering the myriad meanings of energy for science and technology, economics and politics, personal and social lifestyles, the self-consciousness of cultures, ethics and religion. On no other issue is it more obvious that forced decisions come at the intersection of technology and ethics.

THE GLOBAL REALITY

The starting point in any discussion of energy is the recognition that the worldwide emergency in energy is real. Whatever the temporary perturbations that cause a gasoline shortage one month and a glut the next, the continuing global emergency is authentic. It is not an artificial product of blundering by governments or manipulation by corporations. I take it for granted that, like most people, governments have blundered and corporations have manipulated. But even if they had not, the world would still be in trouble about energy.

Resources of energy can be classified as renewable or nonrenewable. The emergency is critical in both.

An example of a renewable resource is firewood. Wood was the chief fuel in the United States until 1880, as it is for much of the world today. As Erik Eckholm points out, "for more than a third of the world's people, the real energy crisis is a daily scramble to find the wood they need to cook dinner. . . . Nine-tenths of the people in most poor countries today depend on firewood as their chief source of fuel."[1] They are consuming that resource much faster than nature and human cultivation are renewing it. In part of Nepal, for example, the collecting of a family's daily firewood, which used to require an hour or two, now requires a whole day's work. Prices of firewood in some areas have risen faster than the more notorious prices of petroleum.

Furthermore, the seizing of every available tree and shrub by families hurting for energy means the denuding of the soil, with its consequent erosion and sometimes desertification. That means a reduction of food as well as of energy.

Obviously the consumption of renewable resources at a rate faster than their renewal brings trouble. The people causing the trouble are often so poor and such modest consumers that one cannot blame them. But they are making agony for themselves and the generations that follow them. In fact, many of them suffer now because of their past consumption and that of their ancestors.

Nonrenewable resources follow a different logic. An example is petroleum. The world's reserves of petroleum represent a hundred million years of solar energy, transformed by biological and geological processes into underground deposits of oil. And that legacy of the ages is fueling the processes of industrial civilization on a horrendous scale. Former President Carter gave the basic facts to the nation in his first major address on energy, April 18, 1977.[2] In the *one decade* of the 1950s the human race consumed *more oil than in all prior history.* Then in the 1960s, people used twice as much as in the 1950s, once again consuming more than in all past history. That kind of consumption uses up irreplaceable resources at an enormous rate and their exhaustion threatens the whole world.

It is not quite accurate to say that the world's petroleum will soon run dry. There will be some petroleum underground longer than there are people on earth, but it will become harder and more costly to get out. The rising costs of petroleum in dollars (or yen or rupees) are obvious, but even more important are the rising energy costs of energy. It takes energy to extract energy from the earth. If the process of extraction uses 10 or 50 units of energy to recover 100 units, that is worth while. When it uses 99 units to recover 100 units, it is less helpful. And when it uses 101 units to recover 100 units, it had better stop (unless it uses a plentiful form of energy to produce a scarce form).

Already the age of cheap petroleum is past. We can only read with wonder stories of how in 1901 on a Texas oil field, a *barrel* of crude oil cost three cents while a glass of water cost five cents. Such a time will not return. And the time is coming when, for all practical purposes, petroleum will not be available for burning. Nobody knows exactly when that will be. It depends on (1) the extent of petroleum reserves yet to be discovered, (2) new techniques of extraction, and (3) rates of consumption, which can rise or decline. Because of these three unknown factors, the estimates on the future availability of petroleum vary greatly. A rough estimate, about halfway between the most optimistic and the most pessimistic, is that the world will face very serious permanent shortages in the 1980s, and that the virtual exhaustion of petroleum can be expected in the early twenty-first century.

I need not waste much time on a peculiarly glib argument that appears occasionally in political and economic oratory. It is sometimes said that the processes of the market will handle the problem: as prices rise, there is greater incentive to explore for new oil wells and to extract more oil from once-abandoned sources. The facts are accurate but not very helpful. In the United States, for example, oil production peaked in 1970 and has been declining since then. Since 1973 rising prices have led to increased exploration and drilling, but known reserves have declined.[3] We can hope for modest reversals of the trend, but we cannot count on them.

There is no getting around the fact that petroleum reserves are finite and are decreasing. And no financial incentives for recovery can overcome the fact that it is useless to go on when the energy expenditures of recovery become higher than the energy recovered.

As the supplies of energy decline, the demand for it rises. Since World War II the worldwide consumption of energy has risen at an average rate of 5.03 percent per year.[4] That rate means a doubling of consumption every fourteen years. The rise in consumption has taken place almost everywhere. Consumption of energy is by far the greatest in the industrialized nations; per capita consumption in the United States, for example, is more than fifty times that in India.[5] But the *rate* of increase, especially in use of electrical energy, is often faster in the developing countries, although this increase makes less of a drain on the world's resources because of the initially low usage. If Ethiopia doubles its consumption, that makes less of a worldwide ripple than a one percent rise in consumption in the United States. But the developing countries, with their low base and their rising consumption, have a very great stake in maintaining the growth of energy production.

One more point of fact is important. What the world craves is not simply "energy" in some total, abstract sense. It wants and needs specific kinds of energy in particular places. When during one harsh winter (1976–1977) Ohio factories closed because of a shortage of natural gas, it was no help to know that producers were flaring off excess natural gas in Middle Eastern oil fields. When people shiver in their homes in northern climates, it is no comfort to realize that nature provides free home heat on the equator. Energy needs are diverse and specific. Even so, one generalization is possible: the energy problem in industrial societies is related primarily to two forms of energy, electricity and liquid fuels.

To summarize, before exploring the chief ethical issues, the worldwide emergency is real. It comes out of the clash between rising consumption almost everywhere and dwindling supplies of the principal resources of renewable and nonrenewable energy.

HOW IMPORTANT IS ENERGY

The first ethical question about energy—and the prerequisite to all the other questions—is a naive yet profound question: how important for human welfare is energy?

Our world assumes that energy is utterly important. That assumption, though true, needs examination. While some consumption of energy is an absolute necessity for all life, the familiar modern patterns of consumption belong to only a recent moment in a long human history.

For most of human existence energy has been mostly food, plus sometimes a bit of heat beyond the gifts of the climate. Granted these two inputs, the human body produced the energy to do the world's work. Even the domestication of animals—by which superior human shrewdness appropriated the superior muscular strength of horses, oxen, camels, and elephants—is a fairly late episode in history. And the familiar contrivances of modern civilization are last-minute appearances: steam engines, internal combustion engines, electrical wiring, telephones, radios, and airplanes. It remains to be seen whether industrial civilization will turn out to be a flashing moment in history or the pattern for millennia to come.

To those of us whose idea of the good life comes from the patterns of industrial civilization, it may be jolting to realize that life could be glorious long before the invention of objects that we regard as necessities. Think of some of the giants of human history: prophets and sages like Gautama Buddha, Confucius, Lao-tse, the Hebrew prophets, Socrates; poets like Aeschylus and Sophocles, Dante and Shakespeare; the builders of the Parthenon, the Gothic cathedrals, the Taj Mahal; shapers of history like Alexander, Julius Caesar, Joan of Arc, George Washington; artists like Leonardo and Rembrandt, Bach and Mozart; scientists like Galileo and Newton. Creative life does not require electricity and gasoline.

But the world has changed. Today most of the human race puts a high value on plentiful energy. It may be that self-indulgence has softened our characters beyond repair. One recent mood, however, is critical of high technology and friendly to spare lifestyles, although that mood is more obvious in the United States than in South America, more characteristic of the satiated rich than of the suffering poor. But it has some persuasiveness in developing countries among people who are deciding that envy of the affluent societies is misplaced.

To move from moods to analysis, we may note some cogent reasons to believe that plentiful energy has value. One reason is that the planet earth, for the first time in history, carries more than four billion people, many of whom live in cities that could not survive without energy-intensive systems of support. Food, for example, must arrive daily by railroad or truck. Any sudden disruption of the energy that keeps such cities functioning would bring disaster, and even a gradual disruption would bring pain and social chaos.

Another reason is that energy-consuming machines do much of the drudge work once done by the lower classes in hierarchical societies. The high culture of past civilizations was usually the privilege of a few. It rested on a social base of slavery, serfdom, or peonage. Many of the values of democracy depend on the release of vast populations from drudgery.[6] Granted, misery and oppression are still the lot of many people, sometimes in the most affluent societies; that is a social and ethical failure that ought to be remedied. Industrial society makes it possible for vast populations to have access to the education and culture that were formerly available only to elites.

Again, energy-consuming technologies have contributed to human health. The data, of course, are mixed. People die from overeating and underexercising. The pollution of high-energy societies produces cancers and pulmonary diseases. Energy-consuming automobiles kill their thousands. More and more people in the affluent societies die of self-induced and socially induced ailments. Yet people in high-energy societies, despite "junk food," usually have more adequate diets than people in low-energy societies. And there is no denying the reduction of infant mortality, the conquests of smallpox and polio, and the many health-serving forces that are now possible for the first time in history. While such progress is by no means directly proportional to consumption of energy—as Ivan Illich and many others have forcefully argued —it is part of a civilizational system that depends on massive supplies of energy. (See Chapter II.)

Thus there are reasons why high-energy societies feel threatened by loss of energy resources and low-energy societies want more energy. But there is no fixed ratio between energy consumption and human good. The benefits and harms of plentiful energy depend largely on the social organizations that appropriate them. One of many examples is employment. In an industrial society like the United States, energy shortages mean unemployment. Scarcer and more costly petroleum brings some reduction in automobile transportation. There are many social benefits to a cooling off of the American love affair with the auto, but those benefits are not most obvious to automobile workers —or to steel, rubber, and glass workers—who lose jobs. It is not surprising that the United Automobile Workers and the National Association for the Advancement of Colored People are more concerned than affluent intellectuals about maintaining high production of energy and energy-consuming devices. Yet in some developing countries unemployment advances with the whole package of changes that go with industrialization, urbanization, and electrification.

Human ingenuity should be able to devise systems for revising the relations between energy consumption and employment in the industrialized societies. It is reasonable to figure that employment would rise if factories and farms bought more human labor and less machine labor. But such a reversal of prevalent practices is not easy to contrive. And it is sure to hurt some people, unless it is brought off with imagination and skill.

By this time the uses of energy have been so built into the structures of civilization—above all in the North Atlantic societies but not only there—that any major threat to supplies of energy produces a social trauma. It is one thing to say that a wiser humanity would not have become so dependent on lavish consumption of energy. It is another thing to recognize that reversal of present patterns of life, without intensifying social conflict and misery, is hard to accomplish.

How important, then, is plentiful energy? Different individuals and societies will give different answers to that question. But I think that wide agreement is possible on four assertions: (1) Meaningful life, even ecstatic life, is possible without high consumption of energy. (2) Yet increased energy is needed in order that much of the present world can rise out of poverty and misery. (3) Although there is no fixed ratio between energy consumption and human welfare, many civilizational values depend upon access to energy. (4) The values served by energy depend upon the social systems that appropriate energy.

DISTRIBUTIVE JUSTICE

The question is as old as human life: how do people divide up economic goods when there aren't enough to please everybody? Aristotle gave the problem the technical name that has become conventional: distributive justice.

The conventional metaphor that goes with the question is the slicing of the pie. Social pies are sliced in many ways. Arguments about the slicing fluctuate in their fury. When the pie is growing, people (even those getting the smallest slices) often feel a greater stake in promoting that growth than in quarreling over the division. When the pie is shrinking, the mode of slicing becomes more urgent. Now that the world's energy pie has slowed its growth, the issues of distribution are becoming more intense.

The issues arise within three important contexts: (1) within particular societies; (2) within the world society; (3) within societies extended into the future.

Justice Within Particular Societies

Most societies use two systems for distributing economic goods: the market and social allocations. The relative importance of each varies with the society.

The market plays a major role in the United States, and it has some role in every society that uses money—that means, today, almost all societies. In a monetary society, people use their money to buy in markets what they want and can afford. The ethical value of the market, a value that has not lacked celebration in American culture, is freedom. People, given even a modest income, would rather decide what to buy than have somebody else (particularly a government bureaucracy) decide for them. As Charles Lindblom has shown in his important book *Politics and Markets,*[7] all industrial societies assign a considerable importance to markets, although not all rely on them or acclaim them as much as the United States.

Social allocations also have a major role in the United States, and they have a greater role in some other societies. That is, the society through its political system allocates some economic goods to people. Such allocations may be hierarchical or egalitarian. Most modern societies have edged toward egalitarian models of allocation. These models qualify the value of freedom, emphasized by the market, with the value of equality. No modern society distributes police and fire protection solely through markets. A very few people and more institutions do, in fact, hire security guards of their own on the market. But police and fire protection, totally in principle and partly in fact, are available to all. Public parks and at least minimal educational opportunities are accessible outside the market. Societies are saying, more than in the past, that unpolluted air and health services are common rights, not solely commodities for sale on the market.

In times of severe shortage of necessities, most societies make some shift of power from markets toward social allocations. Thus during World War II the United States rationed some foods and gasoline.

During temporary water shortages cities sometimes forbid the watering of lawns. It would be incredible to let the market take its course (price rationing), if that meant that some people could buy water to wash their cars and irrigate huge estates while others died of thirst.

The end of the era of cheap energy heightens the ethical problems of distribution in even the wealthiest societies. The market will continue to have a role. It is obvious that artificially low prices of gasoline in the United States—approximately half the prices in Europe—long encouraged carefree waste of energy in this country, and rising market prices are a strong incentive to conservation. Likewise, when price controls are a disincentive to production, decontrol gains some economic usefulness. But when rising prices of fuel mean that some people may freeze in their homes, federal and state governments begin to devise extra-market schemes of allocation, and Congress authorizes a standby plan for gasoline rationing.

The social debate about the relation of freedom and equality is a continuing one in human life. Scarcity intensifies the debate. In the debate, industrial societies will have to give new attention to their ethical values.

Justice Within the World Society

When the issues of distributive justice reach beyond national boundaries to include the world, they become stupendous. The contemporary world is barely beginning to learn how to think about them, and it is far from knowing how to act about them. When the United Nations has a conference like the Conference on Science and Technology for Development (Vienna, August, 1979), the mood is a mixture of bickering petulance, anguish, stubborn complacence, revolutionary ardor, low comedy and high tragedy, and futility.

Once upon a time long, long ago, societies lived on the resources of their own areas. When the resources were inadequate, people migrated. Migration might mean movement into virgin territories; or it might mean wars of conquest or defeat. If, thousands of miles away, there were more prosperous societies, nobody knew that.

Today there is a world market in energy. Sellers depend on buyers far, far way; and, in a sudden shift of power, buyers depend even more obviously on sellers. Energy resources are distributed very unequally —as though Providence either did not care about just distribution or deliberately chose to confront an unready human race with an ethical problem of high moment. The consumption of energy follows patterns different from those of its production, but these patterns are just as unequal. Access to energy depends only partly on geography and proximity to resources; it has a lot to do with power—technological, economic, political, and military.

The American public is bored with hearing that the United States, with about six percent of the world's population, consumes about thirty percent of the world's energy. (Even that figure is down from the forty-seven percent of so recent a date as 1947—not because of austerity in the United States but because of growth of consumption elsewhere.[8]) People can respond to that data in many ways. Two former presidents of the United States boasted that they intended to keep things that way. But some people in the United States think that kind of distribution cannot and ought not continue. And other people elsewhere, angry about it, intend to change it.

Such averages, though important, hide the enormity of inequality. For example, per capita energy consumption in the United States is —or has been within the present decade—331 times that in Ethiopia. Such a figure is hard to grasp, harder to do anything about. Most people have enough worries about energy in their own homes and gasoline tanks, without adding worries about East Africa. But even if the name of Ethiopia rarely crosses their minds, they cannot entirely block out the problem that Ethiopia represents. Ethiopia is part of a syndrome; it includes a recent Ethiopian coup d'etat (1974), increased Soviet influence in the Horn of Africa and around the Persian Gulf, higher military expenditures and taxes in the United States, public discussion of reinstating the military draft. It's that kind of world.

I do not expect that worldwide equality—in relation to energy, food, sunshine, orchids, or symphony orchestras—ever will or should prevail. Different climates mean different requirements and opportunities. Some people may—perhaps wisely—decide that they want a simpler lifestyle than others. But the enormous contrasts between wealth and poverty in this world, especially when publicized by the media of mass communication, are both morally disquieting and dangerous.

Once—quite recently when measured in years but long ago on the calendar of changing intellectual climates—there was a standard answer to the problem: economic development. Technological ingenuity, it was said, would raise the productivity of poor societies. The answer to the contrast between rich and poor was to make all societies rich. There are still authentic hopes for economic development. But the naive hopes of even a decade or two ago have crashed on hard rocks of data. If the world were to consume energy at the rate the United States does, total energy consumption would be multiplied by five—in the face of the decreasing supplies of fuels. That kind of light is not at the end of any discernible tunnel.

The situation is that hundreds of societies are competing for scarce resources, and the most powerful are getting them. If the power involved were blatantly bullets and bombs, the offensiveness of the situation would be overpowering. As it is, the power is most obviously dollars—which, though related to bullets and bombs, are not identical with them. It is unnerving, even to those with lots of dollars, to see the value of those dollars drop, largely because of the energy situation. It is devasting to those without dollars to suffer because energy flows toward the dollars.

Former President Carter—though more sensitive to the issues of energy than his predecessors—sometimes said that the United States, as the most energy-rich country of the world, can summon the will and intelligence to meet its emergency. To much of the rest of the world that reasoning is infuriating. Why does the most energy-rich country import millions of barrels of petroleum *a day,* simply outbidding poorer countries that need it more? To burn so precious a substance as oil, which might make fertilizers to feed crops that save people from starvation, is—to much of the world—an extravagance. To import and burn it on the scale the United States does is an atrocity.

Even the Report of the Energy Project at Harvard University, heralded for its thoughtful emphasis on conservation, proposes that in the late 1980s the United States will be importing nine million barrels of oil a day—a proposal that is dubious technically, politically, and morally.[9]

If we ask whether this society, or any society known to history, has the sensitivity and will to meet such a moral challenge, the answers are not encouraging. But before even considering possible answers, we must look at one more complication that makes the problem even more severe.

Justice Within Societies Extended into the Future

This generation's consumption of energy is a direct threat to the next generation and generations yet to come. To realize that is to take on a perplexing ethical liability. How can societies, already baffled by questions of justice and survival beyond their competence, accept the extra burden of relating responsibly to the future?

There are two valid qualifications upon any such responsibility. First, there is nothing any generation can do to guarantee a good life for its heirs. They must make their own decisions in situations the present world cannot foresee. An exaggerated sense of responsibility for the future is pretentious.

Second, human ingenuity in years to come will discover some new ways of developing energy or living adequately with less energy. Modern technologies, which obviously consume energy on a grandiose scale, also "create" energy. Coal lay undisturbed in the ground for aeons before technology made it into a source of energy. Oil and uranium have become important sources of energy only recently. Nobody knows what successes technology may achieve in capturing solar energy and turning it into electricity and liquid fuels. Nuclear fusion may become practical, safe, and reliable. Theorists and laboratory technicians may tomorrow or a century from tomorrow discover sources of energy now unexpected. It is ethically justifiable to hope and strive for such successes.

But it is irresponsible to count on "technical fixes" that are unpredictable or to accept improbable achievements as an escape from ethical liability. And it is irresponsible to trifle with two scales that loom over present consciousness. The scale of sheer quantity of consumption and expectation, which I have mentioned in the figures from former President Carter, cannot be balanced by any foreseeable discoveries. The scale of time means that unforeseeable developments, with whatever lead times they require, are not matching the speed of depletion of present resources.

Future generations have a peculiar vulnerability to present decisions. Present poor societies are already desperately vulnerable, as copious data on world poverty show. But they can at least complain; the United Nations even offers them a forum for complaints. And they can threaten—to go Communist or commit sabotage or take hostages or destabilize the world of the comfortable. Unborn people can neither complain nor threaten. So the present world—both the complacent world and the miserable world—easily dismiss their problems, perhaps with the cliché: what do we owe posterity? What did it ever do for us?

There are some honest difficulties in thinking about responsibility to posterity. It is one thing to recognize suffering, anger, and ethical claims of existing persons or groups of people; it is something else to think about claims of those who do not exist. Some ethical theories deny the possibility of an unembodied ethical claim.

We can begin to get at the issue by thinking about living generations. Conceivably I and my peers in the latter third or fourth of our life span might reason that present world systems are sustainable for the rest of our lives—granted the inconveniences of inflation and sporadic disturbances of supplies—and that our responsibilities do not extend beyond our own lives. That logic is not attractive to young people. It is not attractive to old people who love their children and grandchildren.

That situation hints at an ethical insight that has been part of many traditions of faith: we human beings are all parts of a community of the human race extending over space and time. John Donne's testimony that "no man is an islande" has temporal as well as spatial meaning. Everybody's identity is bound up with a wider and longer human identity. We cannot destroy the prospects of humane living for others without destroying something precious in ourselves.

Granted, the whole planetary enterprise is a temporary project, and no technological or economic reforms can make it permanent. Still there is a moral numbness in any policies that, deliberately or recklessly, make life worse for people yet to come. To plunder and pollute the biosphere, to change the climate recklessly, to impose on the future a legacy of destruction—these are irresponsible acts. There are already people living in wretchedness because of malicious or careless acts committed before their births. Their pain is a testimony to the reality of moral responsibility toward people yet to come.

DEPENDENCE, INDEPENDENCE, INTERDEPENDENCE

Every society, I suppose, both craves freedom and knows that it cannot be entirely free. Dependence on nature is one limitation on freedom. Dependence on external political powers is a more variable and more offensive limitation. Thomas Jefferson and the signers of the Declaration of Independence of 1776 could not guess how dependent the forthcoming nation would be on other nations by the time it would celebrate the bicentennial of their act.

Reliance on imported energy means dependence. It means that a revolution thousands of miles away can send tremors down Wall Street and a thousand Main Streets. An upheaval in Saudi Arabia, comparable to that in Iran in 1979, could shake life in every household of the United States. Already the costs of dependence on foreign oil include inflation, economic and military insecurity, and painful perplexities about foreign policy. I have never been able to understand why the Pentagon, which is in the business of contingency planning for all kinds of events, did not scream to heaven about this nation's slalom from energy sufficiency to radical dependence.

There is bitter irony in recalling that in 1973 President Nixon announced "Project Independence," a plan with the aim of making the United States self-sufficient in energy by 1980. In the next few years oil imports almost doubled. When conservation and recession finally brought a reduction, imports for 1980 were still higher than in 1973.

If nations learn by experience—a possible but not certain hypothesis—this learning experience could be a step toward maturity. The kind of dependence that is new to this country is an old story to many countries. Often they have quivered in their dependence on our stock and commodity markets, our monetary policy, our political and military decisions. A change of a few cents a pound in the price for cocoa or coffee in New York can shake the economies of other nations. For North Americans, Western Europeans, and Japanese to find themselves dependent on caprices of faraway political and religious leaders can be a thought-provoking experience. It conceivably might lead the most industrialized countries to a more responsible use of power.

Interdependence—rather than either independence or dependence —can be a healthy recognition of reality and an ethical ideal. But interdependence is a shifting variable. Between equals it is one thing;

between unequals it is another. And the gyrating balances of inequality can threaten anybody on any tomorrow. Societies must ask: how dangerous is dependence to the values we most cherish? What changes in ways of life are we willing to make for the sake of greater independence?

Dependence not only threatens security; it also puts loyalties to the test. To admit this is demeaning. In the brave words of Senator Daniel Patrick Moynihan, "American foreign policy is not for sale—not 1 million barrels of oil a day nor 100 million barrels will buy the honor of this republic."[10] But that is political oratory. Certainly American relations with the former Shah of Iran and his conquerors, with the whole Middle East, with Israel, with neighboring Mexico and Canada have been influenced, subtly or drastically, by oil.

The problem is not unique to energy. The United States long ago discovered that it was easier to denounce violations of human rights by some nations than by others. Often its support of foreign dictators, accepted as allies in a world ideological confrontation, has earned the hatred of the people who later overthrew those dictators. The relation between obvious national interests and national ideals has never been easy to work out. The energy problem increases the tension between self-interest and moral posture. We in the United States can readily see how France and Japan, industrial nations that must import almost all their coal and oil, have to walk delicately through international controversies. Our own international and domestic policies must clumsily relate delicacy and self-assertion.

Suppose, to imagine the wildly improbable, the United States were to decide—not as an act of bravado but as a sober moral-political decision—to stop importing petroleum. To do so immediately would mean a major disruption of economies, national and international. But suppose the nation were to set a target date, maybe ten years hence, and in the interim reduce imports of oil, year by year, to zero. If the notion looks impossible, recall that it was only in 1948 that the United States became a permanent net importer of oil. Recall, also, that at some unknown date in the twenty-first century there will be, by all present signs, no significant amount of petroleum for anybody to burn anywhere.

The plan would be costly to this country and its standards of living. It would require major reorganizing of the economy so that the dam-

age would not fall on the weaker members of the society, already
hurting from poverty and unemployment. It would be so hard to bring
off that I see no likelihood of doing it, short of international catastrophes that may indeed occur.

But, to conjecture about the incredible, such a decision would have
two important meanings. First, it would reduce our precarious dependence on distant nations who can hurt us at any time by decisions,
calculated or erratic. Second, it would be a step, small but significant,
toward the impossible but alluring goal of equalizing the world's
access to energy.

Of course, any such scheme would bring new problems. Its internal
economic and political ramifications would jeopardize the interests
both modest and extravagant of many people and social groups. And
it would probably give impetus to the ideology of a "Fortress America," an ideology with its own destructive potentialities.

So I throw the idea into the public arena with a skeptical smile and
a recognition of its unreality, because it is an interesting talking point.
It requires that we ask, in relation to both our securities and our
loyalties, what we want in terms of dependence, independence, and
interdependence.

NO PANACEAS

The starting point of social wisdom in the face of the world's energy
needs is the realization that there are no panaceas in sight. There is
no technical fix that avoids hard social and ethical decisions. There
are many techniques that are helpful, but none provides what the
world craves: increasing supplies of energy at low prices.

There are three major sources of energy: fossil fuels, solar energy
(including hydropower, winds, and tides), and nuclear energy. Geo-
thermal energy, which can be significant in a few locations, is not a
resource for most of the earth. In looking at the three great options,
my aim here is not to put any down, but to make the minimum case
that none offers an easy solution.

Among fossil fuels, petroleum will continue to be used on a big scale
for a while, but it is the finite supply of petroleum that causes the
immediate problem. Most nations in the world aim to increase their
consumption of petroleum, even though they know that supplies will

decrease, not immediately but before long. The collision between rising demand and falling supplies is portentous, especially for the poor societies. There are unrealized possibilities of extracting petroleum from tar sands and from shale, but the process consumes huge amounts of energy and of water, and it creates overwhelming quantities of wastes. There is no getting around the fact that petroleum is a diminishing resource.

Natural gas will presumably last longer than petroleum, but probably not very much longer. And the transportation of it across oceans is far more difficult and dangerous than the transportation of oil.

Coal is the most plentiful of the fossil fuels for some countries. It will last far longer than petroleum. It will be burned directly, will be used to produce electricity, and will be transformed by expensive processes into liquid energy (synfuels). Former President Carter once projected a vast program for synfuels, reckoned to cost up to $88 billion dollars—more than was spent on "the space program, the interstate highway system and the Marshall Plan combined."[11] John Sawhill, the first head of the Synthetic Fuels Corporation, although an energetic advocate of the program, then had to admit: "We've learned that these are complex, difficult projects and we cannot proceed as rapidly as we expected."[12]

Coal and its derivatives present two great difficulties. First, more than ninety percent of the world's known and inferred reserves of coal are in just three countries (the Soviet Union, the United States, and China),[13] and none of these countries has shown much enthusiasm for alleviating the poverty of the Southern Hemisphere, which has almost no coal. Second, coal is exceedingly dangerous, with a high rate of human casualties from its mining, transportation, and pollution. These can be reduced at increased costs. But no technique can reduce the transformation of oxygen into carbon dioxide, a problem with all fossil fuels.

The question of risk is so important, and so characteristic of many modern technologies, that I shall come back to it in Chapter 11. For the time being it is enough to say that fossil fuels, although they will be part of the human future, are no panacea.

Nuclear energy is likewise problematic. The early euphoria about "the peaceful atom" has long ago disappeared. Nobody today expects nuclear energy to produce electricity "too cheap to meter," and nobody repeats former President Nixon's predictions that it will provide thirty to forty percent of America's electricity by the late 1980s. Nuclear energy will be of varying importance in different parts of the world. For obvious reasons nations with little coal or petroleum like France and Japan will push ahead faster with it than oil-rich and coal-rich countries.

The present form of fission reactors, which are producing electrical energy, have a limited future, because they depend on high-grade uranium ores, which will probably last not very much longer than petroleum. Breeder reactors can extend the use of uranium for a much longer time, but at the cost of a new set of hazards. The willingness of industrial countries to use breeder reactors is generally in inverse proportion to their wealth in other sources of energy. Fusion reactors use virtually inexhaustible hydrogen and reduce some risks. They may or may not become practical someday. Experimental fusion has been achieved, but thus far the process consumes more energy than it produces. Commercially practical fusion is not likely to come soon.

The great public arguments over nuclear energy center on its risks. As in the case of coal, I shall return to that issue in Chapter 11.

Given the problems in fossil fuels and nuclear energy, solar energy has become the favorite hope of almost everybody. It is absolutely fundamental, both symbolically and literally. Fossil fuels are simply accumulated solar energy. Nuclear energy, particularly in fusion form, is a miniature replica of what goes on in the sun.

Some of the uses of solar energy are elemental and obvious. Cattle and horses in a pasture know how to gather under a shade tree in the heat of the day and to seek the sun when the air turns chilly. It took millennia for architects and builders to lose that horse sense and construct buildings that ignore or resist the sun. Now there is a new appreciation of the "passive" uses of solar energy in styles of building that cooperate with nature. The economics of such construction look better and better as costs of other forms of energy rise.

The use of biomass—crops that can be turned into fuel oils or burned directly as fuel—is another possibility. Thus far, the production of alcohol, to be used directly as fuel or combined with gasoline is gasohol, appears to consume more energy than it produces; but new methods are more efficient. Some emerging possibilities of bioproduction are promising. But to make a major dent in a petroleum consumption of seventeen to nineteen million barrels of petroleum per day, in the United States alone, is a *big deal*. And, as Lester Brown warns, the future may see a cruel competition for use of agricultural land between the energy-hungry rich and the food-hungry poor.[14]

A major technological break-through has been the development of photovoltaic cells, which convert solar energy into electricity and thus make solar energy a direct competitor with nuclear energy and fossil fuels in many of their uses. A series of technical improvements has reduced the price of this method, which was at first very expensive. Furthermore, as other energy costs rise, this method becomes more attractive. The entry of many major American corporations into the field of solar energy is evidence that the economic prospects look much better than a decade or two ago.

One problem with solar energy is that the sun does not shine at night or even at every noon. So solar systems require methods of energy storage or conventional backup systems, both of which increase costs. The backup systems are the more expensive because they demand capital investments for facilities that are used at a small fraction of their capacity. One asset acclaimed for solar energy is that sunlight is free, widely distributed (unlike coal and petroleum), and therefore decentralized. The picture is of millions of householders gathering their own energy, independent of giant corporations, government agencies, or international cartels. That picture is valid for some uses of solar energy. But to imagine railway systems and great industries running on solar-generated electricity, even in the summer, to say nothing of winters with long nights and cloudy days, is to think of a highly centralized, capital-intensive operation using huge spaces for the collection of solar energy. (I shall return to this theme shortly.)

It is not surprising that expectations for the use of solar energy are controversial. The famous study at the Harvard Business School, *Energy Future,* reports on various projections ranging from seven percent to twenty-three percent for the United States by the year 2000.[15] Since then, CONAES (The Committee on Nuclear and Alternative Energy Systems of the National Academy of Sciences) has come in with an estimate of five percent, unless there is "massive government intervention."[16] Amory Lovins, on the other hand, is far more optimistic.[17] Gus Speth, Chairman of the President's Council on Environmental Quality and a strong advocate of solar energy, writes:

"Achieving the Administration's goal of 20% solar energy by the year 2000 will not be easy, but its pursuit is essential to our long-term energy security, and the best evidence available suggests that it can be achieved at acceptable costs."[18]

Why are there such great differences in the estimates of solar possibilities for the decades just ahead? Partly because of a difference in definitions: the high estimates usually include existing hydropower and the low estimates do not. Partly because of differing enthusiasms of the estimators. Partly because nobody can know what will happen. The diversity of estimates makes difficulties for sound thinking and planning. Most partisans in current debates are likely to pick their estimates to fit their conclusions—not a very sound way of reasoning. But even with the wide range of estimates, there is a visible emerging consensus for a range of seven to twenty percent. Though far from precise, that is much better than arguments assuming either that solar energy will be negligible or that it will easily resolve our problems.

Thus far the progress of solar energy has fallen behind most predictions. Nicholas Panagakos wrote in 1975: "Twenty-five years ago, a Presidential commission on solar energy applications predicted that by 1975 there would be about 13 million American homes heated by solar energy. Instead, today there are only about a dozen."[19] One reason for the delay was the cheap price of oil; another was incredible cultural and governmental lethargy. The recent surge of interest in solar energy gives hope for an increased tempo of action. It is desirable to strive for the higher estimates of solar energy by the year 2000; it is neither reasonable nor moral to count on the higher estimates or let them dull awareness of the world's needs.

The end of waste—in the forms both of inefficiency and of extravagant consumption—remains essential. Here there is some good news. Several eminent studies show that greatly increased efficiency in energy usage is possible.[20] They break the old association of a rise in economic productivity with an equal rise in energy consumption. They make the argument that the United States can continue strong economic growth with modest growth in energy usage. Many large corporations, alert to "the bottom line," are achieving impressive feats of conservation.

The same studies are less helpful on stabilizing or reducing consumption of energy. The reason is that most of the new efficiencies they commend depend on industrial innovations that are most achievable in an expanding economy. Even so, conservation appears increasingly prominent among the "sources" of energy for the future.

Some politicians, arguing that conservation at best postpones troubles by a short time, still insist that increased production is the only answer. But they have trouble specifying realistic plans for that increased production and they fail to reckon with two advantages of conservation. (1) If it brings a society closer to the break-even point where renewable resources match consumption, it is a positive gain. (2) The postponement of trouble extends opportunities for the research and development that offer some promises for the future.

It is foolish to be dogmatic about the energy future: technology may be more or less successful in replacing diminishing resources with new resources. But a modest conclusion is possible. The world's billions of people cannot consume energy on the scale familiar to the wealthiest societies; and the wealthiest societies cannot maintain their present ways undisturbed.

THE LOCUS OF DECISION MAKING

Many social decisions, I said in Chapter 2, seem just to "happen." But always somebody is deciding something. So we must ask of any option: who decides? And, where is the decision made? The locus of decision making is as important as the content of the decision. Often the former determines the latter.

Through much of human history the big social decisions have been in the hands of kings, tyrants, military leaders, bishops, and other members of an elite group within a hierarchical society. As history went on, technological elites became more powerful. But a counteridea has also taken hold in the world: all people should have a share in the decisions that affect their own lives. Democracy has been an effort with some limited success to institutionalize this idea.

It has become banal to talk about the present world's conflict between democracies and dictatorships. Within all forms of government there is the persistent issue of locating the decision making. Which decisions are made in central governments, in regional and local governments, in laboratories, in offices of industry, in labor organizations, in churches, in schools, in homes? On questions of energy, who decides the big questions and the little questions that add up to big questions?

When the World Council of Churches, through its Sub-Unit on Church and Society, made a presentation to the International Atomic Energy Agency at Salzburg (1977), it called for "the widest possible public discussion" and insisted that "every human being has a voice and a stake" in decisions about nuclear energy.[21] Here was a religious testimony that specialists in government and technology did not have the moral right to impose their decisions upon unconsulted publics. The World Council of Churches has affirmed its commitment to a society that is *just, sustainable,* and *participatory.* I have already said something about justice and sustainability in relation to energy. I must now say something about public participation.

A citizen, to participate meaningfully in the major public decisions, needs an education that is overwhelming in scope. Such a citizen needs to know something about economics, including fiscal and monetary theories and their bearing on inflation and unemployment; about military strategies, weapons, and budgets; about biological science and medical practice; about political processes; about the relation of crime to society and to punishment; about a hundred other pressing topics. The question of the relation of technical knowledge and social decisions is at the heart of this book. It comes up in every chapter, and in Chapter 12 I draw together some of the results and propose some conclusions.

For the moment I shall take up only one issue in the larger problem, an issue that has won wide attention in debates about energy. There are obvious advantages in small-scale decisions that people and communities make for themselves. All of us know something about looking out for our own interests; we are less sure that distant officials of government and industry are looking out for our interests. I know how to participate in the operation of my household, but I am perplexed about participating in the important decisions, affecting me, of the White House, the Congress, the giant corporations that produce and sell energy. So the public mood, after a long fascination with big enterprises and economies of scale, has a new interest in decentralization.

Roman Catholic moral theology has traditionally emphasized the principle of subsidiarity. It means that decisions should be made by the smallest and most local body that can competently and fairly make them. That means keeping decisions close to the people involved, rather than bucking them up the line to higher and more distant authorities.

The current uneasiness with distant, powerful authorities—who may not know as much as they claim to know and who may use their knowledge for their own advantage—has expressed itself in the wide public interest in the book *Small Is Beautiful*[22] by the late British economist E. F. Schumacher. It is not the biggest technology but the most appropriate technology that attracts Schumacher. Out of extensive experience in many parts of the world he argues that small and simple technologies are often better—more economical, more reliable, more repairable—than big and intricate technologies. If I rely upon household helps that I can manage and maintain, I escape craven dependence on the distant specialists and organizations that I never see.

Schumacher and many others have applied this theme to energy. In popular discussion it has led to a preference, for example, for solar roof panels on houses instead of reliance upon nuclear reactors, which clearly are not small and manageable by householders.

But generalizations based on examples need examination. I, for one, thoroughly endorse the subtitle of Schumacher's famous book: *Economics as if People Mattered.* I endorse the main title, *Small Is Beautiful,* as a response to intoxication with the big, the elaborate, the grandiose. But not as a universal major premise for all occasions. Big whales are, by most human standards, more beautiful than small cockroaches; people themselves are more "beautiful" than tiny polio bacilli.

On matters of energy the argument for the small and decentralized can be deceptive. Its merit is its emphasis on using the most modest forms of energy that will do a job worth doing. It is most impressive when directed against the enormous extravagance of societies entranced by their own achievements and blind to their limitations. I expect that—if humanity survives—more chastened generations will look at our time as an era of fixated adolescence in the industrial societies.

But there are two problems in decentralization. The first is that it is sometimes simply inefficient. A major example is transportation.

The private automobile is—apart from walking, which has merits worth rediscovery—the ultimate decentralization of urban transportation. As a driver of my own car, I enjoy much more power in decision making than as a passenger on bus, subway, railroad, or airline. I set my own schedule and route to suit myself. I feel in charge. It is this delight in private cars, in a civilization that glorifies individualism, that has led to excessive consumption of energy and the neglect of public transportation. The future of industrial civilization will require greater centralization of transportation.

That will mean also centralized production of energy. The subways of New York, Tokyo, London, and Paris will not run on electricity coming from solar panels on their roofs. Whatever the source, it will be big and centralized.

A study of energy consumption in the United States showed that the lowest per capita consumption of energy was in New York State, the highest in Texas.[23] The reasons are obvious. New Yorkers, though not inherently more virtuous than Texans, are more urbanized; they travel less by car, more by public transportation; they use more apartment dwellings, fewer private houses. The data are not an argument for urbanization; rural life can be economical and desirable. But a world of four billion people is going to need some centralization of energy production and distribution.

The same situation applies to industry. Gerald Foley in his study of British industry between 1960 and 1972 concluded that "the move from labour-intensive methods to highly automated and centralized production systems not only eliminated much dangerous and unpleasant work but resulted in a very large increase in the efficiency of energy utilization."[24] On the other hand, recently some industries in several countries have found some advantages in decentralization, and new techniques in communication increase the possibilities of efficient, economic decentralization. My point is not to argue for either centralization or decentralization. It is to argue against slogans that stop thinking, particularly the kind of concrete inquiry that upsets easy generalizations.

The second problem in decentralization is that it often exaggerates local interests as against wider interests. It is sobering to remember that in the United States the old battle to maintain racial segregation was usually fought under banners of "states rights" and "local determination." Sometimes the more encompassing authority corrects wrongs stemming from the declared interests of local political and economic entities.

In many societies it has become obvious that most people want (1) more energy (2) produced farther away from their homes. People want access to energy (and trains and airplanes and industrial products), but they don't want to live next door to power plants (or railroad tracks or airports or factories). In industrial societies centralized authorities have sometimes ruthlessly overridden local communities for the sake of a real or presumed wider social good. In reaction, local groups in many countries have learned new tactics of standing up against the more centralized authorities. When they win, it is with the thrill of David defeating Goliath. But the hidden reality is that too often the groups that win are those with the political and economic clout to protect themselves, while poorer and less powerful groups suffer.

The issue of the location of decision making is closely related to the prior issue: dependence, independence, interdependence. The basic assumption must be that human life is life-in-community. There is no total independence. The political-economic-technical issue is to ensure people some rights of self-determination, some significant participation in the larger processes on which they depend, some authentic interdependence. To achieve this in matters of energy as in most issues of contemporary life will require both techniques and imagination not yet realized.

4. Food for a Hungry World

Food is absolutely essential to life. That needs no argument.

Furthermore, healthy life requires more than an adequate quantity of food. People can stuff their stomachs daily and still suffer disease and death because they do not get adequate proteins and vitamins. None of this is controversial.

In today's world many people starve or suffer from malnutrition. Other people overeat, waste food, and cut back on overproduction of food. Such facts are obvious.

But after the obvious facts are stated the arguments begin. The simple desire to relieve hunger soon leads to complicated and controversial matters of nutrition, agricultural systems, economics, politics, demography, and culture, until most human institutions and values are involved.

THE SCOPE OF THE PROBLEM

Among many controversies and uncertainties, a few things stand out clearly. Four propositions give a sense of the scope of the problem.

1. The number of people who suffer from hunger is overwhelming. The World Food Council of the United Nations reckons that "close to 500 million people suffer from a significant degree of malnutrition," and the World Bank estimates that "more than one billion people suffer from some degree of energy deficiency related to diet."[1] Some of these people starve to death. More die from diseases that they could resist if they had adequate food. A standard estimate is that ten thousand people a day die from starvation or the consequences of malnutrition. That is the figure that President Nixon used in a message to Congress in 1969,[2] and Nixon did not usually use the figures

of left-wing propagandists. Furthermore, 1969 was a good year for food production—before the droughts and crop failures of 1972–1974 (in the Soviet Union, South Asia, and the African Sahel) that reduced grain reserves so severely and doubled or tripled deaths from hunger. Ivan Bennett, Jr., former chairman of the U.S. Panel on the World Food Supply, said in 1970: "there are today in the world more hungry mouths than ever before in history."[3] And two years later there were many more. A precarious improvement came with the bumper crops of 1975–1978, but the basic problem persisted. The year 1979 brought the special problems of starvation in Cambodia, and 1980 brought the agonies of the eastern Horn of Africa.

Most of us could not bear to live alongside a starving person without doing something to help. But we live in a world where starvation is common, and most of the time we screen the evidence out of our perception.

2. Uncounted thousands of people suffer from mental deficiency because of inadequate protein in their diets during the crucial years of infancy. Between a hundred thousand and two hundred and fifty thousand children go blind each year, especially in the Middle East and India, because of a deficiency of vitamin A.[4] Many, many more endure other disabilities due to defects in diet. Poverty and ignorance cause mental and physical handicaps; then the handicaps add to the burden of poverty and ignorance. A turnabout could change the vicious circle to a beneficent circle.

3. Some people and some societies eat far more than other people and other societies—by a monumental amount. Differences in eating habits that are obvious at any picnic become multiplied by cultural habits and situations. In the most literal sense it may seem impossible that the average person in the United States could eat—day in and day out—five times as much as the average person in India or Southeast Asia. After all, there are limits to the human body's ability to digest food. But the real facts are more impressive than the obvious facts. In some societies people eat a lot of grain. In other societies they eat most of their grain after it has been processed by fowl and animals into eggs, milk, and meat. Even a modest steak usually represents far more grain than its size and weight betray.

4. The problem includes both production and distribution. On the relation between the two, experts argue. Georg Borgstrom writes:

"Let us also put to rest the glib notion that feeding the world is merely a question of distribution. . . . Equal distribution of all available food would only make hunger universal and shared by everyone."[5] But Ivan Bennett argues: "The basic problem of world hunger is that of uneven distribution of the food supply. . . . Statistical surveys show that there is no *global* shortage of food, either in terms of quantity (measured in calories) or quality (measured as *protein*)."[6] This chapter looks later at some reasons for such disagreements. For the moment it is enough to say that both increased production and improved distribution require immense *technical* and *social* (political and economic) achievements. And the burden of the problem will increase with the doubled population that is expected in another thirty-five to forty years.

These four propositions are part of a situation that is both ethically disturbing and dangerous. To be offended by starvation requires no specially ethical conscience. Failure to act to relieve famine "would be gross immorality according to world-wide standards."[7] It was not the most exalted ethic of the Hebrew prophets but the common folk wisdom that said, "If your enemy is hungry, give him bread to eat" (Prov. 25:21). Relief of starvation seems, at first, to be about as simple an ethical responsibility as anybody can find. The world's major religions, including secular humanism, all recognize the point.[8] For Jews (the people of the Passover Seder) and Christians (the people of the Lord's Supper) the central ritual act of faith is the sharing of food.

But in our world such sharing is not simple. World hunger, like all the forced options described in this book, requires attention to two kinds of problems.

The first is technical. A fresh egg in Arkansas is not a fresh egg in the African Horn. To get an egg from Arkansas to the Horn requires a transportation network including innumerable people, elaborate equipment, fuel, and an international economic system as well as infrastructures at every stage of the way. The building of the infrastructures would, ironically, mean paving over some land that now produces food. The whole business adds up to a stupendous achievement and a lot of money. And if the achievement were to come off, it might turn out that moving eggs from Arkansas is not really a good way to relieve protein deficiencies in the diet of children in the African Horn.

The second problem is a matter of ethical will and social institutions. Vague good will is not enough. Even the strongest good will that most people feel at moments of intense concern is not enough. The good will must take shape in institutions—agricultural, economic, political. If it turns out that the affluence of some people in Africa and some of us in the industrialized West is built upon the hunger of other people, then we who are affluent will be slow to act. We may not knowingly want hunger in Africa; we may even give some money to relieve hunger. But we shall be slow to recognize our own complicity in the situation, and we shall find many plausible reasons not to encourage the radical institutional changes that could help.

Both these problems require elaboration. That is what the rest of this chapter is about.

FOOD AND ENERGY

Food is energy. And food requires energy for its production and distribution. In detail, those two statements include some startling facts.

By one way of reckoning, food production in industrialized societies has been a story of dazzling success. Around the world about half the people live on farms and produce food, but in industrial societies a far smaller number of people produce food for all. In colonial North America about ninety percent of the people engaged in farming.[9] By 1900, one farmer was able to feed five people. And by now one farmer can feed almost fifty.[10] Simultaneously, yields per acre have risen dramatically, and the United States is the world's leading exporter of food. Contrary to expectations of the recent past, the United States has turned out to be a world leader in food production while it is failing to compete successfully in what was suppose to be its industrial strength—automobile production.

A consumer in India is likely to spend seventy-five to eighty percent of take-home pay on food, in a good agricultural year. In the United States the average family spends about fifteen percent of take-home pay on food.[11] All this is the celebrated story of agricultural efficiency in a highly industrialized society.

But examine the facts more closely. The farmer who feeds almost fifty people is not a lone individual. This farmer is backed up by industries that manufacture and service farm machinery, other industries that make fertilizers and insecticides, and still other industries that process and distribute food. All in all, it is not one farmer but perhaps sixteen people in many walks of life who feed the forty-five to fifty.[12] Still, there is an impressive demonstration of certain kinds of efficiency here.

But now look at efficiency in a different way. In some tropical areas a peasant growing rice puts into the effort one calorie of energy and draws out fifty calories of food to be eaten by the family on the spot. More generally, in so-called primitive cultures and in some highly civilized societies an investment of one calorie brings a yield of five to fifty calories. That is obviously good productivity. In the United States by 1900 an input of one calorie was bringing an output of only one calorie. And by 1970 the society was expending about nine calories of energy to get one calorie back on the dinner table.[13] That is low productivity.

Even so, that system may be profitable—both to producers and consumers—*if* the calories expended are cheap and plentiful forms of energy and the calories consumed are more scarce and valuable. As long as petroleum, for example, was cheap and abundant, there was no particular problem in the fact that the United Kingdom and the United States consumed, to feed each person, three times the average amount of fuel used *per capita* for *all* purposes in that majority of the world called "developing."[14] Obviously the world cannot imitate this model. Even the wealthiest nations must question it as petroleum becomes more scarce and expensive.

What is in question is not simply methods of farming; it is the whole way of organizing a society. The figures on energy input/output involve not only the growing of crops but the getting of them to the consumer. Only about a fourth of the total energy is expended in raising and harvesting the crop. After that comes the processing and the distribution—the packaging, trucking, the maintenance of freezing temperatures in frozen-food sections of supermarkets, and all the rest. The figures do not, however, include the consumers' use of cars in driving to markets or the costs of garbage disposal—two more costs that have been rising dramatically.

The whole situation calls for a reappraisal of efficiency. In a time of energy shortages and unemployment, efficiency might mean reduced energy consumption and more human labor—just the opposite of what efficiency has usually been taken to mean. If this is true in an energy-rich nation like the United States, it is even more true in countries that have no petroleum or coal.

According to wide report Senator Daniel Patrick Moynihan, in one of his characteristically undiplomatic moments, said to representatives of the Third World: "Food growing is the first thing you do when you come down out of the trees. The question is, how come the United States can grow food and you can't?" He knew, of course, that all countries grow food, but he was proposing that hungry countries might learn from the United States how to grow more. But the facts on energy–food ratios show that the methods used in the United States would be catastrophic if applied to the whole world. They may not work much longer even here.

SOLUTIONS THAT MAKE NEW PROBLEMS

One answer to food shortages is to produce more food. The celebrated Green Revolution of the mid-twentieth century has done that on a grand scale.

Actually, this achievement is the latest stage in a much longer revolution in food production. The most important leap of all came about 9000–7000 B.C. with the beginnings of agriculture through the domestication of wheat and barley. The second great leap came about 6000 B.C. with the domestication of animals. The unknown heroes and heroines of these achievements did more to change human existence than any group of scientists since that ancient time. There have been many more leaps through the centuries. Our century has made its addition, small in the whole picture, but the most spectacular of all in its speed and immediate quantitative results.

The long perspective helps show what is happening. In hunting-gathering societies people fed themselves on seeds, berries, nuts, roots, insects, worms, fish, and animals killed in the hunt. Without agriculture the world might have been able to sustain only twenty to forty million people, less than a hundredth of the number now alive.

Agriculture means a reduction in the number of foods eaten. Instead of picking up whatever is edible, people select a few plants (their favorites or the most productive) and cultivate them. Consumers still enjoy variety; a large American supermarket carries about sixteen thousand products. But out of about eighty thousand edible species, only twelve now provide ninety percent of the world's crops.[15]

Agriculture also means increased productivity. For example, the ancestor of our corn was a grass with an "ear" of edible seeds the size of a thumbnail. Over the centuries hybridization, natural and humanly contrived, and the selection of seeds have produced modern varieties of corn.

This fantastic gain comes at a cost—a cost that people gladly pay but had better think about. The original corn seeded itself and grew without any human attention; a modern cornpatch, neglected for a year or two, is just about useless, although somebody might find a few edible weeds in it.

Furthermore, almost any year is a good year for some crops and a bad year for others. A hunting-gathering society eating hundreds of species may scarcely notice a bad year for a few species. But agricultural societies can really suffer if it's a bad year for corn or wheat or rice. And monocultures invite bad years. The insects that thrive on corn had to do a lot of hunting for their food when corn was one of the many grasses in prairies. Now those insects find that farmers have arranged meals more conveniently for them. So agriculture is more vulnerable to threats like the Irish potato famine of 1846, which brought starvation to an estimated 1.5 million people.

A scientific agriculture learns how to defeat insect predators with pesticides. But insects unpredictably mutate or build up resistance against the pesticides, and the pesticides sometimes do unexpected damage to human beings and ecosystems. In the constant struggle food producers aspire to invulnerability but sometimes unwittingly create more precarious systems.

The Green Revolution of this century achieved some startling successes with its new varieties of wheat, corn, and rice. A dramatic example is the jump in production of wheat in India from eleven million to twenty-six million tons in seven years (1965–1972). Mexico, Pakistan, Turkey, the Philippines, Taiwan, Indonesia, Malaysia, and Sri Lanka are some of the other countries that have used the new varieties of seed to increase food production on a big scale. Worldwide, the production of food since World War II has outrun the population explosion by a modest margin. No wonder Norman Borlaug, the most noted pioneer in the Green Revolution, won the Nobel Peace Prize in 1970.

Like all technical achievements, the Green Revolution brings problems. These are of the usual two kinds: technical and social.

Of the technical problems, the first is that the new varieties of seeds require great quantities of fertilizer to achieve their potential. Without fertilizer they often are less productive than traditional crops. And the dependence on fertilizer comes at a time when fertilizers are rising in cost. They also frequently require irrigation, in a world where water is increasingly scarce (see Chapter 6). And, because they require fertilizer (some of it made from petroleum or natural gas) and water (much of it pumped), they require more energy.

Norman Borlaug reports that China prior to 1960 maintained good soil fertility by careful use of organic fertilizers and compost. But by 1973, in its steps to increase food production, it had become "the world's largest importer of urea and other solid nitrogenous fertilizers."[16] When the OPEC petroleum embargo threatened its supplies of fertilizer, it initiated its own systems of fertilizer production, importing technologies from the United States and Japan, in a program that will mean investments of perhaps $7–8 billion.[17] Even so, China in 1980 signed an agreement to buy about eight million metric tons of grain annually from the United States for a period of four years. Such acts are not possible for the poorest countries. India did not fare so well. Shortages of fertilizer and energy were a major cause in the reduction of India's wheat crop from a projected thirty million to an actual twenty-three million metric tons in 1974.[18]

Another technical problem of the Green Revolution is that the new seeds have not, like traditional crops, built up resistances over the centuries to diseases. Nobody knows how vulnerable they may be to an unpredictable onslaught. And because of their genetic uniformity, they may suffer destruction in a way that more diverse crops would not. Some of the "miracle" rices have proved susceptible to disease. In the United States a corn leaf blight cut the crop in half throughout several southern states in 1970. A large and food-rich country can absorb such a loss (it was only fifteen to twenty percent of the national corn crop), but for some countries it would bring great suffering and death.

These technical risks of the Green Revolution must be weighed against the starvation that it has prevented. They are a warning of the dangers in pushing any system of food production to its limits.

The social problems connected with the Green Revolution are quite different in nature. They are comparable to those in any technological change. To repeat a point that runs through this book, technology is power, and the benefits and harms of power depend upon the people and social systems that use it.

The first social problem is that the Green Revolution often functions to increase the gap between rich and poor in a society. The farmers who gain from it are those with money and know-how. As Lester Brown points out, "In countries and locales where farmers with large holdings have better access to credit and to technical advisory services, rich farmers often get richer and poor farmers often get poorer."[19] Further, while the new crops and more intensive agriculture often increase the number of jobs, sometimes mechanization (available to the wealthy) displaces farm workers, who may then migrate to cities and join the urban unemployed. Government policies often encourage mechanization that is economically harmful to the society as a whole. The whole process may end up by a concentration of land ownership by prosperous farmers and a displacement of tenant farmers and landless laborers.

Such change often discriminates against women. They are, says a U.N. report, "the majority of the world's food producers." However, "they are more likely than men to be malnourished, overemployed, uneducated and demeaned in their roles as agriculture is modernized."[20]

The second social problem is the increased reliance on imports. Many countries must import fertilizers, machinery, fuel, pesticides, and sometimes hybrid seed. These imports increase dependence on external sources of supply. They also mean that the country must export something of value in order to get the foreign exchange to pay for the imports. So the agricultural economy becomes skewed toward exports rather than toward the hungry people at home. The blame does not belong to the Green Revolution; the process was at work long before this century. But the economic mechanisms accompanying the Green Revolution have helped it along.

THE STORY OF LATINAFRASIA

Latinafrasia is an imaginary nation, but it is not unreal. It represents a composite of many countries on three continents. Its story is symbolic of the troubles of much of the contemporary world.

For many centuries Latinafrasia was an agricultural country in which peasants raised most of their own food, buying and exchanging some in local markets. It had a high birth rate and high infant mortality rate, with a total population growing at a manageable rate. Traditional patterns of life persisted from generation to generation.

Great changes came to Latinafrasia in the period of the colonial empires. It does not matter for this story whether the country was conquered by imperial armies or whether it simply got swept into imperial economies. Somebody discovered that this country was a marvelous place to grow crop X. Crop X might be a food like cocoa (cacao beans) or bananas or sugar. It might be an edible nonfood like coffee. It might be a nonedible agricultural product like cotton or rubber or carnations. Such details don't matter. What matters is that a hectare of land in such crops produced more money—hard money, valid in international transactions—than the same land used traditionally for growing local crops.

So the country turned to the new crop. The decision might have been made by a Western European conquering nation, by an American corporation moving into the country and buying land, or by local landowners making contracts with foreign importers. In any case, the use of land followed the money.

With foreign exchange earned by the exports, the nation could buy many imported products. It imported some foods. It imported machinery and petroleum to run the machinery. It imported many manufactured goods. Then, as old-fashioned colonialism went out of style, Latinafrasia built factories so that it could manufacture its own consumer goods, but it had to pay out cash and go in debt for the factories and the energy to run them. It increased its exports to pay the bills and the interest on its rising debts.

Simultaneously, new medical techniques brought a swift drop in infant mortality and a rise in population. Even so, average per capita income and consumption rose. So did literacy and travel. With electrification in urban areas, people bought electrical refrigerators and television sets. Automobiles and trucks led to the building of new roads. Airplanes needed airports and supporting services. Petroleum imports increased still more. The national debt increased and brought greater pressures for exports.

Today Latinafrasia faces several perplexities. The average family no longer grows its food; it buys the food and a lot else that its ancestors never used. Although the country has doubled its population in the last twenty-five years, it has more than doubled its food consumption (in local produce plus imports). But unemployment is high. Some people hover on the edge of starvation. Some children grow up blind or mentally disabled because of inadequate diet.

There are protests. There is crime in urban slums. There is festering discontent. There are riots. An incessant argument goes on between protestors and the elite who run the country's government and business.

Protestors: Why are we exporting this produce (coffee, cocoa, cotton, rubber, bananas, or carnations) when we might be growing food for our hungry people to eat? (Or, why do we export fishmeal to feed chickens and hogs in rich countries when our children are disabled by protein deficiency?)

Elite: These exports enable us to import things we need. We now feed a much larger population than we fed before. We have wiped out some diseases. Life expectancy is longer. We are electrifying. The per capita GNP of this growing country is much higher than it would be without the exports.

Protestors: But the country has become dependent on imports and we cannot control the rise in their prices. And we cannot even control the prices on our exports. (If only we had oil!) A distant commodity market determines our destiny. We're getting a bad deal.

Elite: But we're creating wealth in this nation. Be patient. It will reach you.

Protestors: We don't see it coming. Our family farms are almost gone. A peasant farmer cannot grow cacao or coffee; it's four to eight years from planting to a crop. That requires big capital investment, and it works best on large plantations. So agribusiness takes over the old family farms and employs a few of us. But it replaces workers with machines. Our children go to the cities, where a few hit it rich and the others are unemployed. The rising average income of the nation means a lower income for many of us. The crops that we export bring us roads and cars that the majority of us cannot use and airplanes that very few of us can use. This system looks like a conspiracy of our government and our rich people with foreign countries against most of us.

The controversy goes on, with local variations, in most of the world. It is not surprising that the world press carries almost daily reports of riots, revolutionary plots, or coups d'etat in the many Latinafrasias of this world. It is no wonder that revolutionary ideologies erupt in many places. The wonder is that so many people in centers of power argue that the answer to such ideologies is new weapons and greater military power.

One response to such a world is ethical outrage. But outrage is not a program that will correct the intolerable situation. It is not *necessarily* unwise for a hungry country to direct part of its production toward exports, if it can thereby get needed imports. The U.N. World Food Council has recognized that "the ability of developing countries to earn foreign exchange and thus to import the food they cannot grow is essential to their self-reliance."[21] There is a general, though approximate, correlation between the exports of nations and their economic growth. The troubles come when the international trading game is stacked against the hungry countries and when the exports benefit the wealthy at the cost of the hungry.

Thus any answer to the world's hunger must look at a lot besides hunger. I soon suggest some possible answers. But first I must look at the arguments of those who say that *no* possible answer is adequate.

COUNSELS OF DESPAIR

When the problem is as tough and painful as starvation, there is no use in sentimental gestures that really don't change the harsh realities. And there is no use for misguided benevolence that unintentionally does more harm than good. So it is not surprising that the world hears many calls for hard-nosed thinking that faces the facts.

One such call, which by now has reverberated around the world, came from William and Paul Paddock in their book of 1967, *Famine 1975.* [22] They saw the world careening into an unavoidable crisis of starvation. A 1976 revised edition, *Time of Famine,* reported that events had confirmed most of the earlier predictions.

The Paddock brothers, one an agronomist and the other a retired foreign service officer of the U.S. State Department, saw no possible way of preventing massive starvation. They believed that the United States, with its wealth and technical skills, could not meet the world-wide problem but could do something. Their proposal made famous the French word *triage.*

They took the term from the practice in battlefield hospitals receiving more wounded soldiers than they can possibly help. Medical staff divide the wounded into three groups: (1) those who will die in spite of efforts to save them or relieve their pain; (2) those who can survive without the treatment that could spare them pain, (3) those who can be saved from death by medical attention.

In a tragically cruel logic the staff neglect the first two groups and concentrate on the third. The Paddocks recommended a comparable food policy for the United States. In addition they would quite candidly, without any hypocritical pretenses, "favor nations which have military value to the United States."[23] This nation should neglect the nations that cannot be saved (examples in 1967: India, Egypt, Haiti) and that can make it without help (example: Libya), in order to concentrate on the nations where help can make a genuine difference (examples: Pakistan, Tunisia).

The proposals caused an uproar. Paul Ehrlich hailed them as the only "realistic suggestion" and "national choice"[24] available, and he proposed his own revised version of them. But more than the Paddocks he called on changed patterns of consumption in American society; and he later came to a far more complex understanding of the relation of hunger, population, and economic development.[25]

On the other side, in religious and humanitarian organizations, almost all discussions of world hunger single out the proposal of triage for moral condemnation. They see it as a deliberate hardheartedness that inflicts unnecessary suffering and demoralizes the society that practices it.

But in fairness to the Paddocks I should point out that their declared aim is to use limited resources in the most "humanitarian" way possible for the sake of a " 'better' world for our children."[26] They oppose the American drift to isolationism, and they are ready to curtail American food consumption in order to maintain foreign aid.

Second, I must observe reluctantly that the response to proposals of triage has often been ethical horror combined with practical acquiescence in something worse than triage. Food exports from the United States, as from most countries, go primarily not where the need is greatest but where the money is. For example, the huge grain sales of the United States to the Soviet Union (until the embargo following the Soviet invasion of Afghanistan) were prescribed not by Soviet need but by Soviet ability to pay. Former Senator Dick Clark has pointed out the decreased food aid and increased food sales of the United States in the 1970s. And he has shown that most of the aid went for military and political rather than humanitarian purposes.[27]

Third, I have to say that there are situations of tragic necessity in which triage is morally responsible. The battlefield hospital is an example. I don't *know* how I would act if I were a wounded soldier in groups 1 or 2; I might cry out for relief from excruciating pain. I *hope* I would agree that the doctors should pass me by to help those in group 3. I do not say that prolonging life is *always* more important than comforting the dying, and I assume that doctors will make mistakes in estimating which patients they can save. But in the specific situation I think triage is as good a policy as anybody can design. Certainly it is ethically better than a policy by which the doctors give their services to the highest bidders, to their friends, or to those who promise to side with the doctors against their critics.

But the real issue is whether the field hospital is a valid analogy with the world today. Any analogy that desensitizes the moral perceptions of the wealthy and powerful requires skeptical scrutiny. There may be options better than triage.

Before turning to those, I must look at one alternative even more "tough-minded"—if that phrase is accurate—than triage. It is Garrett Hardin's "lifeboat ethics." When I quoted Hardin with approval in Chapter 2, I said that I had disagreements with him. The time has come to state them.

In a metaphor that has become famous, Hardin sees the affluent industrialized world—and notably the United States—as passengers in a lifeboat surrounded by drowning people who want to clamber aboard. Some passengers in sentimental mercy might help them get in. But the lifeboat is already loaded to capacity. To take on more people will mean that the boat and all its passengers go down. It is better to save some than none. So it becomes morally responsible for those on the lifeboat to resist the others and let them drown.[28]

Hardin makes one other portentous point. He believes that "foreign aid" from the affluent nations actually increases worldwide suffering. By preventing starvation now, it enables people to survive and reproduce, with the outcome that more people starve in the next generation. After twenty-five years of foreign aid, he argues, the number of malnourished people in the world has risen from 1.5 to 2.5 billion people. The seeming charity was really an amiability detrimental to real charity.[29]

Hardin has become an even more conspicuous target of ethical criticism than the Paddock brothers.[30] Before joining the critics, I want to point out two aspects of Hardin's position. First, he is not simply a complacent defender of privileged people and nations; he calls for a radical transformation of the extravagant, destructive economic habits of the affluent societies. Second, he wants his critics to face a rigorous ethical question: do you really advocate prevention of starvation if the consequence is increased starvation? He has every right to press that painful question—just as I have the equal right to ask whether it is the real question and whether the lifeboat is a helpful metaphor for our world.

To start with the lifeboat, suppose the surrounding swimmers have guns and have managed to keep them dry; suppose they can sink the lifeboat; and suppose that in their anger they are ready to sink it whether or not that helps them survive. Robert Heilbroner makes the forceful case that—to shift from metaphor to fact—many angry societies will soon have nuclear weapons and, though they cannot "win" a nuclear war, they will be ready in their desperation to destroy the affluent centers of power. To this possibility Hardin has only the futile answer of increased security measures.[31]

The logic of the lifeboat fails, even in the crudest pragmatic meaning, if the whole human race are passengers on an ocean liner with a gash in the hull. If the ship is going down, there is no comfort for first-class passengers in noticing that the hole is in the third-class section.

Both Hardin and the Paddock brothers have been willing to throw brutally fierce questions into the face of a public that wants to avoid them. I find their challenges less morally offensive than the indifference and moral evasions that characterize the public at large in the affluent world. But I resist their counsels of despair. There are in the situation possibilities that even they, on occasion, acknowledge.

A GLIMMER OF HOPE

Frances Moore Lappé and Joseph Collins are two people who believe that there are effective answers to the world's hunger and starvation. They say so—emphatically and polemically—in their book *Food First: Beyond the Myth of Scarcity.* The core of their case is startling in its promise and its simplicity: "Every country can and must mobilize its own food resources to meet its own needs. . . . *Every country in the world has the capacity to feed itself.*"[32]

The argument is that even the countries with the worst starvation and malnutrition could produce enough calories and proteins for *all* their people if they would produce basic foods (grains and legumes) for everybody instead of (1) raising fodders to feed cattle to produce meat for the wealthy and (2) growing crops for export.

If the answer sounds too easy, Lappé and Collins recognize the difficulties. They say that their answer would require extensive land reforms, assigning land to people who could eat its crops rather than to wealthy individuals and corporations more interested in cash income. And it would require radical changes in national and international economies.

They back up their argument by showing examples of one country after another that has exported food while its people were starving. For example, Bangladesh smugglers have exported food to India, where prices were higher. And in the time of starvation following the 1974 floods, millions of tons of rice piled up in warehouses because people were too poor to buy it. In the African Sahel (the drought-stricken sub-Sahara region), ships brought in food granted to relieve hunger, then left with "hundreds of millions of dollars worth" of "peanuts, cotton, vegetables, and meat." As if to support Lappé and Collins, the Inter-American Development Bank reported in 1979 that while Latin American population was outracing food production, a rising percentage of food (especially beef) was being exported.[33]

Lappé and Collins have not convinced all their critics. They write with the passion of crusaders who have found the villains and enjoy excoriating them. I am not convinced that they have seen the complexity of the problem as clearly as Lester Brown or as Paul and Arthur Simon. Nor am I convinced that "scarcity" is a "myth." But I want to point to a remarkable convergence of findings from people with utterly different ideological positions. The Paddock brothers and Garrett Hardin are at opposite ends of most ideological spectra from Lappé and Collins, so their agreements are worth noticing.

The Paddocks say:

If a hungry nation were to give total time, attention and money to the single, narrow problem of increasing local food production—while at the same time striving to lower population growth—then there could be hope of an escape from the impending famines.

No nation seems ready for such Draconian action.[34]

And Garrett Hardin recognizes that some societies, where people once were drowning in the sea of hunger, have built some pretty sturdy lifeboats. His most notable example is China. Leftists and rightists all over the world are pretty well agreed that China, feeding a fourth of the world's people with an eighth of the arable land, has done an unpredicted and effective job in eliminating the worst of the hunger that once haunted that vast country. And Hardin points out that China's achievements came "without an iota of help from us, and almost none from anybody else," while countries that were getting international help often floundered and lost ground.[35]

Lappé and Collins, from their side, acknowledge that their claims for a realizable self-sufficiency in food for all nations will not hold true indefinitely if populations continue to grow. They differ from the Paddocks and Hardin about the ways to slow population growth—a topic for the next chapter of this book. But the differences do not obscure a widely shared recognition: there are ways of meeting world hunger.

If this means a glimmer of hope, it does not justify euphoria. I suggest two warnings.

First, we should be suspicious of arguments that make us comfortable. Such arguments *may* be valid; truth is not *always* discomforting. But human beings have a great capacity to welcome agreeable arguments and reject disturbing ones, quite apart from criteria of logical cogency. Lappé and Collins, the Paddocks, and Hardin all intend to disturb us and jolt us out of familiar prejudices. Yet all of them provide data—for example, about the counterproductivity of many foreign aid programs—that are welcomed by the most greedy and reactionary forces of our society. Ethically responsible people will not reject accurate data that scoundrels can also use; they will scrutinize the data and ask what other data have been omitted.

Second, none of the answers suggested gives any ground for complacency. Suppose we agree with Lappé and Collins and with the Paddocks that hungry nations could, with proper concentration of resources, overcome famine and give everybody an adequate though not exciting diet of grain and beans. The costs still have to be reckoned. The moral problem of exporting food from a hungry nation is obvious and vivid. The motives may be the sordid gain of the rich and powerful. But there may be other motives. Exports pay for imports. If a country lacking any coal or petroleum cuts off exports, it effectively cuts off imports of energy. That, too, has its human costs, including poverty and death. That is why China, for example, exports pork (its chief animal protein) in order to import grain and fertilizers.

But, without euphoria, hope is possible in the face of world hunger. That hope leads on to suggestions of possible directions of action.

POSSIBILITIES FOR ACTION

An ethically responsible approach to world hunger requires four major types of action. All are as necessary as the legs of a four-legged table. Remove any one leg and the table is unstable.

Technical Advances

The Green Revolution, which began eleven thousand years ago and took a leap forward in the twentiety century, can continue. Already it is trying new directions. Instead of reducing the number of species that feed the world, it is looking at new species or recovering ancient ones that have fallen out of style. Instead of concentrating on miracle grains that give spectacular performance in ideal conditions, it is working on drought-resistant, disease-resistant, pest-resistant varieties.

Soybeans, brought to the United States from Paris by Benjamin

Franklin, are spreading throughout the world. Amaranth, a high-protein grain used by the Aztecs and the Nepalese for centuries, has caught the interest of several major research centers. Triticale, a cross between wheat and rye, looks promising for its high-protein content and its ability to resist cold and drought. The buffalo gourd, grown by American Indians ten thousand years ago for its protein productivity in arid regions, is again the subject of research.

Experimentation is going on, with mixed results, with yeasts, bacteria, and other single-cell proteins. Earlier hopes for algae were too optimistic, but work goes on. A more far-out possibility is the cross-breeding of grains and legumes. Since grains withdraw nitrogen from the soil and legumes restore it, a hybrid might prove productive in poor soils without costly fertilization.

The U.N. World Food Conference of 1974 urged a "major acceleration" in food production of developing countries. Noting the benefits of the Green Revolution, it asked for "strengthening and improvement" of national seed programs.[36]

Another technical issue is the relation of food production to wider ecological systems. For example, the world's fish catch rose from twenty-one million to seventy-five million tons between 1950 and 1976, then went into a decline despite increasing efforts.[37] Overfishing becomes counterproductive—as does the overexpansion of agriculture into forests and grasslands. Better technical knowledge gives the basis for wiser policies of food production.

Nutritional knowledge is also important, both for affluent societies where some people prefer junk foods to healthy diets and for impoverished societies where lives are wrecked because people lack specific vitamins and proteins.

In all these cases technical knowledge is essential to sound choices. But, to repeat a theme, there is no technical fix. The effect of techniques depends upon the social systems that appropriate them.

Population Restraint

Since world food production has been rising faster than world population, population cannot be blamed as the primary cause of hunger. But a hungry society has trouble overcoming its food deficit if soaring food production is matched or (as in some areas) out-run by soaring population. This issue of population is so complex and so important that it is the subject of Chapter 5. For the moment, I can only say that it is one of the four necessary approaches to the problem of food.

Political and Economic Action

The starting point is the bitter, stubborn, ineradicable fact: rising food supplies for the world often are no help at all to the neediest. Even worse, more total food sometimes means less food for the hungriest. That situation requires attention to national and international politics and economics.

The World Food Conference in 1974 concluded that technical factors of food supply, though important, were less critical than political decisions by governments. To this finding, Maurice Williams, Executive Director of the World Food Council, adds: "The economic and technical potential for eliminating hunger and malnutrition exists. However, if the suffering of hungry millions is to be relieved, this potential requires a major and well-directed effort and the sustained political will to see it through."[38]

If the economy of Latinafrasia is dominated by an alliance between its rich people and wealthy foreign nations that buy its products, then increased food productivity won't help the poor. It may hurt them— if, for example, the rich use their income to mechanize farms and throw poor people out of work.

There are reforms that do relieve hunger, and they have come in a wide variety of social systems. Examples include Taiwan and South Korea as well as the People's Republic of China. None of these nations is a model of civil liberties. I would be unhappy in all of them. But they show that countries of vastly different ideologies can win victories against hunger.

One helpful step in some societies is land reform, a term that can mean many things. It has meant breaking up vast estates and distributing the land to families; it has meant merging small farms into huge collectives; it has meant experiments with co-ops and kibbutzim. There is no single pattern. But there is now considerable evidence that people get fed when they do their own farming and have a direct stake in the results. Large plantations with absentee landowners usually do the worst. Land reform is least useful when the land is poor and the people-to-land ratio is bad. According to one study, "Land is already pretty evenly distributed in the bulk of Asian countries—and the holdings are so small that while redistribution may save some of the rural poor from continued destitution, it will certainly not solve the poverty problem."[39] So land reform is no total answer. But in many societies it is a big part of the answer.

Sometimes a society has abundant supplies of food, but some people are simply too poor to buy it. The most bizarre example in the world is the United States. In 1967 the Senate Subcommittee on Employment, Manpower and Poverty heard pediatricians who testified to malnutrition and starvation among children in this lavishly food-rich country. In 1971 the Committee on Nutrition looked at the picture of a four-and-a-half-month-old child of migrant workers, diagnosed as sick from calorie starvation, scurvy, rickets, pneumonia, and lack of vitamin C.[40] In 1973 the Simon brothers reckoned that "11 million U.S. citizens below the poverty line and without food assistance cannot eat what they need," and that millions more "cannot afford an adequate diet."[41]

The need in the United States is not for higher food productivity. It is for urgent steps to overcome poverty. The United States may be unique in the contrast between general food abundance and deprivation of a minority, but in many societies the problem of food is directly the result of a general economic situation that allows searing poverty within a prosperous society. A U.N. report says: "Basically, the main obstacle to meeting the nutritional needs of large populations is one of poverty or lack of 'effective demand'—the ability of consumers to pay for the food and of farmers to market food at prices which cover the costs of production."[42] The need is for "development policies which increase employment for the rural landless and the urban poor and stimulate increased production by small subsistence farmers."

The situation within nations is magnified on the international scale. The answer becomes far more complex. What is the responsibility of food-rich nations for starvation in other nations?

One obvious answer is to send food to the needy. A press headline in 1978 said: "U.S. Grain Surplus Is Providing New Relief for World and Nation."[43] The United States is frequently called "the breadbasket of the world." Lester Brown wrote in 1974: ". . . the United States is now not only the world's major exporter of wheat and feed grains but also the world's leading exporter of rice. Indeed, North America

today controls a larger share of the world's exportable surplus of
grains than the Middle East does of current world oil exports."[44]

Some of these exports have saved people from starvation. But as I
have already said, money and military alliances, not sheer need, direct
most of the exports. Now I want to make the still more fundamental
point that charity is not the best long-range answer to food needs. The
ethical validity of food grants to meet emergencies or to help societies
through economic transitions needs no argument, but emergency
grants are not a permanent answer.

One reason is that the grantors are unreliable. The U.S. program
is a combination of genuine concern for hungry people, the need to
do something with agricultural surpluses, and the desire to assert
American power in the world. Any investigation of the maneuvers
used to get appropriations through Congress shows that. When surpluses dwindle exports go down. Thus the United States suddenly
imposed restrictions on exports of soybeans in June of 1973, relieving
inflation at home and increasing hunger and inflation abroad.[45]

A second reason is that permanent dependence on another nation
for necessities of national existence is painful to national morale. It
does not hurt the United States to depend on other nations for bananas and pineapples. A cut-off of supplies would not threaten the
security of the society. But to live permanently as a suppliant for
necessities is a very different matter.

A third reason is that food exports, designed as much to serve the
interests of exporters as of importers, often do not really help the
receiving societies.[46] Some countries have neglected their own agricultural development because they could import food at low prices on
credit.[47] It used to be the habit of right-wing critics of foreign aid to
collect stories of blunders that resulted in more harm than good. Now
left-wing critics, adding the connivings of agribusinesses to the
manipulations and errors of governments, do the same thing.

For these various reasons there has been in recent years an increasing call, coming from the developing countries, for "self-reliance."
They have felt the hurt of the insecurity and demeaning behavior that
go with dependence. They want freedom and self-respect.

The wealthy countries sometimes hear that cry a little too cheer-
fully. It takes them off the hook of moral responsibility. It feeds the
"new isolationism," which has reduced U.S. foreign aid until this

country now contributes a far lower fraction of its GNP than many less prosperous countries.

The slogan of self-reliance can easily be misunderstood. Life— whether in the family, a society, or the world—can be far richer in genuine interdependence than in either abject dependence or sterile isolation. But there is something to be said for an interdependence built upon some degree of local or regional self-reliance. International trade and investment, writes Gunnar Myrdal, "will generally tend to breed inequality, and will do so the more strongly when substantial inequalities are already established."[48] The increasing cost of international transportation due to the costs of energy adds force to older arguments for some degree of self-sufficiency.

It is not easy to achieve self-reliance, especially in a society that has long been victimized from outside. The change in food dependency will require something like the New International Economic Order called for by the Sixth Special Session of the General Assembly of the United Nations, April–May, 1974. The resistance to such proposals in the powerful nations is obvious.

Changes in Lifestyle

Some people in our world eat lavishly while others starve. Lester Brown states the moral meaning of this fact: "The issue that some of us are forced to confront in a world where we are dependent on common resources of energy and fertilizer to produce food is whether we can realize *our* full humanity if we continue to overconsume in full knowledge that we are thereby contributing to the premature death of fellow human beings."[49]

Anybody can think of a simple response: "Is there the slightest reason to think that, if I give up a marbled steak, a starving infant in India will get the calories and proteins that I have passed by?" This skeptical question has its point. Detached from political and economic changes, revised personal lifestyles make little difference.

But the question is still too glib. One reason, maybe the most stubborn reason, that people resist political and economic change is that they want to hang on to customary lifestyles. And one reason for the hunger of poor people is the familiar three-step process: (1) the world, on the average, gets richer; (2) richer people buy more meat;

(3) grain goes to feed cattle for the prosperous instead of bread for the poor.

Suppose that more of the world's grain went to feeding people instead of feeding cattle. Fewer cattle would mean higher prices for steaks. People would complain about inflation. Somebody in Washington and Buenos Aires and a few other capital cities would try to increase beef supplies in order to quiet the complaints, and more grain would go back to the cattle.

So changed lifestyles, as part of a total strategy, are important. Such a strategy might mean that the United States would import less fertilizer (or less petroleum for manufacture of fertilizer), while India imported more. That could reduce grain production slightly here and increase it greatly in India. (An extra ton of fertilizer in industrialized nations makes far less difference than an extra ton in nations that don't have much fertilizer.) Reduced grain supplies in rich countries would mean less cattle from the feedlots and therefore fewer (or leaner) steaks. Range-fed cattle are a different story; a steer or milch cow and a pasture are still more efficient convertors of solar energy than most sophisticated and expensive machines. Again, reduced imports of cocoa and coffee can mean more food for hungry people in exporting nations—*if* the land is shifted from monocultures to production of foods for people to eat.

A simplified diet in many cases would be more healthful. A lot of people would be better off with fewer cocktails and less cholesterol. Already changes from butter to margarine have improved health and reduced the ecological load of diets in affluent societies.

I repeat that changed lifestyles, isolated from a larger political strategy, accomplish little. Yet they have a purpose. Those who adopt simpler diets may be useful pioneers, showing more timid people that life can be enjoyable without lavish consumption.

And those of us who are not pioneers can try a few acts that are both symbolic and useful. Oxfam, for example, asks willing people to fast one day in the year and contribute the savings to campaigns against hunger. This is not a substitute for other actions. Oxfam is praised by Lappé and Collins as an organization that, rather than merely dispensing relief, enables poor people in poor countries to help themselves.[50]

Similarly, people might adopt a regimen of one or two or three meatless days a week, contributing the cash savings to Bread.for the World, an organization that works on political dimensions of world hunger. The money makes a difference. And the discipline of occasional fasting or regular meatless days does something for consciousness-raising. People who try those tactics find themselves reading their newspapers and exercising their citizenship differently.

I started this chapter by looking at food as the center of one of the most obvious of all ethical issues. Almost anybody can see the worth of helping the hungry neighbor, but answers to the problem of hunger are complex and controversial. They require an intricate combination of approaches. Maurice Williams, reporting to the World Food Council, makes a convincing case that any attempted solution by increased production *alone* or improved distribution *alone* is "unrealistic."[51]

Answers to hunger require scientific, political, and economic skills, joined to ethical imagination and resolute will. That is the nature of forced options in this technologically intricate world.

A Note on India and China

The conventional wisdom among Western intellectuals these days is that China has handled the hunger problem effectively and that India has not. This opinion is the more persuasive because it has overcome a dominant ideological preference for Indian democracy as against Chinese communism. But I add to my chapter this note simply as a reminder that the picture is far from clear.

The Paddock brothers, as I have noted above, in 1967 wrote off India as a country in such great trouble that help was futile. Yet in 1980 Michael T. Kaufman reported in the *New York Times* (August 10, Section 4, p. 22) that, four years after the last shipload of foreign wheat to arrive in India, the nation was producing "enough food to nourish all of its 630 million people"—even after a serious drought. Noting the persistence of hunger, he explained: "Production difficulties have been largely solved; the biggest obstacles lie in distribution." (The Paddocks, I may add, also gave up on Egypt, which is now one of the biggest recipients of U.S. aid because it is a political ally in the troubled Middle

East. This fact may not be strictly relevant in a chapter on food, but it shows how political relationships frequently confound technical expectations.)

In the case of China information is incomplete and conflicting, largely because most sources have a polemical intent. For a time the Maoist government claimed to have overcome China's traditional problem of starvation, and reports from visitors to China (on supervised tours) confirmed these claims. More recently Wei Jingshen, a former Red Guard turned dissident and sentenced in 1979 to fifteen years in prison, has contested these claims. His report, smuggled out of China before his imprisonment, tells of widespread starvation and even the eating of babies during the Cultural Revolution. (Wei Jingshen, "A Dissenter's Odyssey through Mao's China," *New York Times Magazine,* November 16, 1980, pp. 143ff.)

Less polemical accounts fall between the extremes. According to the Hong Kong press, Li Kiannian, a deputy chairman of the Communist Party, said in 1979 that about ten percent of China's population have insufficient food and factory workers have inadequate diet to sustain hard work. (Fox Butterfield, *New York Times,* June 15, 1979, p. D1.) John Oakes has written from Manchuria that "near-starvation—though not remotely comparable to the famines that used to sweep through China—is still reported from the drier western areas of the country" (*New York Times,* September 1, 1980, p. A13). A detailed analysis of data from many sources by Nick Eberstadt concludes: "There is no doubt that China has been able to cut dramatically the proportion of its population doomed to hunger. . . . It would be unreasonable, however, to assume that hunger has been completely eliminated" or "that China is the best-fed poor country." ("Has China Failed?" *New York Review of Books,* vol. 26, no. 5, April 5, 1979, p. 36.)

In recent years, as India has (at least temporarily) become virtually self-sufficient in food, China has increased its imports. On October 22, 1980 China signed an agreement with the United States to buy 6–8 million metric tons of wheat and corn annually for four years, thus establishing itself as the fourth largest food customer of the United States. In March 1981 the European Eco-

nomic Community granted $6.2 million worth of food to China
as a help to the millions of people who, according to Chinese
officials, faced starvation because of drought in Hebei province
and floods in Hubei. Despite these difficulties there is no doubt
that serious hunger is more conspicuous in India, because of
maldistribution, than in China.

The purpose of his note is not to engage in ideological argument about India and China. It is simply to show the fallibility
of human predictions and the difficulty and importance of getting
adequate information to make social and ethical judgments about
the contemporary world—a theme to which I return in Chapter
12.

5. Population and Its Paradoxes

To many enlightened people the rising population of the world is an overwhelming threat of starvation, misery, chaos, and war. To many equally enlightened people such an opinion is incomprehensible or infuriating.

As an entry point to the controversy, consider a discussion that has gone on hundreds of times in recent international or intercultural gatherings. A conspicuous example was the World Population Conference of the United Nations in Bucharest, August 1974. The discussion is many-sided, but to get at it briefly, assume for the moment that only two people are involved. Both are intelligent, educated, and overflowing with good intentions. One is from the imaginary but real country that I have already called Latinafrasia. The other is from one of the industrialized nations of the North Atlantic region.

Northatlantican: Of course, we'll never solve the problem [war, poverty, starvation, housing, education, adequate medical care, or something else] until we stop the population explosion.

Latinafrasian: But population is not the important issue. The real problem is the inequalities of wealth and power.

Northatlantican: How can you say population is not important? The world has to feed an additional seventy-two million people every year.[1] Look at the hunger and suffering of the countries with the fastest growing populations.

Latinafrasian: They are countries that have been exploited and are still exploited by more powerful countries, sometimes in a conspiracy with the wealthy classes inside the country. End the exploitation, and they can handle their other problems, including population.

Northatlantican: Exploitation is wrong, but look at the recent programs to overcome poverty. There have been stupendous efforts, the most successful efforts in all history to increase food supplies all over the world, but they barely keep up with the rising population. The U.N. Food and Agriculture Organization says that in the "developing countries" food production rose 2.9 percent per year, 1970–1978—a pretty good rate when you keep it up year after year like compound interest. But, because of rising population, the rise per person was only 0.5 percent. And in the MSA (Most Seriously Affected) countries, the total rise was 2.4 percent, but there was a per-person *loss* of 0.1 percent.[2] When too many people are born, too many must starve.

Latinafrasian: It's still true that anywhere in the world people can get food if they have money.

Northatlantican: Yes, but that means that when food is limited, those with money get it. That doesn't say that if you passed out money, there'd be enough food for everybody.

Latinafrasian: In many places where people are hungry, farmers would raise more food, or sell more of it locally instead of exporting it, if people could buy it.

Northatlantican: But surely you believe there are limits to the world's capacity to produce food and housing and hospitals and all the other things that people need. We can't continue straining its resources without limit.

Latinafrasian: Who is it who's straining the earth's resources? A U.S. Senator has said, "The average American consumes in natural resources as much as do thirty residents of India."[3]

Northatlantican: I think that the wealthiest countries must moderate their consumption. I favor a moderate population and moderate consumption rather than a crowded planet with people living in destitution. But surely you'll agree that the wealthiest countries are those with stable or nearly stable populations. If the poor countries would limit their populations, they could raise their standard of living.

Latinafrasian: Maybe it's the other way around. With a higher standard of living, they'd limit their population.

By this time in history such conversations have added up to millions of words, some of them stored on cassettes or recorded on paper, others lost in the atmosphere. They raise issues that require exploration.

THE OBVIOUS CASE

The case for some limitation of global human population is obvious, urgent, and irrefutable. Look first, at a few simple human examples. Think of the farming family in a predominantly agricultural country where the per capita GNP is, say, $300. (For comparison, here are a few figures gathered by the World Bank as of 1976: India, $150; Indonesia, $240; Egypt, $280; People's Republic of China, $410; Peru, $800; United States, $7,890; Switzerland, $8,880.)

This family, more fortunate than some others, owns its small farm. It grows most of its own food but sells some and uses the cash to buy other products. In a year of good weather the farm can support five people, but there are eight in the family. All are undernourished. The children are frequently sick.

The neighboring family is, on average, ten years older. The two oldest sons saw that they could not possibly raise their families on the same small farm, subdivided among four sons, so they went to the city to look for work. They settled in a crowded shantytown of a few hundred people where a very few have jobs, others are occasionally hired as day laborers, and many can eat only if they steal.

The city has doubled in population in each of the past three decades. The government has built some new housing, but not nearly enough for all the residents. As it cuts down trees to make houses, alternating floods and drought increase, and food production falters. The government urges the people to practice family planning, and statistics show that the annual rate of population growth has declined from 3 percent to 2.6 percent. The present rate would mean a doubling of the population in twenty-seven years.

The immediate problem of population is the suffering of parents and children in societies that do not supply food, housing, education, and medical care at rates that match the rise in number of people. It is important to realize that population is not the *sole* cause of any of these shortages. A combination of technical skills and redistribution of wealth could overcome many of the shortages, but population is a fundamental part of the situation.

Look, next, at the population story on the big scale. A chart shows what has happened and is happening:

Date	World's Population	Doubling Time
Time of Christ	250 million	
1650	500 million	1650 years
1850	1 billion	200 years
1930	2 billion	80 years
1975	4 billion	45 years
2015	8 billion (projected)	40 years

The figures, of course, are estimates, and various authorities differ on details, but the differences are insignificant compared with the obvious consensus.

Specialists on population have projected present growth rates into the long-range future. One reckoning is that a doubling of the population every generation would mean that in thirty generations there would be 4550 people for every square foot of the earth—including Antarctica and the top of Mount Everest. You can continue the projections until people outweigh the earth or the solar system.[4] Obviously these absurdities will not happen. They cannot happen. The world's worries are about a much closer future—about this generation and its children, not about thirty generations hence. The point of the long-range projection is to show that, whatever the world can now do to meet the needs of people through better techniques and social policies, it *must,* sooner or later, cope with population.

The issue is not *whether* population growth will taper off; it is *how* the change will come about. Must catastrophe be endured or can it be escaped? Will people direct their destinies or succumb to the blind constraints of nature?

Those restraints were effective in the past. Through much of human history smallpox, malaria, and many such diseases have limited population. Some societies have practiced more deliberate methods: exposure of infants and of the aged. (Of the two, the destruction of infants was far more effective. Survival past the age of reproduction makes a big difference for population; prolongation of life after the age of reproduction is, by comparison, trivial.)

Another method has been migration. The Western Hemisphere offered the escape hatch for the first (European) stage of the great modern explosion of population. Migration has often meant wars of conquest. Conquerors thus get more territory for their own expanding populations. Wars of decimation are themselves cruel ways of reducing population. Actually many wars, given the frequent behavior of warriors, have brought surges in population, but the world now knows how to conduct a war that would unquestionably reduce population.

The modern population explosion has come about through triumphs of technology, often linked with humanitarian concern. This human race rejected—and found the technical power to effectively reject—traditional methods of limitation on population. Not increased fertility but reduction of death, especially among infants and children, has brought the burgeoning of the world's population.

Technology can also offer answers. It can match "death control" with "birth control." But, as with all the forced options of this book, there is no sheer "technical fix." If the world is to limit population by humanitarian methods rather than by catastrophes, people must decide to do so.

Other species of life meet natural limits. Populations of bacteria, insects, and some animals can explode at rates that make the human species look puny. But they meet the checks of their own predators. Or they eat so enthusiastically that they exhaust their own food supplies and starve into decline. One amoeba can start a process of division that, if uninterrupted, could in six days produce enough amoebas to outweigh the earth.[5] But the process is always interrupted, usually by a shortage of food.

People have achieved a considerable skill in outwitting natural constraints. They have learned to sustain populations much larger than Thomas Robert Malthus (1766–1834), the gloomy prophet of population crises, thought possible. But they cannot extend the boundaries forever. If human abilities are to triumph over the natural constraints that check amoebas, insects, and animals, then human beings, directing their techniques by moral imagination, must revise and accomplish what nature is always ready to do.

The unique human gift of the ability to foresee possibilities and make choices, along with the other gifts that constitute human dignity, makes creative actions possible. The same gifts make difficulties. People cannot be manipulated in ways that work well enough with other species. An industrialized society will breed about as many cattle or chickens as people decide that they want. It will not be so effective with mosquitoes, but even with them it will have some manipulative successes. However, manipulating human beings is a quite different enterprise. Two persistent human traits—ethical inhibitions of manipulators and rebellion of the manipulated—are part of the picture. Any answer to the population explosion must reckon with both. And that is why the obvious case for restraint of population runs into complications.

THE PECULIARLY HUMAN COMPLICATIONS

To get at the peculiarly human characteristics of the situation, I shall state a proposition that may, at first glance, look outrageously absurd. The most I claim for it is a rough, though utterly important truth. It is this: people on the average have about as many children as they want. And their wants are a combination of social influences and personal desires.

Anybody knows exceptions to the proposition. There are people who ardently want children but are infertile. And there are people who, wanting a sexual relationship, get unwanted children.

The exceptions are impressive enough that the modern population movement in its early stages emphasized family planning, with the expectation that an adjustment of procreation to people's wants would greatly reduce the growth of population. But in the late 1960s the movement came to the conclusion it is mostly *wanted children* who are increasing population so rapidly. Therefore it becomes important to examine why people want the children they want, whether they have good reasons for their desires, and why they sometimes change their desires. A look at the evidence will also, I think, vindicate the proposition that at first seems improbable.

Those who concentrate too exclusively on the population issue, neglecting its cultural contexts, often wonder why people persist in acting against their best interests when the threats of rising population are so obvious. Or they wonder why distribution of contraceptives and propaganda for their use is often so ineffective. They fail to see that people usually act in accord with their interests, *as they perceive them in their cultural situations.* Several factors in the issue deserve mention.

Economics

In an industrialized society children are not usually considered an economic asset. They live through long years of dependency and education, and by the time they become significant wage earners they are likely to establish homes of their own. But in agricultural economies, as in much of past human history, children become economic partners in the family at an early stage. In large parts of the world the family is an economic team with most of the productive work located in and around the home.

I have earlier (Chapter 3) mentioned Erik Eckholm's report that in many of the world's families one member must spend all day collecting that day's firewood for the family.[6] So it makes sense to send the children out to forage for wood. The expanding population makes the problem worse for everybody in the long run, but several children are an advantage for the present.

Furthermore, suppose the society's "social security system" assumes the responsibility of male heirs to care for their aged parents. And suppose also that the society has long had a high rate of infant and child mortality. Parents then have an urgent motivation to produce enough sons that at least one or two will outlive the parents. En route to that goal they produce an equal number of daughters. The whole cultural context supports large families. Six or eight children may seem quite reasonable. (By comparison, eight was the average in colonial America for women who lived until menopause.[7]) If medical innovations have reduced infant mortality, that fact has not yet reshaped cultural habits and attitudes. The population explosion is going full force.

If a distant government then tries to persuade people that small families are better for the society, such arguments may not make connection with the family's immediate ideas of its own welfare or with traditional attitudes. A report from Peking, for example, says that aged people in rural areas, where there is no pension system, depend on their children for support and therefore worry about government pressures for small families.[8]

Demographers often point out that the reduction of infant mortality is one of the most effective ways of reducing fertility in the long run; but its immediate effect is to increase the population. Likewise, they show that economic security for the aged makes small families economically attractive, but the macroeconomic changes are not easy to bring about in impoverished societies.

Politics

Some nations or ethnic groups have political reasons—in the broad sense of that term—for wanting population growth. Their interests, as they perceive them, are hurt by a relative decline of their numbers in relation to their rivals or potential rivals.

For example, the Argentine government in March of 1974 restricted the sale of contraceptive pills as part of an effort to double the population by the end of the century. The Peronist government was worried that overpopulated neighbors might threaten Argentina.[9]

One of those neighbors, Brazil, has four times the population of Argentina. Some Brazilians advocate growth in both population and the economy as a way to join the "big powers." Some ecologists see great harm to Brazil and to many parts of the earth in turning Brazil's tropical forests into farmlands, but that idea is unpersuasive to most Brazilian nationalists.

In a different situation Israel sees itself as a small nation surrounded by large neighbors with burgeoning populations. American Jews, who are mostly urban and well educated, tend to have small families—although some orthodox Jewish leaders have recently called for higher rates of reproduction. In Israel pronatalist attitudes are more persuasive than in America because the political situation looks different.

In the Soviet Union the ethnic Russians dropped to 52.4 percent of the total population in the Soviet census of 1979. The Muslim population—largely Asiatic—has been growing five times as fast as the rest of the population.[10] Some Russians see threats to familiar political patterns in the slippage of Russian strength vis-à-vis other ethnic groups in the Soviet Union.

In the United States black people have reasons, based on a long history of discrimination, for distrusting white people who worry about the growth of the black population. The situation is that black people, on the average, reproduce faster than white people. Any reckoning of the reasons must take account of another fact: the correlation of birthrates with social-economic position is similar in black and white communities, showing that birthrates are related less to race than to social situation. College-educated black people actually have a slightly lower birthrate than college-educated white people.[11] But black people who know their history are likely to distrust the motives of white people who advise them to hold down their numbers. Similarly, on an international scale poor people and colored races distrust propaganda about birth control from affluent white nations. They may, in their distrust, describe the propaganda as an effort at genocide.

All political reasons for increasing population deserve critical scrutiny. Even in terms of crude economic and military power, a stable population with a growing technology may be better off than a growing population plagued by poverty. Population growth may actually stand in the way of security and a higher quality of life. But political dynamics depend not on clear evidence and logic, but on the way people perceive themselves and their world. Some nations and ethnic groups perceive an advantage in a high birthrate.

Ideology

The economic and political factors quickly merge into the ideological. In Chapter 12 I come back to ideology in more detail. At this point it is enough to define ideology as any comprehensive understanding of the world that is directed toward action. Ideology, in this sense, is not undesirable; it is necessary and valuable.

Two major ideologies meet in controversies about population. One is neo-Malthusian; it looks at the limits imposed by nature upon human powers. It emphasizes that a finite earth cannot contain an infinite population or produce all the food, clothing, housing, and amenities to support an ever expanding population. The other ideology is neo-Marxist; it emphasizes the social causes of hunger, poverty, and human misery. (I am using both terms, neo-Malthusian and neo-Marxist, in a very broad sense. Some neo-Malthusians have never heard of Malthus. Some neo-Marxists disagree with Karl Marx on many important issues.)

The neo-Malthusian looks at many human problems and sees the necessity for restraint—in reproduction, in consumption of resources, in pollution. The neo-Marxist looks at the same problems and sees the need for social reforms, perhaps social revolutions.

There is no reason why a person cannot be both a neo-Malthusian and a neo-Marxist. The leaders of contemporary China are both. Throughout this book I am making an argument both for recognition of physical constraints *and* for changes in social structures. The perplexities come in relating the two for the sake of survival and a better human existence.

But the two ideologies often meet in controversy. The reason is that ideologists—and we are all ideologists—tend to see their particular ideologies as all-encompassing interpretations that exclude other ideologies. And they tend to see other ideologies as evasions of "the real problem"—as, indeed, they *may* be.

The dialogue at the beginning of this chapter is an ideological confrontation, abstracted from the many more complex dialogues that go on in our world. The Northatlantican and the Latinafrasian, each using real economic and political information, have built their data into ideological positions that make it hard for them to acknowledge the importance of data in the opposing positions.

Thus in the world discussions of population the more dogmatic of the neo-Malthusians tend to see all dissenters from their position as irresponsible people unwilling to come to terms with obvious irrefutable facts. And the more vehement of the neo-Marxists see their opponents in controversy—especially if they are rich and powerful—as unwilling to accept the social changes that must and ought to come. Progress in such controversy comes only with an enlargement of perception rather than the tunnel vision that afflicts most people most of the time.

Religion

I am here looking at religion as one factor alongside several others influencing population. Elsewhere in this book I think of religion in a more encompassing sense as the total response of persons and communities to the divine in their experience—whether evident in politics, economics, ideology, worship, or ethics. But for the moment it is enough to look at the teachings and practices of recognizable religious communities as they affect procreative behavior.

In India in 1976 I found that the English language press, the only

Indian press that I could read, was carrying daily articles on population. One series was dealing with the religions of India, a different religion each day. Its aim was to show that all the religions endorsed, or at least did not oppose, family planning in the face of India's mounting population. As I remember the series, it fudged on some points: it often emphasized a very general endorsement of or permission for family planning, while neglecting to mention some prohibitions of the most common techniques of limiting fertility.

The worldwide situation is that the major religious communities are relating their beliefs to situations quite different from those that prevailed when their traditions originated and took their dominant shape. Therefore it is not enough that they simply repeat inherited teaching. They must interpret or revise that teaching in the contemporary world. Roman Catholic Christianity is perhaps the most interesting example, because it has specific doctrines and a specifically identifiable teaching authority.

Catholic Christianity inherited from the Bible the general assumption that fecundity was a blessing, perhaps even a sign of divine approval. It also inherited from the Bible an appreciation of the vocation of celibacy, combined sometimes with a nonbiblical, neoplatonic suspicion of the carnal. Moral theologians frequently taught that the intention of procreation was the sole justification of sexual intercourse—with the delights of sex made licit by that intention.

Catholic doctrine no longer requires that the procreation be the primary purpose of the sexual relation or that every sexual act intend procreation. But the formal doctrine, stated by Pope Paul VI (*Humanae Vitae,* July 25, 1968) and frequently reaffirmed by Pope John Paul II, forbids contraception. An impressive group of Catholic theologians has dissented. And Catholic bishops in both the United States and France have affirmed freedom of conscience in relation to the papal teaching.

What about Catholic behavior? It has often been noticed that "the historic transition from large to small families in the West began in two Roman Catholic nations—France and Ireland."[12] In Europe birthrates in predominantly Catholic countries are barely distinguishable from those elsewhere. Birthrates "are lower in Belgium, France, Italy, Spain and Portugal than they are in the United States."[13] In the United States, where Catholics have been expected to have larger families than the national average, the difference had virtually disappeared by 1975.[14] In predominantly Catholic Latin America, birthrates are very high; but one study shows that women who attend mass frequently have slightly fewer children than those who do not.[15] The assumption is not that the mass has a hidden contraceptive efficacy, but that the mass is more accessible in urban than in rural areas.

Incidentally, as the late Dr. André Hellegers points out, the French people, in leading Europe's demographic transition, began the shift to small families "in the early nineteenth century even before the vulcanization of rubber"[16]—and obviously before the IUD and the contraceptive pill. That observation supports my earlier statement that, despite exceptions, people for the most part have about as many children as they want in their cultural situations.

Two groups of people will be disappointed in the evidence that religious teachings have little relation to reproductive behavior: those seriously religious people who want to believe in such a relation and those antireligious people who want to blame Catholicism or some other religion for the population explosion. The kinds of data I have presented do not refute all efficacy of religion. It remains likely that religious attitudes, as internalized within individuals and cultures, make more difference than specific teachings from a remote authority. And it is still the case that some governments have refrained from adopting specific population policies out of a reluctance to offend religious authorities.

At one more important point a religious ethic bears directly on the situation. Abortion is "probably the most widely used method of birth control in the world,"[17] although it may be that the IUD has recently taken first place. It is estimated that in recent times there has been one abortion for every two births. The moral objection to abortion appears in a variety of religious and secular ethics. To discuss the ethics of abortion would take more space than I can give it here.[18] For the moment it is enough to say that those of us who take the population problem seriously do not help our cause by dismissing contemptuously all ethical opposition to abortion.

Culture

Culture is the context in which more particular factors (political, economic, ideological, formally religious) operate. And culture influences the procreative attitudes and behavior of persons.

For most, maybe all human beings the meaning of life has some reference beyond the immediate self. People normally desire some continuation of themselves in future generations. Biological offspring are not the only, but the most obvious form of such continuation. The self-regarding and the altruistic impulses unite in the desire to give birth to and to rear children. Culture is capable of intensifying or sublimating that desire.

One way in which culture operates is through the defining of sex roles. Such roles are variable. A women's liberation movement operating in many cultures is changing traditional sex roles. And such changes are likely to have more effect on population than crusades centering on population alone. People rarely decide to have more or fewer children out of a commitment to some distant good for the human race; they most often decide in terms of their own identity.

If a society has an ingrained belief that "the principal work of a woman is to have children," as a Peronist magazine in Argentina once put it, then women will have a lot of children. To the extent that women internalize such a belief and link their identity with it, demographic information will have little effect on behavior.

Likewise, if men demonstrate their masculinity by proving their fertility, if their status is enhanced among peers in factories and shops by their procreative vigor, that cultural factor will outweigh theories about global demography and even personal poverty. Peer ridicule and approval are powerful forces.

In India one father of ten told Paul Simon, "Children are the one luxury a poor man has."[19] Unpack that statement and you will find in it a sense of personal identity and worth, which is both an internalization of the values of a society and a defiance of the same society's conspiracy to deprive the person of other possibilities. The fact that the man did not mention his wife and that we do not know her opinions is also a part of the cultural scene.

In looking at the economic reasons for wanting heirs I mentioned that high infant and child mortality becomes a force for fecundity. That same reasoning now takes on a still deeper meaning as it bears on personal selfhood. The parents who find their identity in their children want enough children that some will survive the parents, despite the risks that threaten survival.

Cultural habits are not immutable. They can change. And demographic knowledge may contribute to the change. But no pile of facts and no cogent logic, if they ignore the cultural context, are likely to change behavior.

AN ARGUMENT ABOUT MEANS

What can the world do about the perils of overpopulation? What means are effective and acceptable toward the end of moderating the growth of population? Once again, in order to clarify the issues, I shall simplify a many-sided argument by reducing it to two positions.

The "humanitarian" position, to give it a name, accents education, economic development, and the liberation of women, accompanied with the provision of contraceptives for all who want them. It may also, but does not always, advocate easy access to abortion. The thrust of the argument is that people—once they gain moderate economic security, an understanding of the opportunities available to them, freedom from stereotyped gender roles, and access to contraceptives—will see the advantages of small families and will act in accord with their own interests and the public interest.

The other position—it can be called "hard-nosed," although it advocates insist it is not hardhearted—is that purely voluntary methods are not enough to meet the present emergency. Private family interests and the public interest are not obviously identical. *Laissez-faire* is no more adequate for population policy than for the flow of traffic in a city or in the airlanes. What is needed is "mutual coercion mutually agreed on"[20]—the principle already practiced in taxation, compulsory education, and the whole realm of public law.

A juxtaposition of the two positions once appeared in successive issues of the *New York Times.* On September 21, 1969, a story by Harold M. Schmeck, Jr., appeared under a heading, "Family Planning: New Focus in U.S." The report stated that the federal government was assigning high priority to "the related issues of population and family planning," on the assumption that many people would have smaller families if they had access to information and methods. On the following day a contrasting headline said: "Scientists tell Nixon Adviser Voluntary Birth Control is 'Insanity.' " The dispatch by Gladwin Hill reported a meeting where Garrett Hardin and others told Presidential Counsel John Ehrlichman: "In the long run, voluntarism is insanity. The result will be continued uncontrolled population growth."

To reduce the discussion to simplest terms, an imaginary dialogue —abstracted from many real dialogues—will be useful. This dialogue has some resemblance to the one that started this chapter. But that dialogue was about the significance of population as a world issue; this one is about ways of dealing with population.

Humanitarian: Voluntary methods are not only morally superior to coercion, they are the only methods that work. In 1965 Robert C. Cook, president of the Population Reference Bureau, told a Senate committee that in the countries that had achieved an approximately stable population, there had been no legislation to that end—that, in fact, legislation had sometimes tried to encourage a higher birth rate.[21] Philip Hauser, of the University of Chicago Population Research and Training Center, told the same committee: "The fact is that decreases in fertility in what are now the economically advanced nations were achieved completely on a voluntary basis."[22] Roger Revelle of the Harvard Center for Population Studies has shown that social security for the aged and a reduction in child mortality are effective incentives for smaller families—as well as values in their own right.[23]

Hard-Nose: How can you say that voluntary methods are the only methods that work? In the thousands of years of history, whether in primitive societies or the great civilizations, populations have always expanded until they met food limitation. Then expansion stopped through starvation, epidemics, infanticide, or war. This has happened hundreds of times. I advocate a more humane form of coercion.

Humanitarian: But how? Are you going to put mothers and newborn babies in jail? Are you going to fine mothers who are already so poor they can scarcely feed their babies? Or are you going to keep a registry on everybody and inflict compulsory abortions on mothers who transgress the limits?

Hard-Nose: The Internal Revenue Service already keeps a pretty elaborate registry on people. There are many effective disincentives to procreation, used by governments in such differing countries as Tunisia, Singapore, the Philippines, and China. The ultimate sanctions, sterilization of women who have the maximum allowable number of children or compulsory abortion, might never be necessary.

Humanitarian: Your male prejudice is showing. Why do you pick on women?

Hard-Nose: The woman is always present at childbirth, which can be the occasion for sterilization. I might wish the man were, but often he isn't. Sometimes he isn't even known. And although men make women pregnant, abortions are possible only for women. That's not a male prejudice.

Humanitarian: Surgical intrusion in a woman's body is an intolerable invasion of personal liberty—unless she wants it.

Hard-Nose: I already said that ultimate sanction might not be necessary. But if it is, it's not so intolerable as starvation. I think I'm the real humanitarian in this argument, and I don't see how you got your name.

And so the argument goes. Since some details of it hinge on what happened in the "demographic transition" in the industrial West, a look at that process is necessary. Over a period of time the industrialized world went through a radical shift from high birthrates to low. Most of Europe's population growth is now below 1 percent per year (as compared with the rate of 2.6 percent for Africa, 2.3 percent for Asia, 2.9 percent for Latin America, and 2 percent for the world.[24] Several countries are at a rate which, if continued, will mean stable population. The U.S. fertility rate by 1973 dropped to 1.9 children per family. The "replacement level" is usually reckoned at 2.1 children per family. The U.S. population is still growing because of (1) the large number of women at the age of fertility and (2) immigration. But the 1973 rate, *if* held constant, would mean a stable population (apart from immigration) by about 2030.[25]

But the Western demographic transition cannot be a model for the world. There was suffering that nobody wants to repeat, and there was good luck that nobody knows how to repeat.

A series of plagues and epidemics from 1000 to 1600 reduced the population of Europe. The Black Death of the fourteenth century took about half the population of Europe. Despite high fertility there was no growth of population from 1300 to 1600. Poverty, malnutrition, and medical ignorance were reasons for the vulnerability of people to disease.

After 1600 rising economic productivity and rising population went hand in hand. Europe began the most spectacular population explosion of history until that time. There were checks on population: smallpox, typhoid, starvation, war, enforced celibacy among the poor, widespread infanticide. But still population boomed on. The outlet was migration to "the New World"—the greatest export of people in all history.

The present world *intends* to avoid the epidemics that slowed the European population explosion. And, despite nature's ability to produce surprises, medical knowledge may enable the world to make good on that intention. As for migration, that still goes on. But, given present geographical and political limitations, there is no way for billions of people to migrate now as millions did in the nineteenth century.

The demographic transition got under way in earnest by 1820 in France and Switzerland, by the 1850s in Ireland, by 1870 in England. Its great phase was 1880 to 1960.

There are signs, much discussed and much disputed, that the world is now beginning to slow down its rate of population growth. It is certainly doing so in some areas, not in others. If the world were now to begin a demographic transition that would be accomplished like Europe's in eighty to one hundred forty years, that would be far too slow to avoid immense human agony. Ceylon in three years, 1945–1948, "reduced its death rate—thanks primarily to successful measures against malaria—by as much as it took Western Europe three hundred years to accomplish."[26] The pace of change today is swift. The hope is that, given the greater understanding and contraceptive skills of our time, societies can move faster and more humanely to regulate population than any have ever done before.

CHOICES AHEAD

I have said earlier that continued growth of population indefinitely is not a physical possibility. The human race has no choice whatsoever about that fact. But there are other important choices. People can choose between humane methods and catastrophic methods, between action through foresight or surrender to fate. They can also make some choices about the relation of population to consumption: many people walking vis-à-vis fewer people using cars; many people eating grains and beans vis-à-vis fewer people eating meat; a world where people have crowded out animals and flowers or a world where people share resources with other species. There is no one right answer in these choices.

Involved in all these choices will be a fundamental choice that has been going on through all human history: the choice on how to relate individual freedom and social accountability. The dialogue between Humanitarian and Hard-Nose, like the uncountable conversations on which it is based, is in one sense unreal. It makes freedom and social control into abstractions totally opposed to each other. Experience is indeed full of conflicts between the two, but there is never total freedom or total social control. Nor are these two simply ends of a spectrum on which people or societies move one way or the other— although many such spectra do exist. The real issue in social life (the only kind of life there is) becomes the way of relating personal good to public good. Political and ethical wisdom is the discovery of ways in which they enhance each other.

On the issue of population there are policies that permit or encourage freedom. No U.S. government official can tell anybody, "Because you have had three—or ten—children, you must be sterilized." And there are policies that inhibit personal freedom. The Chinese see to it that peasants do not have ten children. But there is never total, abstract freedom unrelated to constraints.

The moderately affluent American family relates the number of children to its income after taxes, to its house (or expectations of a better house), to the age of the parents, to anticipations of whether the government will or won't subsidize college education for the children, and to many other physical and social constraints—as well as to the personal desires of the parents. The American birthrate fell drastically during the Great Depression, rose during World War II and the post-war affluence (so that Americans were proportionally outperforming the people of India in the 1950s), fell again (for many reasons) in the 1970s. Social incentives and constraints—not governmental fiat but very real constraints—were at work all the time.

An ethical concern for human freedom does not require a sheer individualism. Today the world sees a variety of population policies in which societies try to relate freedom to public good. From the many experiments the world keeps learning.

There are a few societies that in recent years have seen dramatic drops in fertility. Perhaps the most conspicuous examples are Japan,

China, South Korea, Taiwan, and Singapore. These societies differ radically in wealth, economic systems, degree of industrialization, and political organization. Among them, Japan is most nearly repeating the demographic transition of the industrialized West, although at a much faster pace. Japan reduced its birthrate by half in a ten-year period—an amazing performance judged by the familiar standards of history.[27]

The other nations differ greatly from Japan. But there are some common characteristics in all these societies *and* in the industrialized West, characteristics usually lacking in the societies with runaway population growth. All have seen a drop in infant and child mortality. All have high literacy and increasing educational opportunities. All have adequate or improving nutrition and rising living standards, with the poor people sharing the benefits. All have low unemployment by prevailing world standards. All have widely available health services including contraception. In all of them population is an issue in public discussion. In most cases there is increased liberation of women from traditional role restraints. And in most cases government has a conspicuous population policy.

But government policy alone is usually futile. In India, during Indira Gandhi's first regime, government propaganda and pressure brought a significant increase in sterilization and other devices for reducing fertility. Popular resentment against this policy was the biggest single factor leading to the fall of that administration in 1977. When Mrs. Gandhi returned to power in 1980, her administration was more timid about confronting issues of population.

China is the most momentous example in all history of a direct, massive attack on the issue of population.[28] Announced public policy aims at Zero Population Growth by the year 2000. There are some claims that the growth rate was cut in half in the seven years up to 1978; other estimates are that the reduction required thirteen years. Some provinces are down to a near replacement rate. The society encourages late marriage and a strict sex ethic. Slogans circulate: "Late, long, few, and fine"; "One is best, two is most." People are taught to esteem daughters. Even postage stamps carry the message of population restraint. Contraception, sterilization, and abortion are available.

Practices vary in different provinces. In Sichuan annual quotas of children are assigned to each factory, district, and commune. Families with a single child get financial bonuses and preferential treatment in housing and education. There are extra taxes for families with more than two children. A directive to Communist Party members in September of 1980 instructed them to have only one child per family.[29] The invasions of personal and family privacy would be considered outrageous in more individualistic societies. Peer pressure is the chief weapon in the campaign.

The Chinese methods are not a model for the world. They would be ineffective and impossible in many societies, but they are instructive. They refute those who say that government pressure and coercion are never effective. But they give no support to those who advocate coercion apart from radical economic reforms improving the lot of the poor.

BEYOND THE IDEOLOGICAL IMPASSE

China, whatever one thinks of that vast nation, is clear evidence that a society need not choose between neo-Marxist and neo-Malthusian assumptions. A synthesis is possible.

The achievements of those greatly varied societies that have changed procreative habits suggest some useful judgments. There is no help either in an exclusive concentration on population or in a cheerful hope that the population problem will disappear if only the world learns to produce more economic goods and distribute them more widely.

When so eminent an anthropologist as Claude Levi-Strauss says that "the only real problem facing civilization today is the population explosion,"[30] he contributes nothing to the solution. His words are unbelievable to people who fear nuclear war, torture by agents of dictatorial governments, racial intimidation, political oppression. Population monomaniacs simply raise the hostile resistance of people whose experience confronts them with other real and painful problems.

But transcendence of the ideological impasse is possible. For example, a meeting of Asians, gathered by the World Council of Churches in Kuala Lumpur, Malaysia, in April 1973, made a forceful criticism of international economic injustices and *then* went on to say: "The problem of poverty and unemployment will defy solution until developing countries severely limit the growth of their populations."[31] The same people would not have said that in a confrontation where Westerners were lecturing Asians about the Asian population problem.

In 1976 I visited ten countries of Asia as part of a study of ethical issues in technological change. I determined never to initiate any mention of population. In all ten countries people living there brought up the issue. For good reasons they resist the frequent efforts to use population as an ideological weapon against them. As an issue requiring understanding and action, they are ready to face it.

There are signs of progress. On rare occasions the dialogue with which I began this chapter is actually reversed. If Northatlantican acknowledges a responsibility for plundering the earth's resources and other people, Latinafrasian can acknowledge a need for changed reproductive habits. And both can recognize that the relation of people to resources and of people to other people is an issue all over the world.

6. Living with Limits

The last three chapters have looked at three problems that raise danger signals for the human race: energy, food, and population. In each case human ingenuity and drive have pushed far beyond expectations of past ages. Societies have developed energy sources, produced food, and learned to sustain populations on a scale incredible to past generations. That fact is a warning against any facile posting of limits. But each case is a warning against facile disregard of limits. In each case the possibilities are finite. Present suffering and threatening catastrophies are signs that the limits may be near.

So the question arises: are energy, food, and population atypical—even though important—issues? Or are they symptomatic? Are there other matters on which civilization presses perilously close to limits?

As one such example, think of water.

WATER

The more you think about water, the more amazing it becomes. Water covers seventy-two percent of the earth's surface. It is, by weight, about seventy percent of the human body. About one hundred gallons of water go into the making of an orange, about thirty-five hundred gallons into producing the daily food of a North American, about four thousand gallons into raising one pound of beef.

Still more remarkable, we human beings today are using the same water that our first human ancestors and their biological ancestors used. A slight part of the world's water has been broken down into hydrogen and oxygen, and recombined; but basically the stock of water has been stable for aeons. Unlike petroleum or coal, water is not "used up" or destroyed. (Technically speaking, energy is never destroyed; that's the First Law of Thermodynamics. But it is dissipated and made useless; that's the Second Law of Thermodynamics.)

The molecules of water in your most recent drink—your coffee, tea, milk, cocktail, or simple glass of water—have probably moved through the kidneys and bowels of people and animals, through dinosaurs and earthworms, through factories and car washes, through streams and steam engines and sewers and oceans. Nature has marvelous abilities to cleanse water—by evaporating it into the atmosphere and returning it as rain or snow, by filtering it under the ground. Technology has some ability to purify water on a much lesser scale.

But this human race has often strained the limits of natural and technical hydrological systems. The failures of great ancient civilizations—in Mesopotamia, Persia, Egypt, India, China, Southeast Asia, and Latin America—were due in large part to soil depletion and exhaustion of water resources, often accompanied by salinization of the soil.[1]

The world today is perilously close to repeating the story. China and India, the two largest nations, are pushing the limits of water resources. All over the world societies are tapping underground water supplies, often with dramatic dropping of the levels of ground water. As Georg Borgstrom reports, Texas and southern California are using up water resources through "a mining of water, Pleistocene in origin and accumulated over thousands of years." As a result of these many processes, "we now face a global water crisis, which in some ways is indeed more crucial than the food crisis and even more ominous."[2]

Since rivers determine their courses without regard for political boundaries, major conflicts center on the uses of their water. Examples include the Indus River (India and Pakistan), the Jordan (Israel and its neighbors), the Colorado (Mexico and seven states within the United States).

In parts of the world, including the southeastern United States, huge government irrigation projects subsidize the cost of food, sometimes extravagantly. Part of the money citizens pay in taxes should be charged, in a proper cost accounting, to their food budgets. One press report states: "Tucson and Phoenix, some analysts argue, are urban luxuries that ultimately will shrivel as the water runs out."[3]

Of course, there is plenty of water in the ocean. And it can be desalted, as it is in several places, most notably in Hong Kong where forty-eight million gallons of fresh water come every day from the world's largest desalinization plant. But the process is expensive, both in money and in consumption of energy. There is a curious water–energy circle: technology could produce more available energy (through coal liquefaction and shale treatment) if more water were available; it could produce more water (through desalinization) if more energy were available.

Water requires hard decisions. Kathleen Wiegner writes in *Forbes,* the magazine that advertises itself as "capitalist tool": "Water stored behind a dam can be used for recreation but not for irrigation, just as water used to irrigate wheat cannot be used to slurry coal or make paper. You can fish in it or you can drop waste in it. You can't do both."[4]

THE INTRICATE RELATIONS AMONG LIMITS

Energy, food, population, and water are four cases where the contemporary world is pushing the edge of danger. There are many more. In 1964 economist Kenneth Boulding pointed out that "the date that divides human history into two equal parts," so far as the mining of many metals is concerned, is 1910.[5] By that he meant that the human race had taken out of mines between 1910 and 1964 about as much as in all history prior to 1910. The nuclear physicist and Episcopal priest William Pollard has written that a number of minerals, a billion years in their formation and concentration in the earth, are being squandered and will probably be exhausted within a century.[6]

Severe shortages are not precisely predictable because nobody knows when new resources will be discovered, but danger signals hang over mercury, tin, helium, copper, lead, chromium, zinc, nickel, and manganese, to name a few. There is deep irony in the fact that the wealthiest nations are the most dependent on such resources. Mesarovic and Pestel note that until the 1940s the United States was a net exporter of materials and until the early 1950s was "virtually self-sufficient in the essential raw materials needed for industrial production." But by 1970 the United States "imported all of its requirements for chromite, columbium, mica, rutile, tantalum, and tin; more than 90% of its requirements for aluminum, antimony, cobalt, manganese, and platinum," and so on. Looking ahead, "according to the National Materials Policy Commission, the United States will, by the year 2000, depend on imports for more than 80%" of the materials used by its industries.[7] Harrison Brown points out that the United States is in a "minerals trap" analogous to its "energy trap."[8]

Such data suggest a new version of "lifeboat ethics" (see Chapter 3). It may be that the presently richest nations in the world will soon be gasping in the ocean, trying unsuccessfully to climb into the life-boats possessed by the presently poorest nations.

To any single shortage an answer may be practical. Technological ingenuity can often devise substitutes or find methods of exploiting progressively poorer ores. The problems come in the great number and variety of shortages and in the relationships between them. It is those relationships that demand attention.

I have already mentioned the water–energy relation. In a way the water shortage is an energy shortage, and the energy shortage is a water shortage. There are many other examples. It used to be said that metals in diminishing supply would be replaced by plastics; but plastics are made of petroleum, which is on the way to becoming scarcer than the metals it was expected to replace. There are great possibilities of recovering scarce metals from the seabed, but that requires huge expenditures of energy. So does massive recycling.

The food–industry–pollution relation is equally serious. The food specialist Ivan Bennett wrote in 1970 that India needed about a million miles of access roads to serve 580,000 villages.[9] But the buildings of roads (and gasoline stations and the whole economic infrastructure that goes with a transportation system) takes land out of food production. It need not do so on the extravagant scale of the United States, which is currently losing four square miles of farmland per day,[10] but it has to take some land. In other ways modern agriculture depends on industry (just as industry depends on agriculture). The Green Revolution requires a huge fertilizer industry to service it. Industry usually means pollution. I used to think that the United States and Germany were the only nations where polluted rivers actually caught fire, but in 1980 the Ba River on the edge of Peking flared up, destroying a bridge and high-tension power lines. Industrial pollution means acid rains that harm crops and kill fish. It means poisoned groundwaters in some areas. Such pollution can be moderated or corrected; but the processes are costly, and they set off further reverberations through the industrial-agricultural system.

It is such relationships that have led to a shift of attention from the risks of specific shortages to the technical-economic-social systems in which the shortages appear. A systems analysis becomes important. And with it comes the growing suspicion, mentioned but not elaborated in Chapter 2, that the dominant industrial systems have a self-destruct apparatus built into them.

PROBLEMS IN THE SYSTEM

Modern industrial systems are built on the assumption, sometimes silently taken for granted and sometimes trumpeted abroad, that there are no limits to human possibilities. The assumption has become a faith that sometimes has a thrilling valor. The Seabees used to say, "The difficult we do today, the impossible we do tomorrow." People with that faith can do things that are impossible for people without the faith. But the faith and assumption are not literally true. It is not possible for the people on earth or the food they produce to multiply until they outweigh the earth. It is not possible to repeal the Second Law of Thermodynamics. The human race has overcome many barriers, but sooner or later it runs into intractable limits.

Modern industrial systems are built on the premise that there are, for practical purposes, no limits to human production and consumption. In the long expanse of human history that is an unusual premise. But the industrial revolution for a while seemed to confirm it.

Economics, once called "the dismal science," turned cheerful. In its popular capitalist versions it assumed that market incentives would encourage ingenuity and productivity without limits. In its popular Marxist versions it assumed that, by eliminating the artificial scarcities imposed by profit-seeking capitalists, society could produce unlimited abundance. Economic development became the way to a better life for the whole world.

In retrospect, it is surprising that the awakening came so late. There has been an almost inaudible undercurrent of warning throughout the twentieth century, but optimism about productivity flourished, especially in the period of remarkable economic growth following World War II. When Harrison Brown sounded an alarm in *The Challenge*

of Man's Future (1954) he was able to point to a small but significant
body of literature on the predatory nature of "machine civilization."[11]
However, such warnings had little influence on the leaders of governments and corporations or on the popular mind.

In the 1960s the murmurs of foreboding became more audible.
Georg Borgstrom spoke with the passion of a biblical prophet on the
problems of food, population, and exploitation of the poor by the
rich.[12] Kenneth Boulding alerted the National Council of Churches to
the perils of the reckless "cowboy" economy and called for an ethic
of moderation, conservation, and recycling.[13] E. J. Mishan in England
combined economic analysis with a somewhat nostalgic mood as he
pointed out the often unrecognized costs of economic growth.[14] Garrett Hardin wrote his controversial "Tragedy of the Commons,"[15]
which quickly became a point of reference for arguments in antholo-
gies and public discussions.

The early 1970s became a time of heightened concern, marked by
a great flow of literature.[16] Two composite studies emerged as light-
ning rods, both warning of danger and attracting bolts of hostility.
The first was *Blueprint for Survival,* a document prepared by a group
of British scientists and philosophers.[17] It argued that present industrial society is not sustainable. "Its termination within the lifetime of
someone born today is inevitable—unless it continues to be sustained
for a while longer by an entrenched minority at the cost of imposing
great suffering on the rest of mankind."[18] Its end will come, either by
catastrophe or by humane and purposeful change. Looking at questions of energy, raw materials, food and population, disruption of
ecosystems by pollution and overexploitation, all combined with social injustices and international tensions, *Blueprint* saw "a profound
incompatibility between deeply rooted beliefs in continuous growth
and the dawning recognition of the earth as a space ship, limited in
its resources and vulnerable to thoughtless mishandling."[19]

The second study was *The Limits to Growth,*[20] produced by an
international team of scientists at the Massachusetts Institute of Technology. It quickly became the most spectacular of all publications on
its theme. One reason was its sponsorship by the Club of Rome, an
international group of scientists and industrialists. Another was the
shrewd public relations that accompanied its launching. Still another
was the combination of a very readable style with an intricate comput-

erized economic model of the world—a point I come back to later. There was also an intriguing irony in the fact that a project so critical of contemporary technological society should come out of M.I.T. and be funded by the Volkswagen Foundation, two organizations that have a considerable stake in technology.

The basic premise of the book is a simple proposition that is virtually an axiom: infinite physical growth is impossible in a finite system. Therefore there are obviously "limits to growth."

The book shows that in many critical areas of human activity growth is moving not at a linear but at an exponential rate. (An example of linear growth: 1, 2, 3, 4, 5. An example of exponential growth: 1, 2, 4, 8, 16.) In early stages exponential growth is no faster than linear growth, but after a while there comes a tremendous speed-up. When there were a hundred human beings on earth, a doubling of the population was (at least on a global scale) not much; it probably gave the race a little more security against hazards that threatened extinction. When there are 4.5 billion people, a doubling of numbers is an entirely different event. During a recent past most American metropolitan areas were able to double electrical consumption in ten years. Now they cannot.

Perhaps nobody would claim that exponential growth (energy consumption, food production, paving over of farmlands, population, pollution) can go on forever. The controversial thesis, then, has to do with time projections. *The Limits to Growth* argues that the moment of truth is near.

The study investigates five principal factors in contemporary world civilization: population, capital (or industrialization), food, consumption of nonrenewable resources (including energy), and pollution. It finds all of them growing exponentially at rapid rates. It finds them interacting, so that the complex of interactions is more threatening than any single process in isolation.

So the report comes to its disturbing conclusions. "If the present growth trends in world population, industrialization, pollution, food production, and resource depletion continue unchanged, the limits to growth on this planet will be reached sometime within the next one hundred years."[21] That situation confronts the world with a forced option. We (the human race) can continue present habits that will lead to catastrophe—in effect, keep driving at accelerating speeds toward the edge of the cliff. Or we can make purposeful plans to modify the world's systems and avoid the collapse—in effect, slow down the machine and avoid the edge of the cliff.

An immediate and resolute change of plans would avoid the crash and minimize the human pain and dislocation. The sooner we start, the easier the change will be. The longer we wait, the more violent it will be.

The need is for a state of "global equilibrium," a "condition of ecological and economic stability that is sustainable far into the future."[22] Here the writers take up the theme that I first mentioned in Chapter 2. In their words, "Numerous problems today have no technical solutions."[23] A far-reaching cultural change is required.

Since the writers are often called prophets of doom, it is important to realize that in many ways they are truly optimistic. They think it physically possible—whether it is humanly and politically possible they do not know—to establish a world system that is:

(1) sustainable without sudden and uncontrollable collapse; and (2) capable of satisfying the basic material requirements of all of its people.[24]

In fact, they are so optimistic that they think it possible to build a world with twice as much food per person as in 1970, a world in which the average income triples—although it is only half the average in the United States.[25] If their goals mean "doom" for some people, they could mean good news for most of the world. But the good news depends less on the scientific possibility of the goals than on the political will to pursue them, and on that question the prospects are portentous.

EVALUATING THE THESIS OF LIMITS

The Limits to Growth and the historical events that quickly followed it—the searing famines of 1973–1975, the petroleum shortages, and the rise in both inflation and unemployment in most of the world —have generated intense controversies.[26] I can best comment on them by noting the main criticisms of the thesis of limits and giving responses to them. Here I am interested more in the general proposition of limits than in any specific book, but *The Limits to Growth* is a convenient reference point. In evaluating the criticisms, I give my own responses; but again the responses of the authors of *The Limits to Growth* are sometimes useful.

Criticism No. 1

The idea of a no-growth society is too grim to contemplate. It could not be achieved without great social dislocations. And the end of economic growth would hurt the poor—both the poor nations and the poor people in the rich nations.

Response

If the thesis of limits is true, there is no gain in refusing to accept it. The debate is about better and worse ways of adjusting to limits.

Yet the pain of the protest deserves serious attention. When Jørgen Randers, one of the four authors of *The Limits to Growth,* presented its thesis to a committee of the World Council of Churches in Nemi, Italy, prior to publication of the book, an Asian social scientist responded: "I'm almost tempted to say that if your case is true, you shouldn't tell anybody." He realized the wry humor of his remark but wanted to show how the idea doomed the hopes of Asia. Africans and Latin Americans who were present seconded his concern. Later American black leaders were to join the complaint. All these people and their constituencies had been living by the hopes and promises of economic development. Now, it seemed, a door was slammed in their faces. They might cynically wonder: are the wealthy nations and social classes now telling us that we can never enjoy the productivity they have achieved for themselves?

Randers immediately replied that he did not want to freeze the present world system of productivity, that he wanted growth for the poor societies and retrenchment for the rich. His reply was unconvincing, not because people questioned his personal good faith but because the world they knew did not work that way.

About four years after publication of *The Limits to Growth* Donella Meadows, one of the authors, reaffirmed all its major arguments, but added: "If I could rewrite any one part of *Limits to Growth,* it would be the last chapter where I do say that stopping growth does not mean freezing income distribution, but I don't say it loudly enough. . . . I look forward to the end of growth because it will raise the distribution question so clearly that the rich people all over the world will no longer be able to ignore it or pass it off by saying, 'Let them eat growth.' "[27]

But the problem—inherent in human nature—remains. The response of almost anybody to a threatening economic situation is a double one: (1) What can societies or governments do to cope with the threat to humanity? (2) How can I look out for my security in the face of the threats? On the basis of long experience the world's poor classes and nations do not believe that Donella Meadows's idealism will be the dominant force in history.

But the issue remains. Imagine a society, normal in all respects except that nobody in it is over forty and the whole society has somehow been shielded from any knowledge of death. People know that animals and vegetation die, but not that they themselves will die. Then the report comes: human death is real and inevitable. People might respond in disbelief: death must not be accepted because it makes too many problems. And, given social inequalities, the problems will be most severe for the poor. They might believe, especially if the news-bringer is a seller of life insurance, that the whole report is a conspiracy designed to make money for somebody else. Or they might believe the report and start actions to assuage the grief of death and modify the social dislocations it causes.

Criticism No. 2

Technology keeps expanding old limits. Like population and production, it also grows exponentially. It has already enabled the human race to overcome many seeming limits of the past. It creates resources as truly as it consumes them. For example, petroleum has been in the ground for millennia; it was modern technology that made it a resource. Technology also enables us to do more with less. Computers and microprocessing of information can now achieve far more with less use of material and energy than their predecessors only a decade or two ago. Recent studies on energy have shown that great savings and efficiencies are possible; GNP is not linked absolutely to energy consumption.

Response

Thus far the growth of technology belongs as much to the problem as to the solution. Technologies are doing the consuming of materials and energy that threatens the human race. A redirected technology can help; it belongs to the "dynamic equilibrium"—not a static equilibrium—that is needed. The kind of technology that does more with less is a help. Unfortunately the examples of such technology are limited, and they are not adequate to the global emergency.

When all is said and done, this is still a finite earth. That means there are limits. Nobody knows exactly what those limits are, and technology may stretch them. But it becomes as important to learn to live with limits as to push them out a little further.

It is, of course, possible that new technologies may appear, as unexpected to us now as petroleum technologies were to the Roman Empire. But it is ethically irresponsible, in the face of the world's crisis, to count on break-throughs that may never come and certainly cannot relieve suffering in this generation.

Criticism No. 3

Some kinds of growth are surely possible. The miniaturizing of computers is an example. It would be better to aim at differentiated growth[28] or selective growth[29] than at "no growth."

Response

I agree with that point. Most of the literature on limits, if studied in detail, allows for those kinds of growth that do not recklessly increase population, food consumption, and pollution, while diminishing resources and arable land. As a matter of fact, *The Limits to Growth* says: "Any human activity that does not require a large flow of irreplaceable resources or produce severe environmental degradation might continue to grow indefinitely."[30] But not everybody noticed that.

Nevertheless, there was an educational wisdom in making growth the target. Growth has been the fetish of industrial society. It has been the illusory promise to the world's deprived people. It has been the rationalization that avoided the demand for social changes. As long as America could talk of financing a "war against poverty" by drawing on the "growth dividend," the nation avoided harder issues. As long as the wealthy nations could prescribe for poor nations the techniques necessary for an economic "take-off,"[31] they could escape some realities of social conflict.

John Kenneth Galbraith has pointed to the importance of growth for the ethos of the corporation. "The primary affirmative purpose of the technostructure [the people who actually run the corporations, though not usually the owners] is the growth of the firm. Such growth then becomes a major purpose of the planning system and, in consequence, of the society in which the large firm is dominant. . . . It is not surprising that the whole corpus of the technostructure is deeply committed to growth."[32] The hostility to the thesis of "limits" becomes obvious in the advertising of such corporations as Mobil and Union Carbide.

It is the idolatry of growth as the solver of intractable social problems that makes it the target of the ecological critics. Therefore their language of "limits to growth" may have been better chosen than a more precisely worded delineation of types of growth. What they are saying is that growth, of the sort the world has come to trust, has limits.

Yet it is important to keep alive any authentic possibilities. Therefore I advocate attention to the "appropriate technologies" that E. F. Schumacher[33] has helped to develop in several developing countries, to the "socially responsible economic growth" through use of "undeveloped human resources" that Peter S. Albin[34] recommends for the United States. There are many ways of combining human ingenuity with changed social structures for the economic benefit of people.

Criticism No. 4

Whatever the value of the general thesis of limits, the specific project of *The Limits to Growth* is too grandiose and ambitious. It depends on a computer model of the world system. The world system is too complicated and contains too many unknowns to be reduced to a model, least of all a model that can be computerized. (E. F. Schumacher, who had himself already sounded alarms about economic growth, joined in this criticism.)

Response

The team that constructed this model acknowledged from the beginning that the model was "imperfect, oversimplified, and unfinished."[35] Why, then, release it to the world? Because the situation is urgent, and it is better to alert the world than to keep refining a model that will always be incomplete. After all, "a model is simply an ordered set of assumptions about a complex system."[36] Any thinking about social systems makes use of models, explicit or implicit. Most thinking about the human future has assumed a model of continued economic growth. There are now strong reasons to challenge that model with a different one.

As for the computer, the basic case in no way depends on a computer. It depends only on the axiom: infinite physical growth is impossible in a finite system. Nobody challenges that.

The extra advantage of the computer is that it imposes a discipline on those who use it and it helps them see the implications of present knowledge. The computer requires (a) that certain assumptions be clarified and (b) that data be fed into the computer. Each of these is important.

(a) All thinking about social futures depends on assumptions. Often these are not stated and therefore cannot be corrected. To use the computer requires that assumptions be stated about many processes; for example, the relation of population growth to food supplies, of industrial growth to consumption of materials (renewable and non-renewable), of industry and agriculture to land use, of industry to pollution. Such assumptions will never be infallible, but the stating of them gets them out in the open where they can be debated and corrected.

(b) The computer requires quantitative data. Nobody has entirely accurate information about the population of the world, or of China, or even of American cities (as the 1980 census showed). There is even less knowledge about undiscovered petroleum or bauxite in the earth. Such unknowns mean that the computer runs will never be accurate. They encourage the familiar complaint about computer processes: GIGO (garbage in, garbage out). But clearly it is better to use the best available estimates of data than to rest content in ignorance or rely on wishful thinking.

From this point on, the advantage of the computer is that it allows quick calculations and a great variety of calculations. For instance, you can do a run with estimated data on reserves of petroleum or bauxite; then you can quickly do another run with a doubled or quintupled estimate. Similarly you can do runs with modified assumptions. One thing this computer model shows is that, on the assumption of continued exponential growth in consumption, even great new discoveries of resources do not extend the functional life of the system by very many years. Present consumption is so fantastically large, compared with all past experience, and exponential growth is so overwhelming, that it soon overtakes a doubling or quintupling of resources. Therefore a moderation of reckless growth becomes more essential for human welfare than an expansion of resources.

Criticism No. 5

A world aggregate model is entirely too simple. It leads to misleading talk about the breakdown of the world system. But obviously a breakdown of the food system in the Sahel does not mean a breakdown in Denmark.

Response

The criticism is correct. The aggregate model is a first step. It is useful to know, for example, that there are limits to the *world's* capacity to provide energy or grow food or sustain human populations, even though some regions will run out of food and other regions will run out of energy and still other regions will suffer pollution at various stages in the process. The second report to the Club of Rome moved on from the initial aggregate model to regional models.[37]

Criticism No. 6

The market system of economics is capable of handling shortages without any comprehensive planning. As specific shortages appear, prices rise. People then consume less of those items and shift to others. Or producers, responding to the incentive of rising prices, increase the supplies. The market system has repeatedly demonstrated its flexibility.

Response

The simplest answer is not *entirely* wrong. It is that the market system, which got the world into its present troubles, is not likely to remove the troubles. To count on it is a little like telling a drowning person to count on rain for help.

Still, that answer is too glib. Market systems help at some points. The rise in petroleum prices has restrained consumption, and it will lead to more restraint. The same rise has led to increased exploration for new supplies. It is probably true that a free market in petroleum, rather than the price controls that operated for a time in the United States, would have hastened the conservation movement, as happened in Europe earlier. But there are two major inadequacies in the market.

First, the market does not look far ahead, and many of the needed actions today have long lead times. OPEC prices, even though they multiplied by a factor of twenty-five or thirty in the decade of the 1970s (even prior to the war between Iraq and Iran, with its consequent price rises), are far from reflecting the greatly diminished supplies and the increased worldwide demand that can be expected in twenty-five years. Yet the answers that will function in twenty-five years need to be initiated now. Likewise food prices, though far too high for many hungry people, do not reflect the probable doubling of the world's population in the next thirty-five to forty years; but people now, night by night, are initiating the processes that lead to that doubling.

Second, market economists (ever since Adam Smith and his "invisible hand") have assumed that private good is roughly equivalent to public good. Sometimes it is: the producers, seeking a profit, direct their efforts to market demand and thereby serve consumers. But the "tragedy of the commons" is that private good sometimes conflicts with public good. It is to the public advantage that I consume less energy; I usually see my private advantage in consuming more. It is to the public advantage that parents generally have small families; the perceived advantage of many parents is in having large families. It is to the public advantage that factories reduce pollution of the air and waterways; it is to the private advantage of many factories to pollute rather than pay the costs of clean-up.

It is such realities that led Henry Ford II to say in a press interview that shortages of raw materials would require increased national planning, while preserving as much free enterprise as possible.[38] One can see many advantages of markets without expecting them to solve all the newly evident problems of industrial civilization.

Criticism No. 7

Socialism can meet the problems of scarcity because it has the ability to allocate resources, direct production, and correct pollution. It is directed toward the public interest rather than private interest.

Response

This criticism is obviously the opposite of No. 6. It was the dominant initial response of socialist societies to the new warnings about limits. It takes us back to the conflict, mentioned in Chapter 4, between neo-Malthusian and neo-Marxist ideologies. Marxism and its contemporary revisions have usually assumed that, with a proper social system and distribution of goods, production can be adequate to human need.

But socialist thinking, both in Europe and in China, is taking more seriously the question of limits. In East Germany there is discussion of *Marxismus ohne Wachstum* (Marxism without growth). The Yugoslavian sociologist Ernest Petric, while insisting that socialism has advantages over capitalism in facing ecological problems, reports on an increasing recognition among Marxists that "there are some objective conditions and ecological limits which cannot be simply abolished either by central planning or any other form of social control."[39]

China, I have noted in Chapter 5, takes seriously the importance of limiting population. Denis Goulet points out that Mao Zedong insisted that austerity was not a temporary evil to be overcome on the way to a materialistic affluence but "a permanent ingredient of authentic socialist humanism."[40] The Chinese press has not hesitated to assert that destruction of forests and grasslands for the sake of increasing food production has contributed to soil erosion and expansion of deserts; and the Chinese have been known to quote Friedrich Engels, Karl Marx's colleague and alter ego: "We should not be overpleased with our victories over nature, since nature revenges itself for our victories."[41]

In 1978 Günter Grass, the West German novelist, said of both capitalism and socialism: "Both believe in ever larger growth. They're twin brothers, born out of the Enlightenment. They were both ideas of progress and now we need to reform them."[42]

Criticism No. 8

The arguments about limits to growth emphasize physical limitations. The reality is that the world will reach social limits long before it reaches physical limits. The world now could feed its hungry people far better than it does if it had the will to do so and the appropriate forms of social and political organization.

Response

I agree, and I have tried to make the same point in Chapter 4. *The Limits to Growth* said as much at several places.[43] But it is still legitimate to call attention to physical limitations and to ask for the institutional changes that will help to cope with them. In fact, the writers of *The Limits to Growth* later emphasized that "by relying on the false promise of growth, social institutions are able to delay facing the very important and difficult tasks of making social trade-offs and defining social goals." They understood their "no-growth argument" as "an appeal for readjusting the composition and distribution of economic output" promptly.[44]

This theme is so important that I come back to it in Chapter 10.

Criticism No. 9

Past alarmists have often been wrong. History is strewn with their erroneous prophecies. Human intelligence and will has repeatedly exceeded the expectations of the doomsayers.

Response

Yes, past alarmists have often been wrong. I use that argument before the end of this book.

But past optimists have also often been wrong—from the priests whom Jeremiah condemned for "crying 'peace, peace,' when there is no peace" to such contemporary futurists as Herman Kahn, some of whose cheerful forecasts have already turned out to look silly. If history is strewn with erroneous prophecies (both gloomy and hopeful), it is also strewn with wreckage of civilizations that have fallen because they did not recognize and act on their problems. It would be quite erroneous to attribute the fall of any civilization, let alone all the past civilizations, to any single cause. But there is plenty of evidence that one major cause has been the relation between their failure to cope with physical limits and their unwillingness to meet the discontents of oppressed social classes both within their borders and outside.[45] Contemporary civilizations and the half-formed world-civilization may be nearing a similar peril.

PROSPECTS

During the 1970s the recognition of limits to growth moved from radical heresy to the conventional wisdom. Or almost so. There was still vigorous dissent, both in intellectual circles and in popular political oratory. But the awareness of limits became a common experience, either as dominant assumption or as nagging worry. There was talk around the United Nations and in the press of the new "revolution of falling expectations."

When the *New York Times* interviewed "some of the world's leading economists" on the fiftieth anniversary of the economic crash of 1929, Robert Lekachman led off the list with the observation: "The era of growth is over and the era of limits is upon us. It means the whole politics of the country has changed. All problems have become distributional. We already see it in a whole set of divisive tendencies: blacks versus Jews; men versus women, and the whole debate over energy policy, which is an argument over distribution."[46] And when *Newsweek* summed up the decade of the 1970s, it used such phrases as "a time of diminution," "a disenchanting age of limits," "the new age of limits."[47]

The reasons for the new consciousness were not primarily the arguments of books by experts, but experiences that touched people in many parts of the world: the Mideast petroleum embargo of 1973 and the subsequent rise in prices of petroleum; the end of euphoria about the prospects for nuclear energy; the famines of the early 1970s, which left people aware, even during the bumper crops of the following years, of the narrow margins on which the world operates; the experience, almost global, of inflation often combined with unemployment, an inflation which many people (including so distinguished an economist as Joan Robinson) attributed to shortages of basic materials needed for industrial growth.

There were, I should note, a series of headlines refuting the grim news about limits. A few of them referred to genuine dissents of technological optimists. But most of them were not justified by the fine print under the headlines. It was reported for example that the Club of Rome was becoming more cheerful. The Club of Rome, in fact, both in its own meetings and in the reports it sponsored, turned to proposals for positive action to meet the human predicament. But to say that it became more optimistic is to neglect (1) what I have above called the "optimism" of *The Limits to Growth* and (2) the great gulf between the proposals for action[48] and the world's willingness to act.

Four public documents have special importance for the issue. The first is *The Future of the World Economy,* a U.N. study by Wassily Leontief, Anne P. Carter, and Peter A. Petri, published in 1977. One of its chief conclusions is: "The principal limits to sustained economic growth and accelerated development are political, social and institutional in character rather than physical. No insurmountable physical barriers exist within the twentieth century to the accelerated development of the developing regions."[49]

The statement, based on intensive studies, is persuasive. But note its qualifications: (1) the "political, social and institutional" limits are, by all present indications, exceedingly stubborn; (2) the study gives no assurances about physical barriers in the *twenty-first* century, and most people now alive expect to live into that century.

The famous historian Geoffrey Barraclough made this comment on the study:

If Leontief is right in his calculation that before the end of the present century, at the present rate of consumption, we shall use up from three to four times the volume of mineral resources that humankind consumed during the whole previous history of civilization, our progress can only be compared with that of the Gadarene swine. But if we in the West pin our hope of escaping from our economic predicaments, and they in the poorer countries pin their hope of development on accelerated growth, every problem will be compounded, and the chances are that disaster, like a galloping consumption, will hit us sooner rather than later, and, like a galloping consumption, will strike us down with no hope of recovery.[50]

The second public document is *North-South: A Program for Survival,* the report of the Independent Commission on International Development Issues under the chairmanship of Willy Brandt. Its subtitle, *A Program for Survival,* shows the intensity of its concern. It sets the problem of resources, population, and starvation in the international context of inequality and threats of war. It is a call to action, not resignation. But as Willy Brandt says in his introduction, it would be "dangerous and insincere" to suggest that the problems of economic recession and international instability "can be overcome with the conventional tools of previous decades."[51]

The third public document is *Global 2000,* a report submitted to President Jimmy Carter by the State Department and the Council on Environmental Quality in 1980.[52] It foresees bitter conflict among peoples for the world's food, energy, water, and other resources, with intense suffering and death for the losers—unless the United States and the world take action not now under way.

The fourth public document is *World Development Report, 1980,* issued by the World Bank.[53] It projects great agony for the world, especially for nations that must import all their petroleum. Bank President Robert McNamara expresses his fear that the rich countries, absorbed in their domestic economic problems, will fail to carry out programs that might relieve the distress of the poorest countries.

None of these documents is fatalistic. All advocate programs of action.

But is the world—are the affluent nations—capable of action?

The most probable actions, judging from recent history, are a lurching from crisis to crisis, each nation looking to its own interests with a few palliatives for others in need. But there is the possibility of some kind of imaginative, resolute action involving both skill and will—both technological and political achievement. Despite the cries coming from repeated U.N. conferences, it will not be a universal world program—not, at least, for a long time. Political rivalries are too great. The expenditure of resources on armaments rather than economic development is too immense. But the precedents of the Marshall Plan and of various U.N. programs show that some actions are possible and get results.

The biggest obstacle is that any useful plans will require affluent societies to reduce some forms, and give up plans to expand some other forms, of consumption. They are already beginning to do that, grudgingly, especially in the case of petroleum. They might learn to do so gracefully according to plans designed to avoid disruption of domestic and world economies.

Reduced consumption does not necessarily mean misery. There is some help for both rich and poor societies, in shifting attention from Gross National Product, which is a poor measure of welfare. The

Overseas Development Council has invented a new indicator called the Physical Quality of Life Index. The PQLI puts together figures on infant mortality, life expectancy, and literacy. Human well-being involves much more than these factors, but these can be quantified. Furthermore, they automatically include some attention to social justice. A nation can have a high GNP even if some of its people are extremely poor. It cannot have a high PQLI if a significant minority die young or are illiterate. Some countries with low GNP have a high PQLI.

GNP is deceptive because it puts all expenditures on the same scale of cash value. A society can increase its use of tobacco and incur consequent cancer deaths; the tobacco and the hospital care of cancer patients both add to the GNP. If it builds unnecessary widgets, thereby pollutes waterways, then pays handsomely to cleanse the streams, it adds to the GNP—the expenditures of both the production and of the clean-up. If one country exports weapons to start a revolution in Latinafrasia and another country exports weapons to put down the revolution, both are adding to their GNP.

The place to start conservation is wherever there is waste or harmful production. That can do a lot, but more will be necessary. And more will be harder.

7. New Frontiers in Genetics

New biological science and technology raise issues quite different from those of the last few chapters. I have been looking into cases where human ambition, aided by technology, threatens to smash into planetary limitations. Biological science, by contrast, is breaking through old limits at a dazzling pace. Federal money for biomedical research in the United States jumped by a thousand times in the thirty years from 1948 to 1978, when it reached $3 billion. Week by week, press reports turn former science fiction into fact. Writers, telling the story of recent events, reach for biblical symbols: *The Second Genesis* and *The Eighth Day of Creation.* [1]

But people, great and small, wonder whether it is good to do all the new things that are possible. Once again, it is a case of forced options.

A new intellectual discipline with the name of bioethics has emerged. [2] The opinions of its practioners spread over a wide range. [3] Its domain are questions of organ transplants, the prolongation of life, the production of test-tube babies, the claims of sociobiology, issues of control of behavior by drugs and electronic means. For the sake of some sharpening of focus, I shall concentrate on only one area within it, perhaps the most important area: genetics.

THE SIGNIFICANCE OF THE NEW GENETICS

Genetics has always fascinated people. Long ago they noticed that offspring—whether of plants, animals, or people—have remarkable resemblances to parents, as well as remarkable differences. For centuries the human race has practiced selective breeding of plants and animals. In the book of Genesis (30:25–43) Jacob, who kept the flocks of his father-in-law Laban, used a genetic trick to get the best of a bargain with Laban—as Shakespeare recalled in *The Merchant of Venice*. By scientific standards the technique was so foolish that it could not have worked without supernatural intervention, which Jacob never claimed. But over the centuries there has been great progress in the genetic improvement of plant and animal stocks. (See Chapter 4 on food.)

Some people have yearned for comparable progress in human genetics. Plato in *The Republic* proposed a public lottery—secretly rigged by political authorities for genetic purposes—to determine the mating of young men and women. Some of Hitler's practices were about as sophisticated. Plato and Hitler, despite all their differences, shared the idea that good soldiers, because of their obviously admirable genetic qualities, should breed a lot of children.

Two major developments marked the progress of modern genetics. The first was the work of the Austrian monk, Gregor Mendel (1822–1884). Working with plants, he formulated genetic laws that show, among other things, why a hereditary trait (like the color of a flower) may "skip" a generation and reappear in the following generation. Human genetics is far more complex, but Mendel's explanation of dominant and recessive characteristics is still important for understanding of some hereditary traits, including some severe ailments.

The second development is the work in molecular biology that is going on now. In 1953 Francis Crick and James Watson discovered the "double helix" in the structure of DNA (deoxyribonucleic acid), the macromolecules that carry the "genetic code."[4] In quick succession have come a series of discoveries that are scintillating in their scientific virtuosity.

To understand the importance of what is happening in genetics, it is useful to note that all the human achievements of the past ten thousand years—probably much longer, but at least the whole history of civilizations—have taken place on approximately the same genetic base, so far as any evidence indicates. People of the modern world are not genetically "superior" to their ancient ancestors. In physical health they are better off, with longer life expectancy, less infectious disease because of medical and nutritional advances; but there is no reason to think they are genetically stronger. If anything, they are weaker because medicine and other arts of civilization do a lot to overcome natural selection. That is, people with hereditary ailments that once led to early death now survive and pass on their ailments to future generations. Mentally the present generation is not smarter than its precivilized ancestors, but it knows more. The inheritance of the arts and sciences is a cultural, not a genetic inheritance.

Now for the first time in history there are possibilities that the human race will intervene effectively in its own genetic development. There is heady talk about taking charge of evolution.

But the prospects are controversial. The history of genetic theory and practice has been a history of mixed superstition, folk wisdom and foolishness, and some bits of science—usually combined with racial prejudice, class distinctions, and imperialistic conquests. Eugenics (the effort to improve the human hereditary stock) of the nineteenth and twentieth century has combined vicious and naive speculations. Current public argument shows that, while the scientific elements have increased, they often still serve old partisan interests. So there are reasons for skepticism and caution about the application of new knowledge.

In Chapter 1 I quoted a statement from Herman Muller so portentous that I want to repeat it here: "Of course we—that is, humanity —will take our biological evolution into our own hands and try to steer its direction, provided that we, humanity, survive our present crises. Have we not eventually utilized, for better or worse, all materials, processes, and powers over which we could gain some mastery?"[5] I do not intend to evaluate Muller's proposals before looking at their specifics, but I am ready to protest immediately against his assumption of inevitability. I want to stake something on the faith that humanity has the freedom and ability *not* to utilize all its powers. The uses of technology are not given necessity, like the orbit of the earth around the sun. They are a human decision.

Marshall Nirenberg, who in 1961 "broke the genetic code" (showed which combination of bases in RNA produce which amino acids), writes as if he were answering Muller: "When man becomes capable of instructing his own cells, he must refrain from doing so until he has sufficient wisdom to use this knowledge for the benefit of mankind."[6] Nirenberg is asking for something rare and difficult: the wisdom to know the limits of present wisdom. He pitches the decisions about genetics into the realm of the other decisions that form the concern of this book—decisions where technological and ethical forces interact.

People today are making such decisions, decisions that were never

required and never possible in all of past history. Three areas of
decision deserve attention here: prenatal diagnosis, selective breeding,
and recombinant DNA.

PRENATAL DIAGNOSIS

Precise prenatal diagnosis of the fetus was not a possibility prior to
this generation, but it is already widely practiced. It is used most often
when parents have reason to think that their children are at risk for
specific, serious genetically transmitted ailments.

A prominent example is Tay-Sachs disease, consequences of which
are extremely severe. The infant, apparently normal, undergoes a
deterioration of the central nervous system, leading to death in the
first five years. The ailment is painful to the child, agonizing to parents. There are no known medical remedies. Whatever can be said
about the possibilities of suffering to enrich life, nobody could wish
Tay-Sachs disease on a family.

I must momentarily digress here because Tay-Sachs raises one issue
that has often emerged in the tumultuous career of genetics. Tay-
Sachs is most likely to afflict Ashkenazi Jews (those of central and
eastern European descent). It appears in one of about every twenty-
five hundred births of such couples. So it becomes a datum for theories
of racial inferiority. What the racists neglect is that various populations are at risk for various abnormalities. I come from a people
(northern and western European) more vulnerable to cystic fibrosis
than Ashkenazi Jews, or than black people, who are more vulnerable
to sickle-cell anemia. We all have our genetic assets and liabilities.
There is mounting evidence that many of the differences between
ethnic groups, once thought to be genetic, are actually cultural. Yet
there are genuine genetic differences. It is foolish either to deny them,
out of an ethical passion for equality, or to build theories of supremacy
on them, out of an insecurity that looks for flaws in other people.

After that digression, I return to my main line of thought. The
reason for choosing Tay-Sachs as an illustration is that it combines
certain characteristics that make it an especially clear example. (1)
Some people carry the recessive trait for the disease. They usually do
not know it, and it does not harm them, but they can pass it on to
their children. (2) It is now possible to test parents or prospective

parents for the recessive trait. (3) When two parents with the recessive trait produce a child, the chances are one in four (in accord with Mendelian principles) that the child will be afflicted. (4) It is possible to test the fetus for the ailment.

There are other anomalies with different characteristics. Hemophilia, the ailment of uncontrolled bleeding, is not so serious as Tay-Sachs, but it greatly inhibits and endangers life, and its treatment is extremely costly. It generally afflicts only males, although females transmit it. In some cases it is possible to predict, on the basis of a test of the prospective mother, that a male child has a one in two probability of hemophilia. It is fairly simple to determine whether the fetus is male and therefore at serious risk.[7]

Down's Syndrome—sometimes called Mongolism, another example of racial prejudice sneaking into the area of biology—is not, strictly speaking, inherited, but it has to do with the genetic stuff of life. The advancing age of the mother increases the risk of the anomaly in the child. Estimates vary, but a common one is that the risk is three out of a thousand when the mother is thirty-five, one out of twenty when the mother is forty-five. A parental test is useless, but a fetal test is practical.

Of the various methods of prenatal diagnosis (including X-ray, intrauterine photograph, and use of ultrasound devices), the most frequent is amniocentesis. This involves the insertion of a needle into the amniotic sac and the withdrawal of some amniotic fluid. Some cells, shed by the fetus, float in this fluid. Either immediately or, more often, after a period of growth in a culture, these cells can be examined for evidence of disorders. The risk of this procedure to fetus and mother, although it cannot be determined with precision, appears to be very slight. If a genetic defect is diagnosed, parents and physicians can begin preparation for treatment of the child after birth. Or, in a very few cases, they can undertake prenatal treatment. More often, if the abnormality is serious, they decide to abort the fetus.

The aims of this process compared to other genetic proposals are modest. It does not set out to reconstitute the human race or create a superrace. Its usual intention is to reduce certain specifiable and very painful ailments.

To some parents this appears a liberating practice. Whereas once they might have avoided procreation in fear, they can now go ahead with confidence that they need not give birth to children with certain untreatable abnormalities. Notice that I did not say they can be sure of a normal child. Of all ailments at birth, only twenty percent are traceable to specific gene defects, and only a fraction of the roughly fifteen hundred recognized gene abnormalities are diagnosable, although the fraction is increasing. A magazine article has the title, "Will the Baby Be Normal?" There is no known or anticipated procedure for answering this question—as there is no agreed-on definition of normality. But there are procedures for discovering some abnormalities. A family whose first child has died of Tay-Sachs disease and who greatly craves another child may now go ahead with another pregnancy, assured that they need not repeat the first experience.

The human and ethical questions arise from the fact that the aim of the process is not, as in most medical practice, the healing of the patient; the "remedy" is the destruction of the fetus. Societies, religions, and individuals differ greatly in their ethical beliefs about abortion. In the United States controversies about abortion divide the society and disturb its political processes. Again, I shall not here take up the whole set of issues.[8] For present purposes it is enough to point out that abortions following amniocentesis are a somewhat special case. Those who oppose all abortion will oppose these abortions. But in a society where abortion is common and is legal for any reason at all, the reasons for abortion of a radically abnormal fetus are probably the most persuasive reasons that can be given for any abortions. One might be morally opposed to abortion for reasons of convenience, yet approve the abortion of a fetus doomed to a short, painful life without realization of most of the qualities that constitute human personhood.

But just as there are special reasons for this kind of abortion, there are special problems connected with it. The arguments for favoring or permitting abortion assume that the fetus, at least in its early stages, is not a person with inviolable human rights. Abortions following amniocentesis usually come in the eighteenth to twentieth week. By this time the woman has felt the fetal movements. The fetus has recordable heartbeat and brain activity. It is approaching viability. The parents know some of its individuating genetic characteristics. It is a he or she, not just an it. Their sense of loss will be greater than with an early fetus.

Biomedical progress may modify some of these considerations. It may, for example, make possible earlier diagnosis and abortion, thus reducing the inhibitions against the abortion. But it may also, as it has continuously been doing, move to an earlier stage the point of viability, thus complicating the issue. (The point of viability was one consideration in the U.S. Supreme Court decision *Roe* v. *Wade,* 1973, establishing a constitutional right to abortion in the early stages of fetal development.) Whenever ethical decisions take facts seriously—as such decisions must in most of the issues of this book—changing facts require reconsideration of decisions.

Another issue is becoming more insistent. As abortion following prenatal diagnosis becomes more frequent, will the occasions for it become more trivial? Will it be used for quite minor genetic deficiencies? There has to be some limit here, because it is "normal" to have a few genetic liabilities—three to eight per person is a frequent scientific estimate. But parents crave "perfect" babies, and definitions of perfection are idiosyncratic. Marc Lappé, an experimental pathologist, states the issue: "What is really at stake is the question of whom we are ready to admit into the human community."[9]

One current controversy centers on the ethical right of a woman to abort a fetus because of its sex.[10] Is gender an abnormality that justifies abortion? Most physicians apparently oppose such abortions, and some refuse to do them, but the number of such abortions is increasing. The Report of the National Council of Churches' Task Force on Human Life and the New Genetics says that abortion because of the sex of the fetus is "destructive of human dignity"—although it leaves open the question in the case of such sex-linked ailments as hemophilia.[11]

Meanwhile research is opening up new possibilities for diagnosis of the fetus. Some specialists predict a day of mass screening of pregnant women, through a blood test (much simpler than amniocentesis), which can diagnose a small number of extremely serious "neural tube" defects. These are malformations of the brain and spinal cord that occur in about two out of a thousand pregnancies in the United States and which apparently occur at random without any past history of the disorder in either parent. Here again knowledge and control are advancing one more step over ignorance and helplessness. But physicians who are performing the tests on an experimental basis warn that the procedure requires a context of medical care and counseling not now available to all patients.

SELECTIVE BREEDING

The next program is more ambitious in the sense that it aspires to a striking improvement in the genetic quality of the human race. The argument about it is at least as old as Plato. Since we plan the breeding of cattle, should we not all the more plan the breeding of people? The obvious counterquestion is: given human dignity and recalcitrance, is it justifiable or possible to mate people like cattle?

In a minor way people have practiced selective breeding for centuries. Many a person, considering marriage, has asked: do I want N—— to be the father/mother of my children? In societies where parents "arrange" marriages, they often—not very scientifically—consider the lineage and heredity of the prospective mates. In societies where individuals choose their spouses, the surrounding social institutions often conspire against interracial marriage or against mixing of Montagues and Capulets, often with genetic hunches and prejudices in the picture.

But the twentieth century has seen new possibilities. AID (artificial insemination by donor) was the first break-through. The usual purpose has been to enable a couple to bear a child even though the husband is apparently sterile. There is generally only minor attention to genetics, in that the physician seeks a healthy donor whose genetic make-up is not radically different from the husband's. Medical students are often the donors; they are frequently available around hospitals, and physicians have an understandable inclination to assume that medical students transmit a fine inheritance. The reports will not die that occasionally a physician uses his own semen, reasoning that he would provide an obviously good inheritance and that he can use the fee as well as anybody else.

AID can become the basis of an intentional genetic program. Just as champion stallions and bulls sire many offspring, so human males, judged to be champions in one sense or another, might do the same. As in the case of animals, human sperm can be frozen to extend its potential use. A few frozen sperm banks are already in operation, usually to preserve semen of men who have undergone vasectomies in case they should later want to become fathers. The use of sperm from such banks is not common, but there are some preliminary findings. A press report in 1971 told of a man, conceived with frozen-and-thawed sperm, who had reached the age of seventeen, was in excellent health, and was an A student.[12]

Herman Muller, already mentioned above, frequently advocated that the sperm of distinguished men be preserved and made available for the procreation of many offspring.[13] His plan would not require any disruption of family patterns or any intrusion on sexual intimacy of husband and wife, except that artificial insemination would become the basis of procreation. Muller realized that many of us males, in our idiosyncratic stubbornness, would prefer to pass on our own mediocre genetic legacy rather than defer to superior human specimens. So he suggested that, if we insist on the traditional way of conceiving the first child, we should be generous enough to seek a better genetic father for the second child.

Muller knew that our evaluations of our contemporaries change frequently. His suggestions of ideal male parents regularly included Darwin; but Lenin, conspicuously present on one of his early lists, was conspicuously absent on a later one. As a cautionary measure he proposed that a period, perhaps twenty years, elapse between the death of the male in question and the release of the frozen semen, thus giving time to evaluate the prospective progenitors.

Muller's dreams have already been realized on a small scale. In March 1980 news was released about a three-year-old sperm bank in California, to which five Nobel laureates in science had contributed their sperm for the sake of "increasing the people at the top of the population."[14] The bank is appropriately named in honor of Muller.

The rules for the Muller sperm bank permit release of semen only for impregnation of wives unable to have children naturally by their husbands. And the husbands must agree. This suggests some social and ethical restraints that are not solely scientific. There is no *scientific* reason why the procedure cannot be used by a married woman without her husband's knowledge, by a single woman, or by one or both of two lesbian partners. The present restraints can, of course, readily be dropped with changing climates of opinion. In the first three years only three or four women have participated. They are reported to be "bright people."

Since Muller's proposals the first "test-tube babies" have been born —an event that raises enough issues to justify a chapter in itself. The process of *in vitro* fertilization was supervised by Drs. Robert Edwards and Patrick Steptoe in England, with the first birth coming on July 25, 1978. Edwards had earlier participated in World Council of Churches studies of the ethics of genetics.[15] His purpose is not a mass genetics program. He combines the scientist's enthusiasm for pure research with the desire for medical knowledge that will prevent some diseases and enable some infertile women to have children. But the possibilities of a major program in genetics are obvious.

The freezing and later thawing for fertilization of ova is more complex than the similar process with sperm, but it is presumably quite possible. The fertilized ovum of a calf has been frozen for a week, thawed, implanted in a host mother, and brought to birth.[16] So Muller's proposals can be expanded. There is apparently no absolute technical obstacle to the establishment of banks of frozen sperm and ova from people selected for their hereditary qualities. Scientific caution would require some experimentation to make sure that neither ova nor sperm are damaged by their long slumber in the deep-freeze.

The feasibility of the whole process has given rise to speculation about "genetic supermarkets" of the future. Husband and wife, assuming the persistence of the family in something like its present form, might consult their genetic counselor and arrange that their child be the genetic offspring of "ideal" parents of their choice.

Returning to the more cautious Muller sperm bank already in operation, anybody might ask a few immediate questions. Who chose the male donors? What did the donors assume about their own merits as genetic fathers? Although they have won Nobel prizes in science, they obviously have not won awards for modesty in their estimate of their own capacities. Why are these people regarded as genetically superior? Why not Nobel laureates in literature or peace? Why not the gold medal winners of Olympic competitions? Or the best Chinese ping pong team? Why not presidents and prime ministers of nations? Why not the top singers at La Scala and the Metropolitan Opera or Nashville's Grand Ole Opry?

If the "genetic supermarket" comes into existence, who will choose the donors? Will there be a competitive market in sperm and ova? Will the "bankers" bid for donors as professional athletic teams bid for

superstars? Will the world's advertisers flood the nations with entice-
ments? In societies where sports heroes draw greater income from
commercial endorsements than from their athletic skills, will they
some day earn even more by marketing sperm and ova? Will there be,
as geneticist Thodosius Dobzhansky used to ask, National Sperm
Banks and National DNA Banks?[17] Will prospective biological parents choose genetic parents according to criteria devised by Nobel
scientists? Or might some prefer, say, Martina Navratilova and
Muhammad Ali? Or Indira Gandhi and Robert Mugabe? Or Jane
Fonda and Deng Xiaoping?

Even technically, there are many questions about the proposal.
Would it result in a narrowing of the gene pool, which in its present
diversity maintains genetic potentialities for life situations not now
foreseen? Would it sometimes result in incestuous matings of siblings
or half-siblings who did not realize their relationship—or would couples with romantic attachments have computerized I.D. cards to
determine whether they might, if they chose, have children in the
old-fashioned way? What psychic burdens would bear down on
youths of distinguished genetic parentage and mediocre achievements? What new kinds of sibling rivalry would arise? How would
Oedipal complexes be directed?

The social and ethical questions are still more problematic. Muller
occasionally thought about these. He wanted his ideal parents to have
good physical health, high intelligence, and above all character. In
character he wanted "brotherly love" and "deep and broad human-
heartedness," along with "independence of judgment and moral courage." In his most thoughtful moments he asked whether contemporary society with its corrupted values would really choose such goals.

He might have wondered more about the relation between genetics
and character. As J. B. S. Haldane says, "We know the genetic basis
of few desirable characters."[18] On this issue it is worth noting that the
one Nobel prize winner who has publicly acknowledged his contribution to the Muller sperm bank is William B. Shockley, professional
physicist and amateur geneticist. His role in the public debates about
genetics, race, and education does not give the basis for much confidence in either his scientific understanding or his human sensitivity
on such issues. To Schockley statistics about IQ have a hypnotic
fascination reminiscent of economist Arthur Okun's observation,

"Stress on IQ is a form of narcissism peculiar to intellectuals."[19] Further evidences of his intellectual and personal qualities emerged when he explained: "In terms of my own capacities my children represent a very significant regression." He knew the reason: "My first wife—their mother—had not as high an academic achievement standing as I had."[20] Evidently genetics, which can be a valid and useful science, has as much to fear from its friends as from its critics.

It is the wider social and ethical implications of genetic practice that led the Section on Biological Manipulation at the World Conference on Faith, Science and the Future (1979) to call attention to "the tragic consequences suffered by many peoples as a result of past eugenic theories and practices." The report rejected any eugenic program for "donor insemination from 'superior people' " on two grounds: first, there is "no concensus" about " 'superior' human qualities"; second, any such program "would require the manipulative power of some experts and raise insoluble problems of who would control the controllers."[21]

Meanwhile anyone interested in selective breeding of human beings would do well to remember an anecdote, perhaps legendary, of George Bernard Shaw. The dancer Isadora Duncan suggested marriage to him, conjecturing that it would produce a wonderful child who would have her looks and his brains. Shaw's reply was to wonder what would happen if the child had his looks and her brains.

RECOMBINANT DNA (GENE SPLICING)

The most spectacular advances in recent genetic science have come in the sphere of recombinant DNA. It is possible to modify the structure of DNA in feats that go by various names: genetic engineering, genetic surgery, chemical hybridization. A more colloquial name is gene splicing.

The process is fantastically intricate. A fertilized human ovum the size of "a millionth of a pinhead" contains "coded information," to use the conventional figure of speech, "equivalent to about a thousand printed volumes of books, each as large as a volume of the Encyclopedia Britannica."[22] A mammalian cell, too small for the naked eye to see, includes (with a lot else) a yard of the double helix of DNA, only twenty angstrom units (seventy-nine billionths of an inch) in diameter.[23] Every human cell has about a million genes, which means the capacity to produce about a million different proteins, although different cells produce different proteins, so that an eye, for example, is different from a finger. To poke into such objects and restructure them is not simply a miniaturization of an appendectomy or even of brain surgery.

Scarcely a decade ago the famous biologist Jacques Monod said: "Not only does modern molecular genetics give us *no means whatsoever* for acting upon the ancestral heritage in order to improve it with new features—to create a genetic 'superman'—but it reveals the vanity of any such hope; the genome's microscopic proportions today and probably forever rule out manipulation of this sort."[24] To Herman Muller, a few years earlier, this sort of achievement looked so remote that he deliberately threw his advocacy to the alternative genetic program already mentioned.[25]

But events have come at a startling pace. It is possible—not by surgery but by chemical or bacterial agents—to reorganize DNA. Already drug companies are learning to make, patent, and sell proteins, hormones, and disease-curing substances formerly unavailable or very expensive. Four examples are insulin, human growth hormone, the antiviral interferon, and a vaccine against foot-and-mouth disease. And nobody knows what tomorrow's newspapers may report.

In this setting scientists are talking seriously about genetic therapy.[26] The hope is to locate within chromosomes specific genes that cause diseases, then to replace them with "better" genes, at first in the somatic cells, then possibly even in the germ cells. The benefits would flow to individuals, families, and the human race.

The advantages of scientific progress are obvious. If treatments like insulin, once costly, become widely accessible at low prices, millions of people will enjoy the gain. And if genetic therapy can eliminate some hereditary ailments without harmful side-effects, that is good. It means the possibility of relieving individuals of painful ailments, as surgery does now, and of relieving future generations of the same ailments, as surgery cannot do.

Inevitably a power so promising is also portentous. Genetic traits undesirable in one physical and social environment may be desirable in another. Dobzhansky, as usual, sees the point: "Does anybody know what will be best for mankind centuries or millennia hence?

... A load-free mankind [i.e., free of the load of genetic defects] may turn out to be a dull stereotype, with no particular physical or mental vigor. . . . No heredity is 'good' regardless of the environment."[27]

It is society, not biology, that turns some genetic characteristics into liabilities. Take skin color, as an example. Dark skin is a biological advantage in some climates; blonds have a hard time of it on tropical beaches. Societies, not biology, have often decreed that dark skin color would mean assignment to a fixed caste, enslavement, barriers to economic advancement, denial of civil rights, lynching. Under such circumstances it is not surprising that parents have often valued light skin color for their children. It is easy to imagine situations where, if the genetic skills had been available, some people might have attempted a "genetic therapy" to lighten the color of their offspring. A culture that is just beginning to learn that "black is beautiful" can begin to see the folly of such "therapy."

Biologist Robert S. Morison once wrote: "The thing that has saved man from his limited visions in the past has been the difficulty of devising suitable means for reaching them."[28] The more adept the human race becomes in technological skills, the more critical becomes the issue of its visions.

In the next few pages I look at two specific perils related to new genetic potentialities: the issues of manipulation and of social-political context. A third peril—that of possible, though improbable catastrophic risks—gets attention in Chapter 11.

MANIPULATION

Manipulation is a scare word, inexact and therefore confusing; yet it points to a real issue. What happens when people regard other people as objects to be designed and readjusted like the objects of laboratory research and industrial production? What happens when they do the same to themselves?

All cultural and religious traditions show some recognition of the mystery of human being. Shakespeare's Hamlet, even in a period of depression about human nature and behavior, exclaims: "What a piece of work is a man! how noble in reason! how infinite in faculty! in form and moving how express and admirable! in action how like an angel! in apprehension how like a god! the beauty of the world! the paragon of animals!"[29]

At what point, in trying to repair and improve this human being, do we inadvertently degrade humanity? People often cry out in protest against manipulation, yet at some point almost everybody welcomes it. Manipulation has become one of the major ethical issues of contemporary culture around the world.[30]

If we think of manipulation as the imposing of certain mechanical procedures upon persons, there is an element of manipulation in all medical practice from the taking of an aspirin tablet to brain surgery. We manipulate our bodies and minds when we practice physical or mental skills like learning to drive or to spell. A self includes physical-chemical processes, and there is self-deception in ignoring that important fact.

Yet a self is not an automobile, to be turned over to mechanics for a carburetor adjustment or to be superseded by new cars without carburetors. And there is something dehumanizing in regarding persons as simply intricate machines.

The issue, of course, is debatable. There are already processes for planting electrodes in animal organisms to receive signals that govern the behavior and moods of the animal. It has been proposed that an elaborate system might be devised for persons, so that a controller at a console could send electrical signals to the receptors, keeping the beneficiary in a state of uninterrupted pleasure. Of such an idea Sir Julian Huxley says, "After all, electric happiness is still happiness, and happiness is very much more important than the physical happenings with which it is correlated."[31] Other people find the idea humanly and ethically offensive. And Sir Julian himself makes his statement as a thinking, feeling human being, *not* as the mechanical reactor to a controller at a console.

Returning to genetic practices, there are ways in which new genetic knowledge can release people from age-old superstition and fear. Genetics, as a human achievement, can be humanizing. But pediatrician Judith Hall points to a possibility and raises a question: "Procreation will inevitably become more and more of a laboratory science in order to obtain normal babies. Are we willing to pay this price?"[32]

Some of the issues come to a focus in the practice of surrogate motherhood. Typical cases involve childless marriages where the wife is infertile. Another woman, either as an act of friendship or as a service for hire, agrees to artificial insemination by the husband. The married couple later adopt the newborn infant. Similar procedures are technically possible following *in vitro* fertilization where the genetic mother for reasons of health or convenience does not want to bear the child.

The commercial aspects of such transactions have led to talk of renting wombs or buying babies. The legal aspects are confusing. The legality of bearing a child for payment varies from place to place. A surrogate mother has been known to change her mind during pregnancy and refuse to give up the child. Laws can be devised to cover these and more complex cases *if* a society so chooses. The choice will depend on how far society wishes to go in separating reproduction from the organic relationships of traditional family patterns.

I know no way of drawing a line and saying: thus far, scientific direction and control are beneficial; beyond this line they become destructive manipulation. I think it more important to keep raising the question, to keep confronting the technological society with the issue. Margaret Mead with her characteristic insight did this a quarter of a century ago, thinking not of genetics but of the whole technological culture in which genetics was soon to become a prominent issue: "Was it possible that modern man might forget his relationship with the rest of the natural world to such a degree that he separated himself from his own pulse-beat, wrote poetry only in tune with machines, and was irrevocably cut off from his own heart? In their new-found preoccupation with power over the natural world, might men so forget God that they would build a barrier against the wisdom of the past that no one could penetrate?"[33]

Such questions set a context of meaning in which persons and societies may think and decide on genetic possibilities.

THE SOCIAL-POLITICAL CONTEXT

I have in this chapter used the conventional terms *genetic defects, abnormalities, ailments,* and *diseases,* as though these words had clear meanings. Sometimes they do. I could easily describe in detail a few characteristics, transmitted genetically, that anybody would consider undesirable in any time and place. These are states of health that are, beyond argument, diseases—that call for healing or prevention.

But I have already said that society, not biology, makes some human qualities into liabilities. As Alexander Capron, a specialist in medical law, puts it, "our definitions of 'disease' and 'health' are social as much as they are medical determinations.' "[34] That insight is frightening. Society already makes great efforts to perpetuate some social patterns and revoke others, including efforts to destroy old prejudices and impose new ones. Education, advertising, and politics are all efforts to communicate a sense of what is normal. A look into any past culture is likely to show that the normal is a confused mixture of characteristics that later cultures partly value and partly reject. What might be the consequences if a culture, notorious for social problems, should set out to impose its peculiar values on generations yet to come?

So disconcerting is the idea that one experimental biologist, Catherine Roberts, abandoned her scientific career because she came to believe that contemporary biology (including genetics) is radically antihumanistic. If contemporary eugenic efforts should succeed, she writes, "the world will forever have with it what it would be better off without—descendants of human beings who are artifically produced according to the whims and fancies and expert advice of one particular generation whose moral code was overshadowed by its enthusiasm for science."[35] Of course, she does not convince most of her scientific colleagues. But there are scientists—an increasing number, I think—who are concerned about the social and political determinants of science.

Even Herman Muller, despite his ambition for genetics, worried about the difficulties in his own proposals. He saw in contemporary society such corrupted values that he could have little confidence that a genetic program would be aimed at desirable human goals. He conjectured about the possibility of a "germinal race" akin to present armaments races.[36] Reading his writings some years ago, I began to imagine a secret meeting of the National Security Council at which the CIA received top-secret reports that the Russians had "cracked the genetic code" and were plotting to produce a race of superwarriors. I plotted a scenario in which the U.S. government would launch an Operation Genewar, akin to the Manhattan Project that produced the atomic bomb. All this, I thought, was playful fantasy. Then one day I read press reports that the Russians were worried that the United States was applying genetics to preparations for war.

Such fantasies aside, the present and enduring fact is that all technological advances take place within a social context. The choice of problems for research, the projected solutions, and the financing of the work all depend upon the ethical sensitivities and the structures of power within the surrounding society. That was the case even when the great scientific pioneers were lonely individuals, often at odds with the dominant powers of their society; it is more the case when science and technology are vast organized endeavors requiring immense financial support from the institutions of society.

Within that broad situation there are two quite specific examples that illustrate the problem. One is genetic screening. Any individual might welcome a voluntary test that could reveal a hidden problem and thereby make possible a healing procedure. A society might have good reasons for compulsory testing that would do the same. Most states in the United States require testing of all newborn infants for PKU (phenylketonuria), because early detection of the ailment makes possible a dietary therapy. But in the early political context of the United States, some states moved to compulsory screening of identifiable ethnic groups, not simply for ailments but for the presence of the recessive genetic traits when there was no medical treatment to follow. The result was the stigmatizing of a people whom society was already stigmatizing in many other ways.

The second example is the patenting of genetic discoveries. In June of 1980 newspapers carried headlines that the U.S. Supreme Court had ruled (by a five to four majority) that patents for new forms of life were legal. Two details were sometimes missed. (1) Patents of living organisms have long been available, as most gardeners know from buying roses and vegetable seeds. The new ruling of the Supreme Court extended the possibility of such patents, available in the United States since 1930, to "a live, humanmade microorganism," produced in the laboratories of the General Electric Company. (2) The Court said only that it understood existing legislation to authorize the patent, that Congress could change the law, and that the decision really belonged in "the legislative process after the kind of investigation, examination and study that legislative bodies can provide and courts cannot."[37]

Nevertheless, the decision set up loud reverberations. It pointed a new direction—unless Congress decides otherwise—that could determine the location of portentous power for a long time to come.

The argument in favor of the patent was that which has justified patents through a long past history: inventors deserve the rewards of their work. People cannot invest the money and energy for research without a chance at getting something back.

Why, then, did so many people respond with a shudder of foreboding? I suppose one reason was that, even in a secularized culture, there is some reverence for the mystery of life, some feeling that what human science can do is so small compared with what nature has already done, that there is an effrontery in establishing ownership and patents. The uneasiness may mount with the first applications, probably soon, for patents on new microorganisms containing human genes.

Then there was the worry about power. In authorizing patents of most inventions, society has some experience in balancing the rights of ownership against the values of diversity and competitive production. In this case nobody knows just what powers have been conferred upon great business corporations. Possibly society will discover, twenty years hence, that it has given away more power than it ever intended. It may also realize that it has contributed, beyond its intentions, to a change in the nature of scientific research: from the legendary selfless search for truth to the competitive, secret maneuvering to outperform a rival.

In Europe, where plant patents have gone far beyond anything that prevails in the United States, the Common Market countries have decided that it will be illegal to sell *nonpatented* varieties of many vegetables. The prohibition might seem an intolerable infringement on freedom in any nontotalitarian society, but it has been invoked to protect patents.[38] One danger is that the limitation of agricultural production to a small number of patented varieties will narrow the genetic diversity that for centuries has made possible adaptation of agriculture to varied changing climates and environments. Warnings on this issue have come from the National Academy of Sciences in the United States, from officials of the Food and Agricultural Organization in Rome, and from scientists at the International Center for the Improvement of Corn and Wheat in Mexico City.[39]

The commercial possibilities of genetic discoveries lead to a strange and wondrous relation between the purportedly noble motives of scientific research and the feverish atmosphere of financial speculation. One evidence is complicated legal disputes—for example, the one between the University of California and the Hoffman-LaRoche

Corporation in 1980—about property rights in discoveries made in university laboratories. Another is gyrations on the stock market where, to take one example, Genentech for a time in 1980 was selling at 8900 times its earnings, because of anticipations about future profits from genetic research. *The Economist* (London) coined a phrase, "Genetics gold rush."[40]

Harvard University faced directly the question of joining with other investors to establish a corporation for genetic engineering and to earn profits from the research already going on in its laboratories. To some the merits of the idea were clear. Why should not a university—which in any case could not survive without income from investments—get the profits from its own research and plough them back into education, rather than let them go to enterprising investors with no scientific motivation? Two counterarguments were impressive. (1) The free exchange of information, traditionally characteristic of higher education and scientific research, fits strangely with the secrecy of competitive business. (2) The explicit relating of investigation to commercially profitable enterprises is likely to skew the direction of free research, already skewed too much by subsidies from government and corporations.

Harvard's initial decision in 1980 was to refrain from the corporate venture. But soon thereafter the German corporation Hoechst A. G. contracted with Harvard's Massachusetts General Hospital to subsidize ($50 million) research in molecular biology in return for exclusive licenses to develop products commercially. Harvard and many other universities will face this sort of question repeatedly.

Genetics is one case, a very important case, where new technologies require new social decisions. Society is groping toward the discovery of methods for making those decisions. Without such methods the momentum of discovery brings about a *fait accompli* before society has reckoned with its meaning. Once again, it is the situation of the forced option. The public and its political representatives in government are not very well equipped to make decisions about genetics. But as scientist Marc Lappé says in a book aptly entitled *Genetic Politics,* "Genetics is too important to be left to the geneticists."[41]

8. The New Dimensions of War

Through all known history war has threatened human beings and their aspirations. The new thing today—the startlingly new thing—is the scale of the threat.

Neither poetry nor prose is adequate to the dramatic terror or the hard reasoning that belong to the problem. There are many important things about war that I shall not try to say here.[1] The sole theme of this chapter is the ways in which scientific technologies, by transforming the dimensions of war, confront the world now with a forced option unknown to past generations.

War is the supreme example of the irony of science and its technologies as they bear on human welfare. Only through scientific achievements can our race win some victories over starvation, disease, and other threats of nature. Yet science and its technologies have now magnified military threats almost beyond comprehension.

The intense irony becomes evident in a remark by Edward Gibbon in his famous work *The Decline and Fall of the Roman Empire,* first published in 1787. After telling much of his story, Gibbon paused to ask whether modern Europe is vulnerable to the fate that ruined Rome. His answer was a hearty *no.* His reasoning is so unbelievable to our anxious time that I must quote him directly. After observing that "in war, the European forces are exercised by temperate and undecisive contests," he went on to explain:

. . . Europe is secure from any future irruption of barbarians; since, before they can conquer, they must cease to be barbarous. Their gradual advances in the science of war would always be accompanied, as we may learn from the example of Russia, with a proportionable improvement in the arts of peace and civil policy; and they themselves must deserve a place among the polished nations whom they subdue.[2]

Out of the debacle of that confidence, so characteristic of the Enlightenment, can we today find any reasons for a more enduring hope? That is the question of this chapter.

THE SCOPE OF THE THREAT

Some of the facts are obvious. They are so overwhelming, yet so monotonously familiar, that they hardly jar anybody into attention. A quick review of a few of them helps focus the mind.

It has for years been the case that a single bomb—one of the bigger nuclear weapons, though it need not be the biggest—carries more explosive power than *all* the weapons used by *all* the combatants in World War II. Scientist Victor F. Weisskopf told a meeting of the American Physical Society commemorating forty years of nuclear fission (Washington, D.C., April 24, 1978): "The arm of technology grew by a factor of a million within the lifetime of one generation." That is a scientist talking to scientists within "the club."

Look at some of the arithmetic. Weapons specialists estimate that all the explosives used in all wars until 1964 add up to some ten megatons[3] (the equivalent of ten million tons of TNT). Add six megatons for the war in Vietnam and note, incidentally, that this means Vietnam was not a small war. That means a sum of sixteen megatons. The present U.S. arsenal amounts to about *seven thousand megatons.*[4] Add in a comparable Soviet arsenal and the smaller ones of a few more countries, and you see that nothing in all past history remotely approaches the kind of destruction that is possible now. And yet nations everywhere—above all the United States and the Soviet Union, but other nations too—are building, planning, inventing, and buying weapons for the sake—it is said—of security.

Notice, also, that the figures above refer to explosive blast alone. There used to be a distinction between high-explosive bombs and incendiary bombs. But nuclear weapons generate so much heat that they are the most powerful of incendiaries as well. What they don't pulverize they set on fire.

Add to blast and fire the effects of radiation. Radioactive fallout would hurt not only the warring nations but all those nearby and some far away. A U.N. study reports: "During the decades after a major nuclear war, fallout would take a toll of millions worldwide, in present and future generations."[5]

To estimate the total destruction is impossible. "The effects of a nuclear war that cannot be calculated are at least as important as those for which calculations are attempted."[6] So says a study of the Office of Technology Assessment of the U.S. Congress.

The disruption of world communication, transportation, and trade is one of the incalculables, but the U.N. report makes some estimates:

The sudden collapse of many of the world's leading trading nations as well as of established mechanisms for international transactions would lead to profound disorganization in world affairs and leave most other nations, even if physically intact, in desperate circumstances. Widespread famines would occur, both in poor developing countries and in industrialized nations. Those starving to death might eventually outnumber the direct fatalities in the belligerent countries. Even non-belligerent States might enter a downward spiral leading to utter misery for their populations, and almost all would suffer a loss of standards corresponding to many decades of progress. Economic conditions such as these might trigger latent political instabilities, causing upheavals and civil and local wars.[7]

In the face of such disaster, there is little comfort in the probability that such a war would not wipe out all human life. It would cause unimaginable suffering. It would destroy achievements of thousands of years. In the proverbial statement of Einstein, "If the next war is fought with atomic weapons, the war after that will be fought with clubs."

It is, in fact, a sober likelihood that civilizations of high technology would be destroyed irretrievably and forever. The reason is that contemporary civilization rests on intricate technological systems built up through centuries. Generations of people, starting with readily available resources and simple technologies, gradually produced the more complicated techniques that enable them to get along when the easily accessible resources are gone. If the elaborate superstructure is destroyed, it is extremely difficult to rebuild the infrastructure. The plentiful firewood, the rich ores lying near the surface of the earth, the unexploited continents are gone or damaged beyond healing. As Harrison Brown puts it, "It is clearly within the realm of possibility that another war would so disrupt existing industrial societies that recovery would be impossible and the societies would either revert to agrarian cultures or become extinct."[8]

By mid-1981 there were two nations with huge nuclear arsenals (the United States and the Soviet Union), two more with deliverable nuclear weapons (the United Kingdom and France), and another two that had exploded nuclear devices (China and India). Nations with a capacity to build nuclear bombs included Canada, West Germany, Israel, Italy, Japan, Pakistan, South Africa, Sweden, and Switzerland. Another ten nations were within a few years of such capacity.

This situation has led to the worldwide debate about "nuclear proliferation," a debate that involves irresolvable ethical dilemmas. An obvious fact is that as more and more nations possess nuclear weapons, more and more are able to use them. The fact has led to the theory of the *nth* nation: the theory that at some point not precisely predictable the proliferation of nuclear weapons means that their use becomes more probable than not.

Out of this concern came the Non-Proliferation Treaty (NPT), approved by the General Assembly of the United Nations in 1968 and signed by forty-three nations. Among the known nuclear nations, France and China did not sign, although neither has acted against the provisions of the NPT. Among other nations a good many did not sign, including six of the "threshold" nations: India, Israel, South Africa, Pakistan, Argentina, and Brazil. The treaty calls for review every five years, and there have been such reviews in 1975 and 1980.

The treaty was a bargain of sorts between nuclear-armed and non–nuclear-armed nations. The former agreed to share their peaceful nuclear technologies with the latter, and the latter agreed not to develop nuclear weapons. Put that way, there was suppose to be an advantage to all involved. The International Atomic Energy Agency was designed to facilitate the exchange of technologies and to inspect nuclear facilities to assure that there was no diversion of materials to weapons. The spread of nuclear weapons among nations is often called "horizontal proliferation," and one aim of the NPT was to stop that trend.

Another aim was to stop the intensification of nuclear armament among nations that already had nuclear weapons. That intensification is often called "vertical proliferation." In Article VI of the NPT the nuclear powers agreed to negotiate "in good faith" toward the goal of disarmament "at an early date." The language was vague and unenforceable. The course of events has brought the exact opposite of disarmament.

A result is increasing discontent, even anger, among the nations without nuclear weapons. They resent the treaty's invidious distinction: one set of rules for the nuclear-armed nations and another set of rules for the rest. Those who signed accepted the temporary discrimination, because the NPT declared the aim of doing away with it. Now they complain: we are keeping our pledge, but the superpowers are not.

Thus it is hard, if not impossible, for the United States or Soviet Union to frame an ethical argument against horizontal proliferation. If, for example, they make clucking sounds about a nuclear test explosion in India, the Indians ask skeptically: does the world really tremble in fear that India may unleash nuclear war?

Yet horizontal proliferation has real risks. Suppose, for example, that in the last decade or two nuclear weapons had been available to Balthazar Vorster in South Africa, Ian Smith in Rhodesia, Idi Amin in Uganda, Pol Pot in Cambodia, Jean-Bédel Bokassa in the Central African Republic, Muammar Qaddafi in Libya, and a few bands of terrorists in Palestine and scattered places. Suppose that the former Shah of Iran had possessed a few nuclear weapons, which then fell into the hands of one or another of the factions that later contended for power in Iran. Surely anybody—revolutionary or dictator, leftist or rightist—wants nuclear weapons kept from *some* of the political powers in that miscellaneous list. I need not make an ethical judgment on the people just listed. It is enough to point to the dangers in the unpredictability of behavior in such a diverse group.

In the present unstable situation any declaration on proliferation by political leaders of nuclear-armed nations is bound to look a little silly. Thus former President Carter's efforts to halt proliferation appeared sanctimonious in view of the huge nuclear arsenal that he commanded. And President Reagan's unconcern about proliferation—granted that in the presidency he moderated the rash statements of his campaign—appeared irresponsible. The truth is that nuclear weapons are a mighty hazard to the world, but those who control them are in a poor position to lecture others about the threat.

One further aspect of the arms race cries for attention. Even if a nuclear weapon is never again used, the competition in armaments is itself damaging. Harrison Brown reckons that "altogether some 375,-000 scientists and engineers are dedicating their research skills to military problems, representing perhaps 40% of the world's total pool of highly qualified research people."[9] The diverting of such skills (and material resources and money) from problems of energy, food, housing, and health services can only cause vast suffering for an already troubled world.

Ruth Leger Sivard, formerly chief economist of the U.S. Arms Control and Disarmament Agency, in her annual study of military and social expenditures, points out:

In rich and poor countries alike, governments neglect elemental social needs in order to expand military power. World-wide, the technology of destruction gets more political attention, and more public funds, than the immediate pressures of the energy shortage, or the profound human suffering in unemployment, poverty, ill-health, and hunger among hundreds of millions of the world's people.[10]

It is, of course, the wealthiest countries that spend the most for armaments. But the poor countries, in their efforts to keep up the pace, have been increasing expenditures faster than the rich countries. As Mrs. Sivard shows, "Developing nations carry three times as much insurance against military attack as against all the health problems that strike people on a day-to-day basis."[11]

The Report of the Brandt Commission, which I mentioned in Chapter 6, states: "The [world's] annual military bill is now approaching 450 billion U.S. dollars, while official development aid accounts for less than 5% of this figure." As one example it reports: "One-half of one percent of one year's military expenditure would pay for all the farm equipment needed to increase food production and approach self-sufficiency in food-deficit low-income countries by 1990."[12]

I should not oversimplify the argument. Weapons specialists sometimes say that one attraction of nuclear weapons, in strictly military terms, is that they are so cheap compared with "conventional" means of destruction. In reply, it should be noted that their true cost includes the human resources that go into their design and construction, as well as the cash and materials that go into the weapons themselves, the delivery systems, the spy-in-the-sky satellites by which nations monitor one another, and the extensive military support systems that surround nuclear weapons. There is also their contribution to the worldwide atmosphere of anxiety and terror that leads many a nonnuclear nation to deprive its people for the sake of a military establishment. Nuclear weapons are the center of a circle whose circumference reaches far into human affairs.

At the World Conference on Faith, Science and the Future in 1979 it was the physical scientists, even more than the theologians and church leaders, who insistently, emphatically pushed for a resolution pleading for "the reduction and eventual abolition" of nuclear weapons.[13] They knew the facts.

ETHICS AND REALPOLITIK

The ethical meaning of the arms race got forceful expression in an important essay by two scientists in 1964. The writers were Jerome Wiesner and Herbert York, who explained that they had both been "engaged for most of our professional lifetimes in consultation on this country's military policy and in the active development of the weapons themselves."[14] (I used a generalization from this article in Chapter 2; now I want to look at its more detailed reasoning.)

The writers were far from typical peaceniks. Wiesner chaired the President's Science Advisory Committee in the Kennedy administration, then became president of the Massachusetts Institute of Technology. York was director of the Livermore Laboratory, organized to work on thermonuclear weapons, and he directed defense research in the Eisenhower administration. The specific issue, at the time they wrote, was the nuclear test ban, but their analysis goes into the whole problem of nuclear weapons.

They start with the assumption: "National security, of course, involves moral questions and human values—political, social, economic and psychological questions as well as technological ones." But, they explain, given their experience, they can best "devote the present discussion to the technological questions."[15]

So they work their way through the technical questions of armaments, using figures, charts, and military reasoning. They then come to the conclusion that *there is no technical way to achieve national security:*

Ever since shortly after World War II the military power of the United States has been steadily increasing. Throughout the same period the national security of the United States has been rapidly and inexorably diminishing.

Both sides in the arms race are thus confronted by the dilemma of steadily increasing military power and steadily decreasing national security. *It is our considered professional judgment that this dilemma has no technical solution.* If the great powers continue to look for solutions in the area of science and technology alone, the result will be to worsen the situation. The clearly predictable course of the arms race is a steady open spiral downward into oblivion.[16]

Thus they find themselves driven back to the very factors they initially excluded: the "moral questions and human values—political, social, economic and psychological questions." And they find some hope in initiating international agreements that "would set significant precedents and lay the foundations of mutual confidence for proceeding thereafter to actual disarmament."[17]

To move the issue into the area of ethics and social change does not make a solution any easier. It raises the perennial question of the relation of ethical visions to the political practice. For centuries people have found their hearts moved by the ancient prophecy in Isaiah 2:4:

> And they shall beat their swords into plowshares,
> and their spears into pruning hooks;
> nation shall not lift up sword against nation,
> neither shall they learn war any more.

But the prophecy has not been fulfilled in twenty-seven centuries.

Political realism is a recognition that societies act in terms of their perceived interests—whether those interests be good or bad in a more ultimate ethical perspective. Through most of history war has served the interests of societies, not always their true interests but their interests as they perceived them. Most independent nations won their freedom through wars. Nations with superior military power frequently conquered nations with inferior military power. So the social question becomes one of relating ethical insight to the *realpolitik* of the world in which we live. In the painful but cogent words of William

Temple, a great archbishop of Canterbury: "We tend to follow one or other of two lines: either we start from a purely ideal conception, and then we bleat fatuously about love; or else we start from the world as it is with the hope of remedying an abuse here or there, and then we have no general direction or criterion of progress."[18] The real ethical decisions that can help the world must somehow relate human idealism, which is unquenchable though not immediately efficacious in the world of nations, to the perceived interests of nations, which in our time include the interests of the Kremlin and the Pentagon.

At just this point nuclear weapons have brought an epochal change. The new realization is that *nuclear war does not serve the national interests of any nation.* This insight is hard to appropriate, hard to fit into national policies formed through a long past. But it is here to stay.

Once it could be argued that war or the capacity to fight war could really accomplish some purposes. Not all purposes, but some purposes, whether such valid purposes as self-defense and the overthrow of tyrannies or such dubious purposes as conquest. The new situation is that nuclear war, in the dimensions described by sober scientific judgment, cannot accomplish any rational social or national purpose. It does not serve the interests of societies and nations. And the armaments race brings "steadily increasing military power and steadily decreasing national security."

But do the political leaders of the nations show any recognition of what is so obvious to experienced scientists? There is strong evidence that they do. Former President Dwight D. Eisenhower, three times in the final year of his presidency, addressed the issue. For example, in Rio de Janeiro in 1960, he said:

Nations now possess power so terrible that mutual annihilation would be the only result of general physical conflict. War is now utterly preposterous. In nearly every generation the fields of earth have been stained with blood. Now war would not yield blood—only a great emptiness of the combatants, and the threat of death from the skies for all who inhabit the earth.[19]

And former President Lyndon Johnson in 1964 said: "General war is impossible and some alternatives are essential."[20] He did not mean, of course, that nuclear war is literally impossible. It might happen. He meant that it is an impossible means of achieving national aims.

Every succeeding president has made the same point, but often in a muted way. In the international game of bluffing, presidents some-times pretend not to fear what they really fear. To acknowledge the known truth may give the appearance, to an antagonist, of weakness. But from time to time the truth shows through the bluff.

For the same reason Soviet leaders are reluctant to state openly the truth that they see, but sometimes they do. Secretary Nikita Khru-shchev frequently described the consequences for the Soviet Union of a nuclear war,[21] and in 1964 he said, "Only a child or idiot does not fear war." His successors, who (like the United States) have used lesser military power, have warily avoided the confrontation that could lead to nuclear war.

So widespread is the recognition of the real situation that Gene Preston, a faculty member at the U.S. Military Academy at West Point, describes most of the cadets there as "nuclear pacifists" and explains:

Many American officers, knowing the devastating effect of strategic nuclear weapons upon civilian populations, and of even subkiloton nuclear tactical weapons on their own troops, long ago sought to define ethical responsibility in a neat dichotomy: in nuclear matters, one is a conscientious objector; in conventional military matters, one is sworn to defend the national interest with one's life.[22]

If the understanding of the purposelessness and potential disaster of nuclear war is so widespread, why then is nuclear disarmament not simple? Why does the arms race continue? Is it simply an absurd desire, in Winston Churchill's pungent phrase, "to make the rubble bounce"?

No, there is a peculiar kind of logic in the arms race. Advocates of peace do not help their cause by ignoring it.

MAD RATIONALITY

Robert Oppenheimer, the famous nuclear physicist, has described the world in a vivid analogy.[23] Imagine two scorpions in a bottle. Each has a deadly sting and can immediately destroy the other. But the victim can in its moment of destruction lash back and destroy the aggressor. So the two scorpions maneuver warily. They annoy each other in all kinds of ways, but stop short of delivering the fatal sting.

Imagine further (to update Oppenheimer's analogy) that the bottle includes many smaller insects with lesser poisonous powers. And some of them are on their way toward developing the venomous sting of the scorpions.

It is a dangerous and unpleasant place to live. Some fighting goes on—some stealing, scratching, and biting. But neither scorpion uses its sting, because it is afraid of the consequences.

The baffling facts are that the bottle would be a safer place to live if each scorpion lost its sting, but it would not be a better place if there were only one scorpion, who could fearlessly terrorize everybody. Because there are two scorpions, each behaves with some restraint.

In today's world of nations the logic of deterrence is that each of the superpowers, with an ability to destroy most of civilization, knows that use of its power will bring retaliatory destruction. The system has the name Mutually Assured Destruction, with the acronym MAD. There is a MAD rationality in the system of deterrence.

The system has one achievement to its credit. The world saw only twenty-one years between the two world wars. The interval since the end of World War II (1945) is already more than half again as long. (At least, World War III has not started as I write this, and if it starts —on a nuclear scale—before this book is published, I assume that nobody will be reading this.) The interim has not been a time of peace. By Harrison Brown's accounting, there were some ninety-seven wars in the first quarter-century (1945–1969) after World War II.[24] There have been more since then. Some of these wars were greater in scope and destruction than many of the famous wars of past history. But none of them was *the* world conflagration. The balance of terror has worked to the extent of preventing a nuclear war.

That is no reason to expect that it will work forever. A rash act, an accident by either of the superpowers—and increasingly, by other nuclear nations—can end the system once and for all. In the words of a U.N. report, "So long as reliance continues to be placed upon the concept of the balance of nuclear deterrence as a method for maintaining peace, the prospects for the future will always remain dark, menacing and as uncertain as the fragile assumptions upon which they are based."[25] MAD rationality is a shade better than mad irrationality. But at best it offers a fleeting alternative to total irrationality, an insecure interim in which the world might move toward sanity.

Ethically the MAD system is an atrocity—even if, as I think, it is momentarily preferable to some alternate atrocities. Each of two superpowers restrains itself because of fear of retaliation. But that fear depends on the perception that the adversary really is able and ready to retaliate. If either is convinced that the other cannot or will not retaliate, the way is opened to exercise arbitrary power with impunity.

Political scientist Hans Morgenthau once described the situation as follows:

The United States and the Soviet Union have continued to threaten each other with nuclear war, although this threat has always been implausible in view of the radical difference between nuclear and traditional violence. Thus in the successive Berlin crises and the Cuban crisis of October, 1962, the United States and the Soviet Union tried to convince each other that they were irrational enough to incur their own destruction by supporting their respective positions with nuclear violence, assuming at the same time that the other side would be rational enough not to provoke such an irrational reaction. . . . Deterrence has thus far worked only because there has remained in the minds of both sides a doubt as to whether the other side was really bluffing.[26]

I can think of no circumstance that would justify willingness to unloose nuclear destruction—except the MAD rationality that such willingness is the momentarily effective bar to nuclear destruction. Such a position is intolerable to any form of ethical rationalism. Yet many people are today in that agonizing position because they would rather prevent war than preserve their own rational consistency or virtue. Those in that unhappy position have responsibility to do whatever they can to get out of it and into a better position.

The absurdity comes to a focus in the debate about counterweapon weapons. In the MAD rationality each adversary, in effect, holds hostage the cities of its prospective foe, because nuclear weapons can destroy whole cities in a moment. If America—so the logic goes—can in minutes knock out Moscow, Leningrad, Kiev, and the other major Soviet cities, and if the Soviet Union can simultaneously knock out Washington, New York, Chicago, and the other major American cities, neither side will be so suicidal as to initiate nuclear war. Politicians, military commanders, and whole nations become, like the West Point cadets, nuclear pacifists.

But then a new logic enters the picture. Suppose one nation develops weapons and targets them with precision on the weapons—not the cities—of its adversary. Then it might let go its weapons, destroy the weapons of its foe (and incidentally quite a few people), and remain immune to counterattack. This reasoning ignores the likelihood that the victim nation, when its warning systems tell of approaching weapons, will let go its own weapons *before* they are destroyed.

In classical political and military ethics—often disregarded in the name of military necessity, but still asserted wherever conscience refused to succumb totally—the targeting of a city was a crime, whereas the targeting of an enemy's weapons might be a justifiable act. Some analysts—for example, Paul Ramsey—still maintain that position. But for others the antiweapon nuclear weapon is a new stage in the disintegration of ethics. The reason is that the deterrent is justifiable only on the expectation and belief that it will have some effect in preventing war—that it will not, in fact, be used. The antiweapons weapon is planned with the expectation that it may indeed be used in a "limited nuclear war." But the very premise of a limited nuclear war is so dubious, given its destructiveness to objects, people, and the global atmosphere, that any step in that direction is an invitation to disaster.

The same logic applies to justifications of "small" tactical nuclear weapons as contrasted to large strategic weapons. Former President Carter's Directive 59, issued in 1980, was widely understood as a change in American policy. Actually, at least since the Kennedy administration, U.S. policy had included such weapons. The Carter directive brought it to public attention again. And insofar as it made the notion of nuclear warfare more acceptable, it contributed to the disintegration of a restraint important to the whole human future.

It can, of course, be argued that the worst of the fire bombings of cities in World War II killed more people than died at Hiroshima or Nagasaki and than some future uses of tactical nuclear weapons might kill. But the wrongness of some atrocities does not justify the wrongness of others. And the argument obscures the fact that, if Dresden marked the top rung of one ladder of destruction, the "smallest" nuclear weapons are the bottom rung of another ladder of far greater proportion. Nuclear weapons mark the threshold of a qualitatively different kind of warfare. There is no reason to suppose that any pair of nations crossing that threshold will stop at other thresholds. That is why John Bennett, after a lifetime of studying issues of war and peace, concludes: "There is no way of stretching Christian ethics, or any other humane ethics, to justify . . . the initiation of nuclear war, even if the intention is to keep it limited."[27]

The question is how the human race gets out of nuclear MADness. No one can guarantee that there is an answer. But to turn to possibilities of an answer is the responsibility of our generation. In that sense we are one of the few landmark generations of all history.

WHY CHANGE IS SO HARD

In a world where the leaders of the great nations acknowledge the futility of nuclear war, why is change so hard to achieve? Since a major war is not in the national interest of anybody, and since escalation of the arms race increases insecurity, why don't the nations change their ways?

The answer, insofar as there is a rational answer, is that weakness also is not in the national interest of anybody. Repeatedly in recent years the weakest have been invaded, outbluffed, victimized.

The pattern of international relations corresponds to familiar game theory. If all parties were to reduce their arms, everybody would be safer and more prosperous. But if only some do, they become vulnerable to those who do not. So nations—especially the two with greatest military strength—live in fear of each other. And fear magnifies the worry about their own weakness and the power of others.

That is why right now voices in Washington are urging increased expenditures on armaments to "catch up" with the Soviet Union, while voices in Moscow call for efforts to match U.S. armaments. In the controversies about military superiority, it almost seems that the debaters elaborate their arguments and then make up the statistics to support those arguments. The citizen, who is personally unable to count bombs and missiles, becomes bewildered at the clash of claims.

On closer examination, the difference turns out to hang less on the statistics—granted their imperfection—than on the way they are reckoned. And on this point any citizen can understand the argument. It has three aspects.

(1) It is hard enough to reckon parity between two nations—for example, the United States and the Soviet Union—but even that

barely begins to get at the strategic issue. The Soviet Union feels a need to match the United States *plus* the NATO forces *plus* China, all of whom it sees as real or prospective enemies. And the United States feels insecure unless it alone can match the Soviet Union and all its allies in Eastern Europe, Africa, Latin America, and Southeast Asia. Any conceivable parity between such rival constellations of power is a logical absurdity.

(2) Arguments about parity soon come to specifics. If one power has greater throw-weight and another power has more missiles, each feels a need to catch up with the other, and such mutual escalation can be infinite. Similarly, parity is geographically conditioned. Is the worry about parity in the Persian Gulf or in the Caribbean, in Poland or in Latin America, in Afghanistan or in Angola? The old doctrine of spheres of influence was an inadequate way of meeting such issues. But when two great powers extend their influence throughout the world, there is no way that each can achieve equality with the other *everywhere*.

(3) Each power is worried, not only about its rival's present capacities, but also about potentialities. Each hears rumors that its adversary may be developing a capacity for a first strike, a successful antiballistic missle, a deadly laser beam, a killer satellite—in short, some breakthrough that will upset the precarious balance of terror. So each strains to develop the answer to every conceivable capacity that the other may attain. And that possibility is, again, a logical absurdity.

It is such fears that bedevil attempts to modify and reverse the arms race. The problem is obvious in all the Strategic Arms Limitations Talks (SALT). Each side wants the other side to hold back on those weapons in which the other side is strong. Contrariwise, each side, in proposing limits, wants to catch up with the other side at every point. Hence the limits are set so high that the agreements encourage more armaments rather than less. Obviously that method won't accomplish much.

On June 12, 1979 I sat in the East Room of the White House while President Carter and National Security Adviser Zbigniew Brzezinski gave the reasons for SALT II. This was one of a series of meetings in which they sought (and finally failed) to rally support for the proposed treaty that had been developed in the Nixon–Ford administrations and completed in the Carter administration. I found Carter and Brzezinski impressive on that day in their logic and mastery of facts as they responded to questions. The heart of their case was the importance of instituting SALT II—inadequate though it was, as both said—as a step in an agreement that could lead to further steps.

But there was a troubling and unavoidable paradox in their presentation. They were defending SALT II against those who thought it went too far and those who thought it didn't go far enough. So they used two arguments: (1) There's nothing sentimental about SALT. It does not depend on our trust of the Russians. We have adequate instruments of inspection to monitor Soviet compliance. (2) SALT can be a stage toward a safer, more trusting world.

That is a hard paradox to maintain: working toward trust while relying on the institutions of distrust. But I don't know any way, given the present condition of the world, to sidestep that paradox.

The reasons for distrust are not sheer fantasy. Each side is trying to restrain and undermine the other. The United States has seen Soviet coercion in Hungary, Czechoslovakia, and Afghanistan. Andrei Sakharov, the Russian scientist and advocate of civil rights, has said that the United States must maintain military strength as a prerequisite to negotiations for disarmament.[28] Francois Mitterand, the socialist president of France, is more explicit in his warnings against the Soviet Union than his more conservative predecessor, Valery Giscard d'Estaing. From the other side, the Soviet Union has seen the United States support the effort at the Bay of Pigs to overthrow Castro's regime in Cuba, plot against socialist regimes in Latin America, and fight furiously in Vietnam.

The problem is to break the vicious circle of fear and hostility, to build actions that will restore trust and confidence in a world where reasons for distrust are real and great.

POSSIBILITIES FOR CHANGE

The need is for a massive multilateral reversal of the arms race. Nothing less will do.

Unilateral disarmament on any grand scale is futile for two reasons. First, it simply won't happen. Neither of the scorpions will give up its sting and leave the other one sole master within the bottle. Second, it is doubtful that it ought to happen. When only one nation had nuclear weapons, it used them. The one thing more dangerous than the balance of terror is a monopoly of terror. Unilateral renunciation of nuclear weapons may be a valid option for some nations; it is not an answer to the world situation.

I do not expect my position to convince either those militarists who reject any possibility of arms reductions or those pacifists who advocate radical unilateral disarmament. But at least I can show that my advocacy of multilateral steps is not paranoid nationalism. In the ludicrous event that the Soviet Union should ask my counsel on disarmament, I would give them the same advice that I give Americans: seek multilateral disarmament. In fact, in 1963 when the United States had nuclear superiority, I took the position—an unusual and unpopular one at that time—that the world would be a little safer if the Soviet Union achieved approximate parity of military power with the United States.[29]

But if massive unilateral action is not helpful, unilateral initiatives may be. A society that has celebrated individual initiative as heartily as ours should not reject out-of-hand the possibility of national initiatives. I see four kinds of action that the United States and its allies —or concerned people within these countries—can initiate. All of them rest on the "moral" and "human" base that Wiesner and York found necessary to prevent our "spiral downward into oblivion."

Break the Pattern of Dogmatic Ideological Thinking

There is a peculiarly religious dimension to international conflict today, as much as ever in the past. Psychologist Gordon Allport in his famous book *The Nature of Prejudice* wrote:

The role of religion is paradoxical. It makes prejudice and it unmakes prejudice. While the creeds of the great religions are universalistic, all stressing brotherhood, the practice of these creeds is frequently divisive and brutal. The sublimity of religious ideals is offset by the horrors of persecution in the name of these same ideals.[30]

It is a further paradox that in this secularized world international conflicts are as intensely dogmatic-religious as in the days when the gods of traditional religion led their peoples into war. Herbert Butterfield, the distinguished British historian, puts it this way:

But the greatest menace to our civilization today is the conflict between giant organized systems of self-righteousness—each system only too delighted to find that the other is wicked—each only too glad that the sins give it the pretext for still deeper hatred and animosity. The effect of the whole situation is barbarizing, since both sides take the wickedness of the other as the pretext for insults, atrocities, and loathing; and each side feels that its own severities are not vicious at all, but simply punitive acts and laudable measures of judgement.[31]

The issue here is not religion versus irreligion. It is whether the religious element that is implicit in all great loyalties shall be simply a projection of partisan ideology or shall have some transcendent dimension that relativizes all partial claims and calls into judgment all ideologies.

Move the World Toward the Point Where Everybody Has a Stake in Peace

Here we start with the fact that neither the United States nor the Soviet Union will rationally wipe each other out; and no other nation will seek to wipe out these two. The act of destruction of an enemy means self-destruction. It serves no national interest.

Still, it may happen. It may happen by accident or by miscalculation in the global game of "chicken." The game that has gone on in Berlin, Cuba, Southeast Asia, and Afghanistan may get out of hand. But each side has a stake in avoidance of the great conflagration. Each side, though under severe irritation from time to time, has shown some restraints.

But some people and societies do not recognize a stake in peace. In some nations there are people who, seeing nothing to lose, might unloose the bombs that others have thus far held in reserve. Just as there are terrorists so desperate that they lose regard for their own survival, there may be governments in nations so desperate that they will accept universal destruction rather than continue in their angry despair.

Violence is not always an act calculated to gain an end. Rollo May wisely writes: "For no human being can stand the perpetually numbing experience of his own powerlessness. . . . Violence is the ultimate destructive substitute which surges in to fill the vacuum where there is no relatedness."[32]

One step toward peace is to nudge the world in the direction of a situation where everybody has a stake in peace. For this reason crusades for disarmament that concentrate solely on disarmament are self-defeating. Questions of food and resources—all the issues of earlier chapters in this book—are important to peace.

I am not arguing that in a more just world all incentives to warfare will disappear. That is one illusion of some decent people who love justice and peace. The trouble with it is that prosperous nations make war as readily as poor ones, and they do more damage because they can buy bigger weapons. All I am here maintaining is that nations with a stake in peace will not rationally bring about their own destruction. And even irrational self-destruction is less likely among people who have some stake in peace.

Initiate Serious Disarmament

I have been saying that there is little help in agreements on "arms limitations," when the limits are far above present realities. The need is for actual reduction. But the skeptical question is obvious: if nations (in particular, the U.S. Senate) cannot agree on limiting their expansion of arms, is there any reason to think they can agree on reduction?

The answer is: the method has been tried, and it has worked. Granted, it was not tried on a big scale, and it did not work for long. But for a short while it happened.

William Epstein, formerly director of the Disarmament Division of the U.N. Secretariat, has summarized the story: ". . . in 1963–64 both the United States and the Soviet Union carried out budget reductions, not by agreement, but unilaterally by what Khrushchev called 'the policy of mutual example' and the Americans called 'reciprocal unilateral acts.' And there were no charges of bad faith on either side."[33]

What then went wrong? In the aftermath of the Cuban missile confrontation of 1962, Khrushchev lost his job and his successors decided to increase armaments. The escalation of warfare in Vietnam turned the international atmosphere more sour, as the Soviet invasion of Afghanistan has done more recently.

It is time to try again. A formal agreement is not necessary. There need be no haggling over details, no bargaining over inspection (which both parties know how to do without each other's consent). The United States can begin with a deliberate act, sending notice to the Soviet Union—whether an official message or some informal "signal" is a matter of diplomatic tactics—that a reciprocal action will bring a further initiative from our side. Nobody needs to worry about signing an agreement, because mutual interest is a better guarantee than signed documents and sanctions. It is a matter of judgment whether the first steps are done with a skillful dramatic sense, so as to rally world support, or quietly, so as to avoid any atmosphere of showdown. But it does matter that they be done as a deliberate act, with a purpose of starting a sequence of acts, so that they do not appear as merely the irresolution of an undisciplined people who are tired of paying taxes.

As one possibility the eminent scientist Victor F. Weisskopf has proposed to both the United States and the Soviet Union, that they start a "Peace Race" by reducing their weapons by an initial ten percent *without waiting for an agreement.* He reasons that the act might bring reciprocal action, but that, even if it does not, the remaining weapons are still an overwhelming deterrent. In fact, he says that the nation who begins this process will thereby be a little more, rather than a little less, secure. It is significant that Weisskopf's proposal, submitted in response to questions from *Tass,* was printed in full in the *Moscow News* in Russian, English, French, and Spanish editions.[34]

A more startling idea comes from George F. Kennan, one of America's most experienced and distinguished diplomats. He advocates that we "cut surgically through all the exaggerated anxieties, the self-engendered nightmares, and the sophisticated mathematics of destruction" characteristic of SALT negotiations in order to try a new venture. The United States, he urges, might "propose to the Soviet government an immediate across-the-boards reduction by 50% of the nuclear arsenals now being maintained by the two superpowers . . . all this to be implemented at once . . . and to be subject to such national means of verification as now lie at the disposal of the two powers."[35] He sees in the proposal no real risk and no reason to worry about precise compliance at fifty percent, because "there would still be plenty of overkill left." His hope is that this first step would lead to another reduction, and then another.

There would still be plenty of problems left, but the initial action —with its easing of insecurities and its lifting of economic burdens on both sides—could mark a change in the direction of history.

Anybody can think of a hundred variations of scale and detail. The point that matters is this: initiatives *are* possible.

Maintain the Belief in an Open Future

The greatest obstacle to change—greater even, I think, than the atmosphere of distrust—is the sense of futility and fate that suffuses most of the human race. It produces a stifling apathy, not the apathy of contentment but the apathy of futility.

Against this apathy Western religious traditions, especially those rooted in the Hebrew and Christian scriptures, bring a conviction of the openness of the future. It is the belief in the freedom of God and his human creatures, the conviction of the possibility of repentance and change of ways.

Recent history suggests vindications of this belief. The worst does not always happen. Think, for example, of the prediction of C. P. Snow, the Englishman famed for achievements in science, government, and literature. Addressing the American Association for the Advancement of Science in December of 1960, he warned about the proliferation of nuclear weapons and said: "Within, at the most, 10 years, some of those bombs are going off. I am saying this as responsibly as I can. *That* is the certainty."[36] His concern was right, but his certainty was wrong—at least by more than ten years. His worst expectations may be realized any year, any day; but destruction is not inevitable.

History shows unexpected turns of events. Who during World War II would have predicted the present friendly relations of the United States with West Germany and Japan? Who would have predicted that Richard Nixon, who made a career of exploiting Communist phobias, would finally make his claim to a decent place in history on the basis of his rapprochement with China? I do not say that these past changes make the next step easier; in fact, they came about because of the shared rivalries with the Soviet Union. So a greater reconciliation—or even a cautious willingness to learn to live together in one world—will be harder. All I maintain is that historical inevitability is not an absolute barrier.

The reasons for investing some courage and imagination in the effort are momentous. As George Kennan writes in an earlier context, we face "truly apocalyptic dangers" that "threaten to put an end to the very continuity of history outside which we would have no identity, no face, either in civilization, in culture, or in morals." Our concern, he continues, must therefore be "to see that man, whose own folly once drove him from the Garden of Eden, does not now commit the blasphemous act of destroying, whether in fear or in anger or in greed, the great and lovely world in which, even in his fallen state, he has been permitted by the grace of God to live."[37]

PART III

PERVASIVE SOCIAL, ETHICAL, AND RELIGIOUS ISSUES

9. The Freedom and Accountability of Science

Science is a social activity, operating within society and affecting society. In our time it has become a huge activity involving big investments, big organizations, big consequences. Society has a stake in its methods and findings. But the society that supports or harasses science, that gains or suffers from its achievements, hardly knows how to relate to its intricacies. So questions of freedom and accountability, troubling enough in all human affairs, become acute here.

The Committee on Scientific Freedom and Responsibility of the American Association for the Advancement of Science (AAAS) reported in 1975: "Faith that scientific and technological progress was supremely desirable has given way to far more troubled and more ambivalent attitudes."[1] As both the promises and the perils of science increase, the public concern about science intensifies.

To explore this issue requires some attention to the relation between science and technology, a subject that I have bypassed in preceding chapters. The two may be very different, or they may approach each other to the point of virtual identity. One tradition, stemming from Plato and Aristotle, separates them sharply. The pure scientist is concerned for "truth," for understanding, for the elegance and beauty of theories. The artisan or technologist performs useful functions in the world. The difference relates to the contrast between "knowledge" and "know-how." In the classical Greek tradition the distinction involved some snobbery in favor of the scientist. The modern world often inverts the snobbery, disdaining pure theory but wanting "more bang for a buck."

A different tradition minimizes the difference between the two enterprises. If "knowledge is power" (Francis Bacon), the contrast between knowledge and know-how fades. If science is a way of solving problems (John Dewey), then "pure" and "applied" science very nearly merge.

It used to be said that technology, as the application of scientific knowledge, was dependent upon science. Today the advance of science as often depends upon the technologies of observation (think of telescopes, microscopes including electron microscopes, X-ray photography, dosimeters) and of experimentation (think of cyclotrons and spaceships). As one writer on science puts it, "Science is helplessly opportunistic; it can pursue only the paths opened by technique."[2]

James B. Conant, once chairman of the National Defense Research Committee and later president of Harvard, warned of the "storm signals of controversy" about "the relation of pure and applied science to each other and to industry and commerce." He advised teachers of science to "point out that some modern writers have declared that 'Science is the product of economic conditions of society, and its social function is to benefit the ruling classes of society'; and this group have minimized any distinction between pure and applied science or between science and technology. On the other hand, such contentions have been vigorously attacked as representing a false interpretation of history and a pernicious ideal for the future."[3]

Although I can criticize the opinion that Conant quotes, I recognize its importance. For the moment, it is enough to say that social decisions have more to do with the convergence than the divergence (equally interesting for other purposes) of science and technology. Therefore this chapter, like most of this book, does not dwell upon the differences between science and technology except at one or two points. And the chapter concentrates on two issues: the relation of science to its social context, and the question about ethical limits to scientific research.

THE SOCIAL CONTEXT OF SCIENTIFIC INQUIRY

One of the glories of science, both in the popular mind and in the scientific profession, has been a certain kind of "objectivity." Scientific inquiry follows the evidence where it leads. Scientists have often abandoned or modified inherited beliefs because evidence showed those beliefs to be wrong. It does not dim the luster of scientific "objectivity" to point out that the direction of the scientific enterprise is constantly influenced by societies—by their desires, their fears, their whims.

The AAAS Committee on Scientific Freedom and Responsibility was utterly clear on this issue:

> It is often said that science is ethically neutral and value-free. Such statements, in our opinion, are seriously misleading and in some respects quite false. It is, of course, obvious that a scientific discovery, once published, is available for anyone to use; it can be used in exceedingly diverse ways, with consequences that may be good or bad, or commonly a complicated mixture of both. The *activities* of scientists and technologists, however, are conditioned and directed at every turn by considerations of human values. This is true over the whole range of activity, from the most basic research to the applications of science in technology.[4]

Following the lead of that paragraph, let us start with the most obvious issue: the uses made of scientific achievements. Society, not scientists alone, decides what to do with the results of science. *Individuals* decide; it was millions of individual decisions, influenced by institutional pressures as well as by personal desires, that led technological societies for so many years to maximize the sciences and technologies of petroleum and to minimize alternatives. *Corporate groups* decide, as industrial corporations (whether privately or publicly owned) choose to push some technologies and ignore others. *Governments* decide as they legislate about public safety or spend money for public services.

The scientist has little influence on the uses of scientific discoveries. Albert Einstein is a dramatic example of a scientist who had the power to influence policy at one stage but lacked it at another, later stage. Worried by the progress of Nazi Germany toward an atomic bomb, Einstein, though a pacifist, on August 2, 1939, sent his historic letter to President Franklin D. Roosevelt, urging experimental work leading to the atomic bomb.[5] That letter had clout. Einstein's later efforts for peace and disarmament had no such clout.

Although in this case we may regret the results, the transfer of power from scientists to society is inevitable—and for the most part desirable. It would be a weird and inconceivable world in which the discoverers-inventors of chemical processes, electricity, radio and TV, autos and airplanes would tell society what it could and could not do with these achievements. Scientists have a special responsibility to give the public scientific information that may influence policy decisions. Beyond that, scientists have the responsibility of all people to participate in the social process.

A case of major importance, both intrinsic and symbolic, was the decision of the U.S. Congress in March 1971 to stop funding the supersonic transport plane (SST). SSTs are functional: France and Great Britain operate them. But they are expensive and wasteful of fuel. Their damaging effects to the atmosphere are alarming, if not precisely known. And they benefit, at most, a tiny fraction of a society. Congress did not forbid them; it voted to quit paying for their development and thus effectively stopped them. Garrett Hardin hailed this decision as a blow against the two dogmas of "Progress":

1. *The Dogma of Aladdin's Lamp:* If we can dream of it, we can invent it.
2. *The Dogma of the Technological Imperative:* When we invent it, we are required to use it.[6]

The dogmas are still being tested week by week in the political and economic decisions of many societies. The important point is that societies can and do decide about such things.

It is not only in the *uses* of science and technology that the social context of science is important; the *direction* of scientific research is also socially influenced. Although it is still possible for an idiosyncratic scientist to pursue an idea against the prejudices of the public and the scientific establishment, most scientific and technological work is a social enterprise. And all of it is influenced by a social-historical situation.

At present the most plainly visible influence of society on science is at the point of funding of research. Most science in our time is not a matter of an insight coming to an Archimedes alone in a bathtub. It involves costly laboratories, complicated equipment, big organizations. I have earlier given three examples of the ways in which money and power direct research: the relative distribution of scientists among technologically advanced and developing countries (Chapter 2), the U.S. funding of biological research (Chapter 7), and the worldwide percentage of scientists working on military projects (Chapter 8).

The chief sources of funding are governments, industrial corporations, and philanthropic foundations. All of them spend money in light of their interests and their values. There is no other possible way for them to decide. Resources are always finite; possibilities for research are infinite. Every decision to involve money or energies of people in one project is a decision not to pursue some other projects.

So societies and organizations within societies are always determining priorities. If they are supporting research, they want to know what they are paying for. That is an inevitable concern, and a quite legitimate one, even though it is often pursued in foolish ways.

The values that direct research are themselves scientific, in part. Some projects are worth financing because they have greater possibilities of discovery—and, in turn, greater possibilities for initiating further processes of discovery—than others. But another important factor is the social value of the anticipated discoveries. Funding authorities are always asking: how important to the purposes of the society or the government or the corporation is this research?

In the summer of 1981 a small international consultation of scientists and other concerned people addressed this issue with respect to just one kind of research: genetics. It reported:

The issues of economic ethics that affect all of society appear also in the area of genetics. A starting point is the financing of expensive research. How much of the resources of a society should be allocated to exotic biological research as compared with prosaic health delivery systems? Surely a rich society can afford some expensive research. Even a poor society can put some financial and human resources into research. If past societies had not done that, the world might still fear smallpox. But as research gets more sophisticated and expensive, issues of its funding and the distribution of its benefits get more complex.[7]

The issue is complicated by the serendipity of science, something often forgotten by politicians. When the United States entered a spate of budget cutting in the early 1980s, the political impulse was to cut back on basic research and concentrate on applied research. Such a policy, scientists quickly reply, will dry up the sources of later applied research.

The history of science is rich with examples. To take a single one, Michael Faraday in 1825 initiated a series of Friday Evening Discourses at the Royal Institution. Once a month London aristocracy gathered for dinner in evening dress, then heard an eminent scientist explain and demonstrate his work. Faraday himself in 1840 used a magnet, a spiral coil of wire, and a galvanometer to show how the approach of the magnet induced a flow of current through the wire. Somebody in the audience questioned the scientist: "Mr. Faraday, the behavior of the magnet and the coil of wire was interesting, but of what use can it be?" Faraday answered: "Sir, of what use is a newborn baby?" Faraday's newborn baby has since become a giant industrial technology.

Scientific research has unpredictable consequences. Perhaps some research should always be a "luxury" so far as utility is concerned. Even so, the organization and direction of research, including the decision to support some luxuries, involves the values of the culture involved. Those values require constant scrutiny. Societies are always deciding how to respect the creative freedom of scientists and how to require of them some accountability to the people and institutions that support them.

ETHICAL LIMITATIONS ON SCIENTIFIC RESEARCH

The question is: are there ethical barriers to scientific research? The answer is: yes, obviously. Everybody understands that.

But the answer is so offensive, so subject to abuse, that nobody should get to it in a hurry. It comes only as a qualification on a basic belief in freedom of inquiry.

Science has an inner logic of its own, an autonomy in its character. When external forces, religious or political, have sought to dictate what scientists should decide or have prescribed what they might publish, the results have usually been ridiculous. Church authorities still apologize for early rejections of Galileo and Darwin. (It is not necessary to argue that Galileo and Darwin were in every respect right; the point is that religious voices went wrong when they tried to impose scientific conclusions.) Political authorities made the same mistake when, for example, the Soviet government sought to establish the genetic theories of Lysenko because of ideological reasons.

The commitment to freedom of inquiry enshrines a very high value —a value that itself has an ethical and religious quality. Isidor Rabi, a Nobel laureate in physics, once expressed this well in a conversation. I can quote him only approximately from notes I wrote down that same evening. "Science simply operates on the faith that knowledge is good and that ignorance is something to be overcome. You can't really vindicate this faith empirically. It is a faith." Rabi went on to relate it to the first chapter of the Bible, "Let there be light." Sharing that faith, he showed an unquenchable desire for knowledge and endorsed the quest for it.

To a very great degree, I identify myself with that faith. When I question some aspects of it, I join a great many scientists who are asking similar questions.

I start with the point I have already made: some *applications* of science are socially undesirable and ethically wrong. Once again I refer to the Report of the AAAS Committee on Scientific Freedom and Responsibility. After pointing to the benefits of technology, the report says: "Conversely, we reject the doctrine of the so-called 'technological imperative'—the notion that, if something is technically possible, we must go ahead and do it. Thousands of projects may be technically feasible, including perhaps the destruction of all human life on earth. Even among those projects that appear attractive at first sight, careful appraisal may lead to the conclusion that some will do more harm than good."[8] I think, and hope, that such a judgment is not controversial, although it may encompass many specific controversial judgments on specific projects.

At this point, one argument runs that if certain technological projects are harmful, the scientific knowledge behind those projects is harmful. The strongest statement of that position that I know anything about comes from, of all people, Herman Kahn. I am surprised at his statement because, in general, he has far more confidence than I in the technological future. Yet he has proposed an "index of forbidden knowledge," a term apparently derived from the Vatican's historic Index of Prohibited Books. It is not always easy to know when Kahn has his tongue in his cheek, but his statement, in an extended press interview in 1971, appears to be quite serious. He said:

Now this is a very hard thing for me to say—10 years ago I couldn't have said it, five years ago I began to think it—but the knowledge and technology that are now becoming available are very hard for society to absorb, so we may well need an index of forbidden knowledge. There is a whole list of things that are either causing or may cause serious problems in the next 10 or 20 years. Not all should be on the index, obviously, but there are a great many that should.

When pressed on the issue by his interviewer, Kahn reaffirmed his opinion:

Whatever the intellectual dangers of an index, they pall in comparison with the danger of not having one. A society that hasn't the moral capacity to absorb new knowledge without putting itself in mortal peril has to have restraints imposed upon it.

As examples, Kahn mentioned secrets of military technology that the U.S. government does not share with its closest allies. But, since military competition has always had rules of its own, his more remarkable example is from genetics: "Genetic engineering has in it the makings of a totalitarianism the like of which the world has never seen."[9]

I suppose a great many people may actually wish that the human race had not discovered and would not ever discover the secrets that make nuclear weapons possible. Such hopes show how far our generation has moved from the confidence of Gibbon (see Chapter 8) that advance in the knowledge and arts of weaponry has an assured civilizing effect. But any implementation of Kahn's proposals brings its own difficulties. His example of military knowledge does not really "forbid" knowledge; it only says that our side doesn't want the other side to know what we know and intend to keep on knowing. Any example implies that somebody or some organization will decide what knowledge is permissible; and such an elite is not inherently more trustworthy than the counterelites whom it would deprive of knowledge. So I cannot accept Kahn's proposal. But I do go on to suggest some ethical limitations on scientific research.

Human Pain and Cruelty

Anybody can think of some experiments that would produce knowledge, perhaps quite useful knowledge, but at the cost of impermissible human pain. Presumably the decapitation of people under controlled laboratory conditions might add to knowledge of human physiology and the way the organism responds to stress. Many less drastic experiments might show how people respond to pain, but at the cost of cruelty to human beings. Scientists in the Nazi regime performed some experiments of this sort in concentration camps, and their work has become a symbol of human degradation, even though it resulted in some actual advancement of knowledge.

Experimentation on animals is more controversial. Most medical ethics endorses the testing of drugs on animals before their testing on people; the assumption is that human life represents a higher value than animal life. That position is challenged today, but it remains dominant. However, when the press reported experiments that blinded baby rabbits in order to test the irritation caused by human cosmetics, many people objected. The assumption of the experiment was that rabbit life had negligible value. Many people who can eat rabbits (or cattle) with untroubled conscience object to wantonly blinding them for a trivial purpose.

But to return to the less controversial, there is surely knowledge not worth the costs in human cruelty. Perhaps the most notorious case in American scientific history is the experiment on syphilitic black men in Alabama in the 1930s. Here physicians of the U.S. Public Health Service deliberately withheld treatment from four hundred black men in order to study and observe the effects of untreated syphilis. The cost was intense pain for the victims and sometimes infection of their wives and unborn children. The nation's social and legal conscience was so offended by this action that an out-of-court settlement in 1974 awarded $10 million to the victims—most of whom by then were dead.[10]

The problem in all these cases is not in the knowledge, which might be valid and useful. It is just that the knowledge is not worth the cost in cruelty.

Violation of Human Dignity

In order to harm a person it is not necessary to inflict cruel physical pain. There are many ways of assaulting that mysterious and elusive quality that goes by the name of human dignity or the sacredness of personality. When the search for knowledge requires the manipulation of human beings, even though that manipulation be gentle, ethical questions arise.

As an example, think of a large-scale, controlled experiment on identical twins. Many scientists are trying to discover the relative functions of heredity and environment in shaping human personality. If identical twins are separated at birth and reared in different environments, researchers can then study the differences between the twins and get some clues as to the ways in which heredity and environment operate. There are a very few cases where something like this has happened. Anyone can imagine an experiment on one hundred pairs of twins, designed to discover what happens to people of identical heredity who live in environments with major calculated contrasts. The resultant knowledge would be theoretically important and practically useful. But there is an ethical barrier to manipulating people that way, even if the experiment should be carried out gently and with maximum regard for the physical well-being of all the twins. A moral restraint prevents the treating of people as though they were automobiles on a test run or rats in a laboratory.

I would raise similar questions about some kinds of sexual experimentation, even though the barriers are falling fast in this area. The difference is that the experimentation is done with adult volunteers, not with infant twins who have no voice in the decision. Even so, to attach electronic instruments to people in order to measure their physiological responses to sexual intercourse seems to be dehumanizing. The knowledge secured is valid—although limited, because it excludes the spontaneity of affection that is one major meaning of sex. But the intrusion on human dignity is severe. I do not propose to make such experiments illegal, but I have a few questions about people who conduct them or participate in them.

Similar questions arise in the scientific community. Catherine Roberts, after a career as a microbiologist in the Carlsberg Laboratories in Copenhagen, came to urge a "credo of self-restraint" for biologists and a "de-emphasis, if not renunciation, of the corrupting aspects of present-day biological research." Her criticism are directed, in part, against specific remediable practices, including cruel treatment of animals. But they extend to something far more inclusive, because she believes that "the biological visions of reality that are now being attained are dehumanizing and demoralizing in the extreme."[11] Her convictions, as I mentioned in Chapter 7, led her to abandon her career in biological research. Without faulting her for that decision, I maintain the hope that some biological researchers with humanistic sensitivity will stay with their profession and seek to influence it. Every advance in the treatment of disease is, in its first stages, an experiment. Past experiments on people have led to treatments, now routine, that relieve much human misery, but there are always ethical problems in experimentation on persons. Therefore, governments, hospitals, and professional organizations have set up elaborate procedures for developing codes and guidelines for experimentation on human subjects. In the United States there has been a National Commission for the Protection of Human Subjects of Biomedical and Behavioral Research and a President's Commission for the Study of Ethical Problems in Medicine and Biomedical and Behavioral Research. The National Institutes of Health have done extensive work in the area. The Department of Health and Human Services (HHS) has issued regulations governing all experimentation in institutions that get federal financial support.[12]

One of the primary principles in all such codes is the "informed consent" of the subject—or, in the case of infants and persons whose sickness prevents a rational and informed decision, the informed consent of some surrogate for the subject. It cannot be assumed that the subject is as scientifically competent as the researchers. But there are two critical reasons for the requirement of informed consent. (1) The researchers in their zeal for scientific discovery may not give primary concern to the interests of the subject. (2) It is a requirement of human dignity that the subject have a right to decide.

In assessing whether knowledge is worth the human cost, either in the inflicting of pain or in the eroding of human dignity, the problem is complicated because often nobody knows precisely what the cost will be. It is the essence of experimental method that there are many unknowns. Risk is part of the bargain. Because the issue of risk has come up so often in this book, Chapter 11 deals with it as an ethical issue.

Knowledge That Will Be Misused

The first two ethical limitations above have dealt with the pursuit of knowledge that, while desirable in itself, may not be worth the human costs of acquiring it. Now we must ask a different question: is there some knowledge that is so likely to be misused that it cannot be considered inherently good?

W. H. Auden, satirizing the belief that knowledge is an absolute good, once pointed to two extreme examples: the gossip column and the cobalt bomb. The former represents the invasion of human privacy, an important issue, but one that has little to do with the freedom and accountability of science. The latter symbolizes all the kinds of scientific discovery that have destruction as their purpose or that, if not destructive per se, are virtually sure to be misused.

One answer is to separate the acquisition of knowledge from its application, endorsing the first but sometimes questioning the second. Such a distinction has some helpfulness but leaves many problems unsolved.

Consider, as an example, biological warfare. The revulsion against it on ethical grounds is, no doubt, enhanced by the fact that plagues and epidemics do not recognize national boundaries, and biological warfare may hurt its initiators as much as its intended victims. But for whatever reason the Geneva Protocol of 1925 forbids the use of biological and chemical weapons; and the Biological Weapons Convention of 1972, which only half the nations had signed by 1981, forbids the development, production, and stockpiling of biological weapons. I have talked with numerous biologists who have told me that, on ethical grounds, they would refuse to do research on bacteriological warfare.

But what about the basic biological research that will have unknown consequences? It may produce knowledge that can then be applied for the healing and the inflicting of disease. When I once raised this question with a scientist who had done important government work, he estimated that three-quarters of what had gone on at Fort Detrick, for the sake of research on bacteriological warfare, was indistinguishable from work at the National Institutes of Health. A conscientious scientist might refuse to do work on bacteriological warfare, yet not refuse to work at the NIH, even though his discoveries there might conceivably be applied someday to warfare.

Some scientists in Nazi Germany stopped or sabotaged scientific research because they were sure that the political authorities would use their findings destructively. At the 1969 meeting of the AAAS in Boston, a young man "demanded" the right to speak from the platform, as was a common custom in those days. He turned out to be James Shapiro, a member of the Harvard team that has recently isolated a gene for the first time. On that day he publicly renounced his scientific career. In his colorful language, which I jotted down at the time, he said that so long as men like Nixon and Agnew supervise the uses of scientific knowledge, scientists should quit giving them the findings that they will abuse. Shapiro later spent some time in Cuba, then returned to the United States to continue scientific work—whether out of approval for the successors of former President Nixon or not, I do not know.

I did not agree with Shapiro's reasoning on that occasion. But I do agree that there are some social situations in which it is ethically responsible to avoid kinds of research that will inevitably be misused. And I do not have to go back to Nazi Germany for examples. There are times and places in which research on the relation of IQ to ethnic identity will be so immediately abused that a scientist might well turn attention to other projects. This is not to say that knowledge is evil; in fact, knowledge on such subjects has in the long run done far more to overcome prejudice than to sustain it. It is only to say that there are times and places in which even accurate knowledge will be so misused that silence is better than publication. I know and admire a social scientist who is now holding up publication of research data because he is sure they would be used to harm people. He expects to publish them when some contemporary controversies subside.

So, with a few qualifications, I affirm, with Isidor Rabi and many a pioneering scientist, that knowledge is better than ignorance, that verifiable findings are better than errors, and that scientific inquiry demands freedom. And I reaffirm my own contention that there are ethical limitations on scientific research.

The reason for such an ambiguous position is the double nature of science: it is both a method of acquiring and correcting knowledge and an organized activity influenced by the values of its practitioners and their surrounding society. Anyone who forgets either side of the picture misconstrues the nature of science and of our human world.

10. Faith and Doctrine Reconsidered

This chapter addresses explicitly the religious concerns that have been implicit throughout the argument of this book.

Issues of ecology and global justice touch upon the deepest human hopes and fears. They are matters of survival. They concern the preservation of all that is worthwhile, the possible creation of a future better than the past. Their substance is the relation of people to one another and to the nature from which they spring and of which they are a part. All this is the most elemental stuff of religion.

There is today a widespread sense that prevalent religious beliefs and attitudes have led the world astray. Or, to put it the other way around, that the feverish drives of competitive industrialized society have corrupted religion. In either case, religion, as experienced by much of the world today, is not the answer to the problem; it is close to the heart of the problem.

Our generation sees, more easily than some generations before us, two aspects of the religious problem. (1) There can be no simple assumption that religion is good. Religion makes and intensifies problems as much as it resolves them. It heightens conflicts as often as it relieves them. The quality and content of religious commitment are crucial. (2) Religion is not a vestigal remnant of a primitive past, now vanishing beneath the tides of enlightened rationality. On the contrary, the victory of a kind of technical rationality is part of the human problem. Even so, there is no help in merely mouthing old religious answers to questions that the past never faced in their present form and scope—in some cases questions that the past never faced at all.

So there is a widespread questioning of religious faith and of the doctrines that are its intellectual expression. I am referring not only to the continuation of the skeptical questions raised by the eighteenth century's confident criticism of traditional beliefs and the nineteenth century's frightened gaze on nihilism. I am here focusing on the new charges that the modern religious ethos, both in its conventional and its corrosive forms, has led humanity astray.

In this examination I am not assuming that religion can be reconstructed at will. Most religions know that grace is mysterious, that faith grasps people as truly as people grasp faith. There is something trivializing in the assumption that, in the light of contemporary history, a society or a church can operationally revise beliefs to meet the latest crisis of militarism or ecology.

But suffering—which is familiar to much of the world and, by all the signs, will become familiar to more of the world—sometimes awakens sensitivities. It may recall people to elements in tradition that they have neglected. It may jar them into new insights. It may even engender hope.

THE NEW CRITICISM OF WESTERN CHRISTIANITY

Looking for the sources of the dangerous potentialities in technological civilization, some inquirers have found an answer in the Bible and the dominant interpretation of it in Western Christianity. In a brilliant and provocative address at the 1966 meeting of the American Association for the Advancement of Science, Lynn White, Jr., a medieval historian, set forth the case. White's address, later printed in the AAAS journal, *Science,* and reprinted in many places, soon became one of the famous essays of the century.

White asserts: "The victory of Christianity over paganism was the greatest psychic revolution in the history of our culture." Even in a presumably "post-Christian age," he said, the consequence of that revolution is imbedded deeply in the consciousness of a society that subordinates nature to human wishes. "Especially in its Western form," says White, "Christianity is the most anthropocentric religion the world has seen." And the reason goes back to that original "psychic revolution." "By destroying pagan animism, Christianity made it possible to exploit nature in a mood of indifference to the feelings of natural objects."[1]

Arnold Toynbee a few years later addressed the same theme. Prior to monotheism, he writes, human beings saw nature as a goddess,

"Mother Earth"; and vegetation, animals, and minerals "all partook of nature's divinity." But "monotheism, as enunciated in the Book of Genesis, has removed the age-old restraint that was once placed on man's greed by his awe." The consequence is that nature "is taking her revenge on us unmistakably in our time."[2]

Historians and philosophers have for a long time suggested that the relation between Christianity and technology is more than coincidental.[3] Animistic religion confers on nature taboos that prevent scientific inquiry, while polytheism denies the all-encompassing rationality that science embodies. For the most part Christian theologians have welcomed this idea. In fact, the exultation over it rose to a paean just before White, Toynbee, and others made their attack. In 1964 Arend van Leeuwen, for example, acclaimed Christianity for its gift of liberation "from the fetters of 'sacred' tradition, together with the renewal of society in the direction of a truly secular and man-made order of life."[4] The next year Harvey Cox commended biblical faith and Barthian theology for undermining myth and ontology with the result that "man's freedom to master and shape, to create and explore now reaches out to the ends of the earth and beyond."[5] Both van Leeuwen and Cox had a fine sense of human responsibility for justice, but they had a grandiose idea of human power in relation to nature. And *that*, said White and Toynbee, is exactly what went wrong in the modern Western consciousness.

But a different sensitivity was already awake in Western religious feeling and thought. Joseph Sittler, in his much-acclaimed address at the 1961 Assembly of the World Council of Churches (New Delhi), called attention to the *theological* importance of "the care of the earth, the realm of nature as a theater of grace, the ordering of the thick, material procedures that make available to or deprive men of bread and peace."[6] Process philosophies and theologies had for some time emphasized the relation of human nature to the rest of nature, and Paul Tillich had made intimate connections between human being and all of being. Now theology began with new eagerness to reexamine the relationships between God and the natural creation in the biblical and theological traditions.[7]

To a generation nurtured on theories of economic causation there was something unusual in the attention to religious foundations of economic and technological behavior. Theologians were not sure whether to be pleased at the importance assigned to theology or to be resentful at the blame imputed to it. In either case they did what theologians like to do: they went back to their sources.

They, as well as their critics, looked again at the first biblical address of God to his human creatures: "Be fruitful and multiply, and fill the earth and subdue it; and have dominion over the fish of the sea and over the birds of the air and over every living thing that moves upon the earth" (Gen. 1:28).[8] Was this an arrogant projection of human ambition onto God and the whole cosmic order? Georg Borgstrom, writing in the vein of White and Toynbee, says:

The image of man as the master of the Creation given divine sanction to multiply and fill the earth, and to subdue nature in order to fill his own needs, is thoroughly unbiological. Even worse, this misinterpreted double mandate actually started man on his calamitous collision course with nature.[9]

If so, it may be that this is the only scriptural command of God that human beings have wholeheartedly and universally obeyed. But in the biblical account, this gift of dominion is promptly qualified. God, after planting the garden of Eden, put Adam in the garden "to till it and keep it" (Gen. 2:15). Here is a role of custodianship, in which dominion is immediately joined to responsibility. John Calvin, who is sometimes accused of laying the spiritual foundations for predatory capitalism, said of this passage:

. . . we possess the things which God has committed to our hands, on the condition, that being content with a frugal and moderate use of them we should take care of what shall remain. Let him who possesses a field, so partake of its yearly fruits, that he may not suffer the ground to be injured by his negligence; but let him endeavour to hand it down to posterity as he received it, or even better cultivated. Let him so feed on its fruits that he neither dissipates it by luxury, nor permits it to be marred or ruined by neglect. Moreover, . . . let every one regard himself as the steward of God in all things which he possesses.[10]

The German theologian Gerhard Liedke has shown that the early chapters of Genesis actually communicate a profound ecological sensitivity.[11] The "dominion" of Genesis 1, he points out, is not in any sense predatory. On the contrary, God prescribes a vegetarian existence in which there is no bloodshed (see Gen. 1:29–30). But sin brings bloodshed to the world. Only in the revised covenant for a world infected with conflict and sin does God permit the eating of flesh. And even here, with an awesome awareness of the importance of life, people may not consume blood, which represents "the life" of animals (see Gen. 9:4). All this, as Liedke says, is not a "rudimentary natural science" and not an alternative to an evolutionary understanding of animal and human origins. It is a story that communicates a set of meanings, an idea of the relation of human to nonhuman nature, a piety towards the whole of creation.

A look at the whole of the biblical tradition confirms in part the judgment of Lynn White: monotheism means that the earth is not the habitat of spirits and demons. The taboos that prevent scientific inquiry and practical use are lifted (even though the biblical people did not do much scientific inquiry or technological manipulation). But as Sittler says, in the Hebrew scriptures nature is "continuous with the reality of God as Creator":

God is made known to man in the matrix of space, time, and matter, which are the substance of that mortal theatre in which God deals with his people in their historical actuality. . . . Our modern view of nature as by definition not having anything to do with the divine is in complete hiatus with the Old Testament view. There nature comes from God, cannot be apart from God, and is capable of bearing the "glory" of God.[12]

And in the New Testament it is "the whole creation" that groans for redemption, including human beings who wait for the redemption not merely of their spirits, but of their "bodies" (Rom. 8:22–23), which belong so obviously to the world of nature.

The biblical tradition expresses the relationship of God, the human creation, and the nonhuman creation (both animate and inanimate) in many themes and counterpoints. God instructed Noah to save birds and beasts and reptiles, no less than his own family, from the flood, then made the rainbow a sign of the divine covenant. The book of Jonah ends by affirming God's concern for Nineveh's "hundred and twenty thousand persons . . . and also much cattle"—a final touch that has always seemed an absurd anticlimax to anthropocentric readers. In the Psalms, "The heavens are telling the glory of God" (Ps. 19:1). This God is concerned for wild asses, storks, cattle, wild goats, lions, and the innumerable creatures of the sea (Ps. 104). Sun and moon, stars, sea monsters, snow and stormy winds, fruit trees and cedars, beasts and cattle—along with "young men and maidens, old men and children"—praise the Lord (Ps. 148). Job looks with amazement at crocodile and hippopotamus—of no conceivable use to him—as evidence that God did not create nature solely for human use. Jesus sees the lilies of the field and the birds of the air as signs of God's creativity and providence (Matt. 6:26, 28–29).

From these scriptures have stemmed many theological traditions. One is the Eastern orthodox, represented in Dostoevsky's Alyosha Karamazov, who exultantly embraces the Russian soil and ponders the meaning of the grain of wheat as a symbol of death and resurrection. Another is that of Martin Luther who, in his sacramentalism, insists that finite objects of nature are "capable of" embodying the infinite God.

Religious beliefs that demean nature—like religious beliefs that demean people or some races and classes of people—involve a very selective reading of scripture. That recognition, of itself, solves no problems. *All* readings of *all* scriptures in all religions are selective —just as anybody's reading of a newspaper (like the writing of the newspaper itself) is selective. Selectivity is inherent in human perception, but cramping and harmful selectivity can be corrected by more illuminating selectivity.

The fact remains that the religion described by Lynn White and Arnold Toynbee is part of the Western heritage. Its origins include a selective appropriation of the biblical tradition, a rejection of parts of that tradition, and many other sources.[13] And a religious error, heresy, or perversion requires a religious correction. As Paul Goodman puts it, "To meet the historical crisis of science at present, for science and technology to become prudent, ecological, and decentralized requires . . . a kind of religious transformation."[14]

But what religious answer will do? Arnold Toynbee proposes a return to the pre-monothesistic pantheism that, he argues, "was once universal."[15] Its universalism is questionable, but Toynbee has in mind a vague pantheism exemplified in "primitive" animism and in the great religions of Asia.

There are two problems in Toynbee's recommendation. The first is that pre-monotheistic cultures had their ecological disasters. In the neolithic period people destroyed many living species. Slash-and-burn methods of tribal societies ravaged natural environments. Ancient

China, India and Pakistan, the Mediterranean, and South America still show signs of ancient depredations. Civilizations decayed following the depletion of fertility of the soil, the destruction of water resources, the wasting of forests. René Dubos, after summarizing some of the evidence, concludes: "All over the globe and at all times in the past, men have pillaged nature and disturbed the ecological equilibrium, usually out of ignorance, but also because they have always been more concerned with immediate advantages than with long-range goals."[16]

The second problem with Toynbee's case is that history is, in some important respects, irreversible. Although modern generations can recover some insights from the past, we cannot revert to that past as though nothing had happened in the interim. My guess is that the "disenchantment" described by Max Weber[17] cannot and should not be totally undone. People today know too much to repopulate the world with spirits and demons.

I call this a guess because nobody knows for certain. A historical understanding of life helps us to realize that many of the "absolute certainties" of our time are cultural whims that will be no more enduring than the shattered absolutes of many past ages. The ancient Greek world went through its disenchantment in the thought of the Sophists, the Skeptics, and Democritus, all of whom were forgotten by the new civilization that rose in the West. But those philosophers were mere intellectuals; their work did not get built into the social structures of life in the manner of modern science and technology.

Conceivably contemporary scientific methods and technological ambitions, even though imbedded deeply in social orders, will give way to a vastly different form of culture, better or worse. But the world needs more, not less technology—although a technology radically redirected from many of its now dominant modes.

Furthermore, innocence lost is not recovered. Something better than innocence may follow it. Thus a disenchanted culture may find that nature has a reenchanting power. Writers like Lewis Thomas, Loren Eiseley, and René Dubos have shown us that. Some poets and artists never forgot it. But the future, including the future of religious insight, will not be a simple undoing of the past. I think Toynbee knew that, even if he did not always say it forcefully enough.

Lynn White's recommendation is quite different from Toynbee's.

Although like Toynbee he finds helpful insights in the Eastern religions, his main hope for the West is a recovery of the Christian insights of St. Francis of Assisi. In "a democracy of all creatures," says White, St. Francis saw "Brother Ant and Sister Fire, praising the Creator in their own ways as Brother Man does in his":

His unique view of nature and of man rested on a unique sort of pan-psychism of all things animate and inanimate, designed for the glorification of their transcendent Creator, who, in the ultimate gesture of cosmic humility, assumed flesh, lay helpless in a manger, and hung dying on a scaffold.[18]

Critics of White[19] have often not recognized his subtlety or his humor. Anyone who could in a speech to the AAAS nominate St. Francis as "a patron saint for ecologists" has, along with his seriousness, a sense of humor. Interestingly Pope John Paul II, if not any scientific organization, on April 6, 1980 formally proclaimed St. Francis the patron saint of ecology.

René Dubos makes an interesting counterproposal to Lynn White. Finding St. Francis too "romantic and unwordly," he nominates St. Benedict of Nursia as "a patron saint of those who believe that true conservation means not only protecting nature against human misbehavior but also developing human activities which favor a creative, harmonious relationship between man and nature."[20] The Benedictines and their Cistercian branch combined prayer and economically productive work. They developed windmills and watermills, manufactured various articles out of the agricultural products that they grew, made wilderness and pestilential swamps habitable, pioneered in various technologies, yet related their lives and rituals to the rhythms of days and seasons. Dubos concludes: "Reverence for nature is compatible with willingness to accept responsibility for a creative stewardship of the earth."[21]

The new appreciation of nature is profoundly valid in its answer to anthropocentric religion. But the mystique of nature has its problems, too. Some rhapsodic descriptions of the intricately coordinated ecosystem are reminiscent of the traditional argument from design for the existence of God, with the major difference that the former attribute to evolutionary development what the latter attributed to a creator-architect. The trouble with both is that too many things go wrong in nature—certainly in terms of human values. Nature can be a "sign" to faith—a sign that in its beauty and mystery awakens gratitude and awe. But nature—I mean the nature known by experience and empirical scientific inquiry, not the abstract "Nature" of the Stoics or Spinoza—does not offer criteria for human justice. Its ecology shows evidence of competitive struggle for survival and of cooperative communities, of waste and conservationist recycling, of terror and of beauty.

It will not do to say with Barry Commoner, "Nature knows best." Commoner, of course, is not a literalist. He is not producing evidence that nature "knows" anything at all. He interprets his own aphorism to mean: "any major man-made change in a natural system is likely to be *detrimental* to that system."[22]

One reply to Commoner (actually published before Commoner's book) comes from P. B. Medawar: "It is a profound truth . . . that nature does *not* know best; that genetical evolution, if we choose to look at it liverishly instead of with fatuous good humour, is a story of waste, makeshift, compromise, and blunder."[23]

Certainly nature does not do what is humanly best. Nature's way to preserve the species is to encourage many births to match high infant mortality. A more human way is to reduce human deaths and, accordingly, births.

To be human is to live in a relationship with all of nature, yet to act purposefully in relation to nature both within oneself and "out there." It is to delight in a qualified "dominion"—to rejoice in the elimination of smallpox and the near elimination of polio without forgetting that human life is still mortal, to modify natural environments while recognizing that nature will outlast all terrestrial life. To be human is also to accept a responsible stewardship for an environment given to our race, not created by us. There need be no irreverence in recognizing, with Genesis 2, that even a garden planted by God can be better for some human care.

SOCIAL DISCIPLINES AND ULTIMATE MEANINGS

The looming time of troubles will require a human discipline both pragmatic and moral. Its pragmatism will need to be tough-minded, attentive to technology and economics, if societies are to move from profligate to sustainable forms of existence. Its morality will need to address issues of distributive justice in the face of most of the world's poverty and need. It will also require the imagination, rare in all times and almost totally absent in modern industrial societies, to practice some restraints now for the sake of future generations.

Whether such a discipline is possible, nobody knows. Already public officials are thinking—on occasion the thoughts break into the open—about future wars for resources. Past history has seen many such wars. But in an age when war quivers on the brink of nuclear holocaust, it is, more strikingly than ever before, neither a pragmatic nor a moral way of meeting human need.

The needed social disciplines must be related to commitments involving the meaning of life—commitments not of a few prophets and saints, but commitments socially shared by many people in diverse societies. Georg Borgstrom puts it in these words: "A common battle against starvation, disease, and misery, and above all against ignorance, this primarily in our own midst, requires a radical change in the goals of human strivings."[24] Such talk about radical change in human goals is the perennial stuff of religion. Today it is increasingly the subject of natural and social scientists as they work on issues of energy, food, population, and war.

Among contemporary tracts for the times, one of the most powerful is Robert Heilbroner's *An Inquiry into the Human Prospect*. After investigating the issues of ecology and distribution, he emphasizes the importance of a social system "that will offer a necessary degree of social order as well as a different set of motives and objectives." And he proposes—somewhat to his own surprise because his personal preferences are quite different—a social order "that blends a 'religious' orientation with a military 'discipline.' "[25]

One might think of the Jesuits or the Salvation Army as examples, but Heilbroner has in mind not elite orders of volunteers but vast societies. His principal example is contemporary China: "I think we can discern in Chinese society certain paradigmatic elements of the future—a careful control over industrialization, an economic policy calculated to restrain rather than to whet individual consumptive appetites, and, above all, an organizing religiosity expressed through the credos and observances of a socialist 'church.' "[26] He personally loves the freedoms of thought and action that belong to the ethos of liberal democracies, and he would like to preserve those as far as possible. But he finds a more disciplined order necessary to steer society away from its ruinous ways.

In his closing pages Heilbroner reaches explicitly into the religious and mythical dimensions of existence. He looks for the figure who has given the modern age its "driving energy." His choice is an intriguing one. Not Caesar, Napoleon, or Washington. Not Adam Smith or Karl Marx. Not Galileo, Newton, or Einstein. Not Moses, Jesus, or Calvin. Heilbroner points to Prometheus.[27]

Prometheus was the Titan of Greek myth, the divine being who out of love stole fire from Zeus and made it a gift to humanity. Prometheus was the daring innovator who taught the human race numbers, language, invention, the arts. Zeus in his jealousy ordered Prometheus chained to a rock on Mount Caucasus in a lonely place where he could share no companionship. Day after day throughout centuries a vulture gnawed at his liver, which grew back every night. Prometheus could have gained his freedom by acquiescing to the will of Zeus, but he chose to resist in courage and defiance.

Ancient Athens celebrated the spirit of Prometheus in the tragedy of Aeschylus. Shelley made Prometheus the symbol of courageous and loving hope:

> to hope till Hope creates
> From its own wreck the thing it contemplates;
> Neither to change, nor falter, nor repent;
> This, like thy glory, Titan, is to be
> Good, great and joyous, beautiful and free.[28]

"Some of that Promethean spirit," writes Heilbroner, "may still serve us in good stead in the years of transition." But it will not be adequate. "For it is only with dismay that Promethean man regards the future."[29] So Heilbroner looks elsewhere for a symbol for this age. And he turns to another Greek Titan, Atlas, who was condemned to carry the sky on his head and hands. For Atlas there are no exciting adventures, no glamorous achievements. He does his duty, wearily enduring. Heilbroner's conclusion is that "the spirit of conquest and aspiration will not provide the inspiration" we now need. "It is the example of Atlas, resolutely bearing his burden, that provides the strength we seek."[30]

The recollection of Greek tragedy is appropriate to a society that, though radically different from the Hellenic, has its own tragic character. But this society has other roots. Those who stand in the Hebrew and Christian traditions will notice that both Prometheus and Atlas were, in their distinctive ways, suffering servants. Their mention will call to mind the suffering servant of the biblical tradition.

In the pluralistic world of contemporary existence no one tradition will move the human race. The General Assembly of the United Nations, to take one example of an international, intercultural gathering, will not respond to a plea for a Jewish, a Christian, a Muslim, a Buddhist, or an orthodox Marxist loyalty. But religion is always concrete. Religion-in-general is too vague and nondescript to influence individuals or societies. Any religious address to the world comes out of concrete religions, which contribute their insights to the common life of the world, for whatever resonance they may evoke. With that understanding I call attention to the suffering servant of the Hebrew scriptures and to the faith of the New Testament that in some profound sense Jesus of Nazareth was and is that suffering servant.

To endorse this Jesus as the answer to human problems is a cliché so weary, a proclamation so often corrupted, a rhetoric so thin that it may seem to offer no meaning at all. And Jesus said nothing specifically addressed to the issues of global organization in the face of today's problems of ecology and distribution. Yet in the concrete details of his life and mission are accents of peculiar power for the contemporary situation. I suggest three.

First, Jesus, faithful Jew that he was, met temptation by repeating a saying from Deuteronomy: "Man does not live by bread alone" (See Deut. 8:3, Matt. 4:4). Yet it was Jesus who at the Last Supper broke bread with his disciples. It was he whom the disciples, after the resurrection, recognized "in the breaking of the bread." Here is neither a dreary materialism, insisting that bread can satisfy the human spirit, nor a lofty idealism that thinks bread unimportant. Humanity does not live by consumption of material goods alone, yet consumption of material goods is utterly important to human existence. The production and distribution of food and energy are religious issues.

Second, Jesus had a concern for human justice. Echoing words from Isaiah, he preached "good news to the poor," "release to the captives," and liberty to "those who are oppressed" (see Luke 4:18). Human survival, though the prerequisite to other human values, is not in itself an adequate value. Meaningful life in shared community *is* a real value.

Third, Jesus showed the possibility of joy in living. Prometheus and Atlas in their solitary grandeur never had fun. (I don't blame them; nobody in their situations could have fun. Jesus on the cross wasn't having fun either. But fun is part of life.) We cannot imagine Prometheus or Atlas turning water into wine at a wedding. They could not rejoice in the lilies of the field, the birds of the air, the warmth of human companionship. The beatitudes all begin with the word blessed. The first one has been translated: "How happy are the poor in spirit, for theirs is the kingdom of heaven."

Margaret Mead once said it beautifully. She blurted it out in her spontaneous way, and happily a tape recorder was turning. "Prayer does not use any artificial energy, it doesn't burn up any fossil fuel, it doesn't pollute. Neither does song, neither does love, neither does the dance."[31]

THE EFFECTIVENESS OF FAITH

But does religious faith really make any difference in the course of the world? Or have economic and technological drives acquired a momentum that drives everything before them?

Karl Marx assigned religion to the ideological superstructure that conceals the real forces that make history, although even he believed that Marxist commitments could make some difference in events. Max Weber argued that religious belief does influence history. The twentieth century discovered the fanatic power of such pseudo-religions as Nazism and Fascism. Then it later discovered the continuing fury of traditional religions, for example, in Iran, the Middle East, and Northern Ireland. In such cases the ostensible religious forces often veiled the working of economic, technological, and demographic forces that fed the conflicts. But at a minimum, powerful historical forces gather a religious aura around them. And all signs indicate that religious commitment itself—for better or worse—is one force in social change.

However, religious faith does not have to claim great historical efficacy for itself. Faith is not faith in religion. It is faith in the reality to which or to whom faith responds religiously. The Hebrew prophets

pointed to the judgment of God in the threat of the Assyrians and the
cries of the poor. They did not expect the religious community to
initiate major changes; they called on people of faith to recognize
divine activity and get with it. That does not mean that they saw all
events as the activity of God. Any belief in divine action in history
had better give attention to demonic acts or to the "principalities and
powers" described in the New Testament. Faith seeks to discern
divine judgment and grace in history, then to act accordingly.

A secular way of putting this is to say that creative and momentous
social change usually requires both pressure and a vision. Either alone
is likely to be insufficient.

Idealism alone is usually not enough. Even change for the better
looks worse to some people and groups in power, and they resist it.
In the United States, from the time of Jefferson and before, there were
people who knew slavery was wrong. But slavery did not end until
pressure overthrew a system. The same was true of segregation. It has
probably been true of every liberation movement in history.

But pressure alone is usually not enough. It meets resistance. It
generates counterpressures and backlashes. Or it wins bitter victories
in which revolutions, as the saying goes, devour their own children.

Creative change can come when pressure is joined to vision. A
leader—a Martin Luther King, Jr., for example—can organize pressure against a system, while verbalizing a dream that has at least some
allure for the society at large. A Supreme Court and a federal government, responding to both pressure and dream, can join the forces of
change.

Saul Alinsky, the veteran community organizer of the generation
just past, commented about the issues of ecology:

Until the question gets immediate, you're not going to get into action. You
can't sit down and rhetorically say you've got to get down to zero population
growth. Man has never operated on that rationale. Until the threat is right
there, until those fangs are right there, people will not get organized. This is
unfortunate but it's the way man is.[32]

The news is that the pressure is on, the fangs are beginning to show.
The poor world is crying out as never before. Even the rich world is
feeling inconvenience, sometimes pain. Faith and reason in close
union have the opportunity to alert a world to what is happening.

Sometimes they can help a world realize that what seems an unpleasant necessity can actually be a good. They have begun to do that—the job is far from done—in the case of racial equality in some parts of the world. They can do it in other cases.

There are signs of a changing awareness among large numbers of people. A Harris poll in 1975 showed a sixty-one to twenty-three percent majority of Americans who thought it "morally wrong" that this country consumed so much of the world's energy and other resources. A larger group, sixty-eight percent, thought that the American public was "highly wasteful." And ninety percent agreed that "we here in this country will have to find ways to cut back on the amount of things we consume and waste." A substantial majority, sixty-four to twenty-nine percent, expected a reduction in living standards as the cost of reducing waste.[33]

Those figures do not mean that most Americans are doing much about the issues mentioned. It is far easier to murmur an answer to a pollster than to move a political system or even change personal habits. Yet the poll shows an education in maturity that would have been incredible two decades earlier. The difference is this: when the pressures—say, of inflation—force people to adjust their ways of living, they do not simply respond in anger at Arab nations or the administration in Washington or devils somewhere else; a significant number are saying that the change is inevitable and morally right. And that, whether or not stated in formally religious terms, is a religious reorientation.

Religious communities can relate to both the pressures and the visions that bring social change. Sometimes and in some places they can add to the pressure. This is not a likely role for the Christian church in China just now or for the Bahai community in Iran. It was a responsible role for religious communities in the American civil rights movement and the opposition to the war in Vietnam. Always religious communities can maintain the vision—the hope for a better world and the trust that their efforts in that direction are a response to divine creative and redemptive purposes.

THEOLOGICAL RECONSTRUCTION

For good reasons Christian theology in this century has emphasized the political world. Gigantic political movements have threatened human freedom. The opposition to Nazism and imperialism, the liberation movement of American black people and Latin American oppressed classes, the conflicts against tyrannical regimes in many a land —all these have raised up heroes and martyrs. Theology has given major attention to human rights, liberation, and justice. Understandably, theologies of politics have won more attention than theologies of nature—or theologies that find politics inseparable from nature.

The ecological crisis has forcibly called attention again to nature. At first, some critics took the ecological interest to be a competitor to political interests, a diversion of middle-class people from concern with social problems to a concern with their own comfort. But increasingly theology is finding that political decisions have ecological consequences and ecological problems call for political responses. There is, for example, no answer to world hunger that does not involve changes in the human relation to nature *and* changes in political-economic processes.

In the summer of 1981 the World Council of Churches' Working Committee on Church and Society met in Jos, Nigeria, inviting a number of African scientists and church leaders to join in the meeting. The chief topic of discussion was, "Faith, Science and the Future— the African Context." In this African setting there was no muting of political-economic interests. Everybody was aware of South African apartheid and tyranny, of the legacy of colonialism, of the skewing of African economies by dependence on multinational corporations, of the relation of oil-rich and energy-poor countries, of hunger and population pressures. But the strong African presence brought to attention theological themes often forgotten or subordinated in European and American meetings. I quote three paragraphs of the conference report:

African experience makes us realize the neglect of some important concerns in recent and Western theologies. The dominant theologies have often separated history from nature, concentrating on the former and almost ignoring the latter. They have often focused attention on eschatology in the form of directing human hope and effort toward a future radically transcending the past and present.

Such theologies have declared liberating messages that are crucially important to humanity in our time. We profoundly appreciate the interest of theology in "the secular," in scientific possibilities, in the ability of God and his human creatures to create a new future.

But if theology emphasizes the future to the erosion of tradition, it may unintentionally legitimate a naive belief in the benefits of change created by science and technology. African experience is a testimony to the continuing importance of reverence for the sacred in the common life. The churches in Africa sensitize us to the continuities of life, to the steadfast faithfulness of God. They remind us that God's promises are known in the rhythms of nature —"seed time and harvest, cold and heat, summer and winter, day and night" —as well as in the promise of the radically new. They tell us again that God is Creator and Sustainer as well as Transformer of the world.[34]

In this and many other ways the industrialized world and its religious communities are being shaken out of their provincialism. Whether the shake-up is too little and too late, history will tell.

11. Living with Risk

The point of thinking about peril is not to revel in misery, but to work toward helpful responses. Today there is a wide consensus that the human enterprise stands at greater risk than at any time since this race won its first precarious security from extinction by wild beasts and weather. That consensus excludes a few technological optimists, but a look at their cheerful projections of two or three decades ago makes their errors all too obvious. It excludes a few despairing fatalists who think that doom is inevitable. For the rest of us the question is: how do we learn to live with risk?

At four stages in this book I have edged up to issues of risk: in Chapter 1 (hypotheticality), Chapter 3 (energy), Chapter 7 (experimentation on DNA), and Chapter 8 (war). Each time I have deferred the discussion of risk, as such, until I could come at it in the broader perspective of this chapter.

The issue has become crucial because human beings have outwitted nature—to a point. The ecosystem puts limits on other species; if they flourish too extravagantly or ruin their environments, nature soon strikes back. Human beings, however, have learned to maneuver around many natural limitations. Much of this progress is humanly gratifying. But as Harrison Brown puts the issue, "Industrial man now lives in a complex and largely synthetic ecological system, new in the human experience and inadequately understood."[1] It is not so much nature as our own blunders that we fear.

Technological progress has been, humanly speaking, a good bargain—to a point. To take a single evidence, not an all-inclusive but an important one, the average human life span in the United States increased from forty-seven to seventy-three years in the first eight decades of this century.[2] And in poverty-haunted India, according to

Nick Eberstadt, the life expectancy of about fifty-three years is "higher than that of nineteenth-century European nobility."[3] The increase in life span, with all that it signifies about health, must be placed against the evidences of technological mishaps.

But such evidences there are. Consider just a sampling of reports that a headline reader might have noticed in the three years 1978–1980.

The year 1978 began with reports of explosions of dust in seven American grain elevators, killing sixty-two people in one month. In February a train wreck in Tennessee led to a huge propane gas explosion and fifteen deaths, and in March apparent sabotage of another train in Florida released chlorine gas, killing eight people and forcing evacuation of thirty-five hundred. In April, fifty-one workers died in the construction of a coal-fired power plant in West Virginia. In July the explosion of a truck carrying liquefied gas killed two-hundred Spanish campers. Throughout the year there were 51,500 motor vehicle deaths in the United States.

In 1979 the most famous accident came in March at the nuclear reactor at Three Mile Island in Pennsylvania. There were no immediate deaths, but the world shuddered with the fear of catastrophe. Far away in the Ural mountains an explosion, apparently in a military biological plant, released bacteria into the atmosphere in April and May; in the following months reports leaking out of Russia said that a thousand people died. In August the flash flooding of thirty-one villages in India, following a dam failure, killed thousands. It was a bad year for air accidents: Bombay, January, 213 dead; Chicago, May, 272 dead; San Diego, September, 143 dead; Antarctica, November, 257 dead.

March 1980 brought the deaths of 123 men when a storm overturned a floating hotel in the North Sea oil field off Norway. Soon after, an explosive chemical fire terrorized Elizabeth, New Jersey. And a few days later a broken valve released toxic fumes nearby, leading to the evacuation of a two-square-mile area. In July the U.S. Environmental Protection Agency released a report on acid rain and its dangers to plants, fish, animals, and people; and in the following months Canadians complained about U.S.-originated acids in their rain. In July another railroad accident, this time in Kentucky, ignited toxic chemicals and required the evacuation of four thousand people. The next month a leaking valve on a tank truck, carrying nine thousand gallons of propane, on the George Washington bridge caused panic for several hours. Nobody was hurt, but two thousand people were evacuated, and traffic jams extended over thirty miles. In September Brazilians discovered a rising rate of stillbirths and deformed fetuses in the industrially polluted "Valley of Death." Controversies over industrial wastes at Love Canal on the edge of Niagara Falls filled the press and airwaves. In the United States more than 56,000 people died in transportation accidents during the year.

If such a recital is wearying, it shows how the assault of such news has deadened sensitivities. I repeat: all these incidents are part of an industrial system that has, on the average, increased life expectancy and safety for most people. But it has brought risks of its own. And these risks nourish the anxiety that this style of civilization is pushing its luck too far, playing with forces it does not understand, and building up perils of catastrophe beyond anything yet realized.

In a news conference in May of 1980 Louis Harris, the pollster, reported his findings on public attitudes in the United States about risk.[4] Among the results were these: (1) most Americans feel that they face more risks now than twenty years ago; (2) a majority think that the risks of technological society will increase; (3) most think that the safety of technological society will require restraints on advanced technology; (4) but most corporate leaders think governmental safety regulations can safely be reduced; (5) in spite of their feeling about risks, most people think that the benefits of technological innovation outweigh the risks.

Such a melange of attitudes is characteristic of modern societies. Risk is a subject that is becoming important for social decisions.

RISK—GOOD WORD, BAD WORD

Risk is a word that in ordinary conversation evokes mixed feelings. The language of capitalism glorifies the risk-taking entrepreneuer, yet wistfully calls stocks "securities." In retrospect, risk looks great when it wins, foolish when it loses. The quarterback who calls the risky play that wins the game, rather than the safe play that preserves a tie, is a hero. But if the same quarterback in the last seconds of the game throws the daring pass that is intercepted instead of dully downing the ball to protect a one-point lead, he is a goat. Life, unlike the football game, does not have simple rules and a precise system of scoring, but historical experience shows the deep human ambivalence about risks. Risk often is a good word. Most national heroes are risk takers. America remembers Patrick Henry who in 1775 said: "Give me liberty, or give me death!" It celebrates annually the Declaration of Independence, whose signers in 1776 pledged "our Lives, our Fortunes and our Sacred Honors." The experiment of "government of the people, by the people, and for the people" was—and still is—a risk.

The stories of faith also honor risk takers. Moses led a people through the hazards of the desert and, when they longed for the "fleshpots of Egypt" and the security of slavery, goaded them on in a more dangerous existence. None of the prophets used the motto, "Safety first." Jesus, described in the New Testament as the "pioneer of faith," took the risk of the journey to Jerusalem and the confrontation with political and religious authorities.

St. Augustine, reviewing Roman history, recalled that Cato urged the destruction of Carthage for the sake of Roman security. His political opponent, Scipio, opposed this policy. "He feared security, that enemy of weak minds." Cato prevailed, and Rome, "delivered from its great cause of anxiety," relaxed and degenerated.[5]

At the Fifth Assembly of the World Council of Churches (Nairobi, 1975) delegates used as a worship book a special edition of the WCC "magazine about renewal in the churches," the magazine named *Risk*. Clearly, in many historical and theological traditions, risk is a good word.

But risk is also a bad word. Any risk puts somebody or something of value in jeopardy. Risk destroys some good. Not every single risk is destructive; some risks turn out well. But any sequence of risks means some losses. If there are *no* losses, that means the risks were only apparent, not real.

Part of the pathos of finitude is that nothing in creation is permanent or secure. If faith looks to an ultimate redemption, that comes from an infinite power who transcends our finitude. In this cosmic history, life and its values are in jeopardy. It may even be that the greatest perils of all come out of strained efforts to attain a security that is impossible—out of the trust in "men and horses" that Isaiah ridiculed or the confidence in money or fame or nuclear weapons that pretend to alleviate but usually heighten anxiety in our time.

But if life with its opportunities is mortal, the careless destruction of life and its goods is still a crime. Heedless jeopardy of life and health are an offense against people. Irresponsible risk taking is an act of ingratitude for the gifts bestowed upon our race.

So language, when it connotes that risk is both good and bad, carries a profound meaning. The ambivalence is continued in two other phrases that have become widespread in recent years: "acceptable risk" and "trade-off." Both are disturbing terms because they communicate a calculating mood and they may seem to trivialize the harms that follow on risk. But both point to perennial ethical issues in human living.

Acceptable risk recognizes that persons and societies accept some risks, reject others. To enter an automobile or to walk across a traffic-crowded street is to accept a risk. To go to work, to marry, to rear children, to walk on the streets of cities, to carry money in a wallet, to protest against the wrongs of an employer or a government, to accept a new idea or to suppress it—all these mean the acceptance of risks. For that matter, to stay at home and do nothing is to live at risk. In a normal year 27,000 Americans die and more than four million are disabled by home accidents. Such risks can and ought to be reduced, but they cannot be eliminated.

So even cautious people accept some risks—partly because the expected gain outweights the estimated risk, partly because of habit, partly because no life is risk-free. Perhaps the greatest risk is to be born. Infants have no choice about accepting that risk. At best, parents, grateful for life with all its risks, accept the risk for their children. At worst, accident imposes the risk, but some people, accidentally conceived, become grateful for their lives.

Human history is a story of societies accepting some risks, rejecting others, and in the process deciding that some risks are acceptable. The difference today is that the stakes are more momentous than in the past and that our generation approaches risk with a uniquely contemporary self-consciousness.

The concept of the trade-off is likewise a troubling one. At worst, it reduces tragic personal decisions to quantitative reckonings: how many lives will you trade for a military victory, or the construction of a great bridge, or the convenience of the automobile? But the trade-off, again, is a consequence of the finitude of life. No person can maximize all the potentialities of a life, develop to the full the athletic, artistic, intellectual possibilities. To become a violinist, a novelist, a molecular biologist, a ballerina or an All-American football player, a mathematician, a juggler, a sculptor, a comedian, a historian—few people achieve any of these aims and nobody achieves them all. Individuals cultivate some possibilities at the cost of neglecting, maybe even crushing, others. Societies do too.

The concept of the trade-off can be misused. Societies acquiesce too easily in trade-offs between full employment and inflation, work and relaxation, freedom and social controls. Often a more imaginative policy can harmonize values that appear to stand in conflict. A sensitive ethic tries to widen possibilities and integrate a variety of values.

But possibilities still remain finite. Many a society has discovered that it cannot afford both guns and butter on the scale it once thought possible. Many a church or university, wanting to do many good things, has had to choose painfully its priorities. A world, confronting limits in resources and ability to sustain increasing populations, must put at risk or renounce some goals that were once taken for granted.

KINDS OF RISKS

If risk is inevitable, choices among risks are possible. People may risk themselves for the sake of others, or they may for their own sake put others at risk. They may sacrifice enduring values for capricious satisfaction, or they may subordinate momentary desires for the sake of long-range goals. They may risk health for pleasure, peace for greed, serenity for ambition, safety for thrills, social harmony for personal gain, future generations for present advantage. Or they may reverse any of these choices.

Some distinctions among kinds of risk can clarify the issues involved in choices among risks.

Inadvertent and Malicious Risks

Life is risky partly because of mistakes. Most misfortunes are unintended. Technology magnifies the scope of some mistakes. In a horse-and-buggy age no one accident in transportation could kill 582 people, the number who died in a single air crash in Tenerife in 1977. As systems become more intricate and complex, errors have more far-reaching effects. The failure of a single valve, an error in military intelligence can disrupt the lives of thousands of people. Perhaps in past ages kingdoms could be lost for the want of a horseshoe nail. But now more than ever, it seems, industrial societies depend on giant systems that nobody entirely understands.

Technology also can build in safeguards against accidents, redundancies to correct particular failures. Much of technology functions pretty well to make life more safe and more comfortable. When systems misfunction, the ethical issue is usually not evil intent. It is rather overconfidence, carelessness, the culpable failure to pay due regard to the welfare of people and ecosystems.

But some crimes are intended, and technology enhances the possibilities of malicious acts. Terrorists could always seize hostages and inflict brutality, but nuclear terrorism is a new possibility. Sabotage now has potentialities unknown to the past.

The vulnerability of modern metropolitan areas is frightening. Power blackouts, entirely unintended, have twice disrupted life in large areas of New York City, reminding populations that the city could not survive an extended power outage. An act of sabotage could conceivably damage the system beyond any quick repair. In the summer of 1981 vandals, opening a valve in an aqueduct, caused the rupture of two 48-inch water mains supplying most of the water for 600,000 people in and near Newark, New Jersey. For a few days, in a touch-and-go situation, the city took emergency measures for conservation and rushed repairs. People sweltering in 90-degree temperatures realized once again their dependence on repair crews upstate, pipe producers in Maryland, transportation systems, and experts who understood intricacies that most people knew nothing about. They learned that the damage would cost upwards of $2.5 million. Four teenagers were soon arrested for the crime. Apparently it was a prank.

The real wonder is that in a world with so many angry and frustrated people, far worse acts of sabotage are not more common. One reason may be that the most angry and despairing people lack the skills for the most effective means of sabotage. Or it may be that even when bitterness approaches insanity, some deep inhibitions prevent the most massively destructive acts. In any case this is a precarious world.

Obvious-Immediate and Hidden-Distant risks

The simplest risks to cope with are those that produce obvious, immediate dangers. The risks of drunken driving are well known. If drunken drivers forget them or pretend that they are not drunk, even they understand the risks when they are sober. Societies take steps— half hearted in the United States, wholehearted in Sweden—to prevent drunken driving. The act and its consequences are closely related. Drunken drivers risk *themselves* (along with other people), and the jeopardy is immediate.

More difficult to handle rationally are those risks that lead to dangers farther removed from the risky acts. The link between the smoking of tobacco and cancer or heart-disease is remote enough that (1) many years of research were necessary to establish the connection convincingly and (2) many people choose to accept the distant liability for the sake of immediate gratification. In cases of genetic damage induced by chemicals or radioactivity, the consequences may not appear for one or several generations, and even then may not be traceable with certainty to the cause.

Some large-scale social acts have long-deferred effects. DDT at first appeared to be a contribution to health. Gradually evidence appeared that it can persist for aeons in the ecosystem and the food chain, at great cost to many living species and at considerable cost to human beings. It was fairly simple for the United States to outlaw it and find substitutes. Lingering DDT will still do harm for a long time to come, but it will not become more prevalent. However, malaria-plagued societies still use DDT. They are more concerned about saving people than about saving birds. And they have an incentive to save people now, even at the cost of long-run dangers.

Some risks of very great proportion remain only hypothetical. A case in point is the rise of carbon dioxide in the atmosphere. An increase of seven percent in the period 1958–1981—and perhaps of fifteen percent, in the past eighty years—is due chiefly to the burning of fossil fuels (which combines oxygen with carbon) and the destruction of forests and vegetation (which break down CO_2 into carbon and oxygen). A fairly well substantiated theory holds that a continuing increase of CO_2 will, through the "greenhouse effect," heat up the earth. It appears that the ninety-six percent CO_2 atmosphere of Venus is largely responsible for the surface temperature there of 900 degrees Fahrenheit. If the earth goes only a little way in that direction, there will be trouble. A change of seven degrees Fahrenheit, which might easily happen in the next fifty years, would disrupt patterns of rainfall and start the melting of the polar icecaps.

But what can motivate a human race to make a major renunciation of present comforts because of troubles that *might* appear in fifty years? It is possible that other causes are now cooling the earth's temperature. Some cold countries might welcome a warming effect. Uncertainty and conflicts of interest interfere with any resolute action now. At worst, people might reason, we can wait a while and see if the earth really heats up.

The trouble with that is that the heating process is probably irreversible. A more densely populated earth, consuming more energy than now, will not be able to make a quick cut in consumption. Age-old forests, quickly destroyed, cannot be quickly replaced. And the melting of polar regions is cumulative. The disappearance of white ice and snow, which reflect solar heat back into space, and the appearance of green and black earth, which absorb solar heat, means that every change of this sort tends to increase the pace of future change. A long-deferred slowdown is probably no slowdown at all.

Ethical motivation is weak when people cannot see the consequences of their actions in their own lifetimes. The people who put the ecosphere at risk are not those who suffer from the risks. Furthermore, the contribution of any one individual or family to the total effect is infinitesimal. Yet the contribution of society is great.

There are many similar processes going on—all less than certain but risky enough for concern. The use of chlorofluorocarbons (in aerosol spray cans and refrigeration units) and the flying of supersonic aircraft (military and civilian) is almost surely depleting the protective layer of ozone in the atmosphere and hence exposing the earth to increased ultraviolet radiation, thereby causing cancers and genetic damage. The overfishing of the seas is apparently depleting the world's food supply. Overfarming and overgrazing contribute to the spread of deserts and reduction of croplands.

In most such cases the evidence is less than certain, the link between present acts and future danger is not entirely clear, and the people who take the risks are not those who suffer the worst consequences.

Any correction of reckless acts therefore requires a wisdom and ethical sensitivity that are rare in human experience. And if the most affluent and educated societies are not capable of action, there is no reason at all to expect that the most impoverished societies will act.

Spectacular and Chronic Risks

Some hazards are so spectacular that the world pays attention. Some greater hazards are so chronic, so routine that they are barely noticed. That contrast often skews ethical judgment.

Any air crash that kills 140 people will get attention around the world. If it happens in the United States, it will produce a headline in almost every newspaper, an announcement on almost every newscast. But there will be no news ripple if United States automobile deaths for that day add up to 140 because *every day,* on average, that number of people die in car accidents. A public does not want to be bored by repetitious reports of what happens as regularly as dawn and dusk. It is more interested in the weather.

There is *some* rationality for the attention to the spectacular. If the cause of the air crash can be determined precisely, perhaps a single correction can prevent repetitions. By comparison, no one action can prevent the many auto accidents each day.

Furthermore, human beings are inherently symbol-making creatures. They feel, think, and act symbolically. The dramatic risk has symbolic power. A careless risk that jeopardizes many people becomes a more potent symbol for the contempt of life than an assortment of humdrum risks that add up to the same factual results. A society is not wise to disdain symbols.

So those who are concerned for people and human values will not neglect the spectacular and symbolically powerful risks. But they will realize that more people are hurt, day in and day out, by chronic risks. And that realization will influence their actions and policy decisions.

PROBABILITY AND MAGNITUDE: AN EXAMPLE FROM BIOLOGY

Two quantitative questions enter into every reckoning about risk. The first is: how likely is the danger? Sometimes (to recall Chapter 1) the answer is well known. A broad base of experience has produced knowledge about the relative risks of traveling by car or plane, of playing professional football or running a corporation, of overeating or taking a bath. If you and I don't have this information, some insurance actuaries have it. In other cases the answer is not known. Every innovation pushes experience into areas where experiential data are scarce. The innovation may actually make life more safe, but there is initial uncertainty.

The second question is: how much is at stake? This is very different from the first question. The probability of catching a cold during any given winter is high for most people; the probability of cancer is much lower. But people worry more about cancer, because more is at stake. Power failures are less frequent in great industrial cities than in Asian villages, but they bring greater danger in the cities. Thomas Sheridan, Professor of Mechanical Engineering at M.I.T., points out "the tendency towards ever larger, more complex, more capital intensive, more centrally and more tightly computer-controlled systems where the costs of failure are large, though the probabilities of failure may be small."[6]

The two questions arise simultaneously in some major new ventures of the human race. Some new discoveries bring the hope of high benefits together with elements of unknown risk.

A classical case is the work of molecular biologists with recombinant DNA. Scientists saw great possibilities of gaining new knowledge, producing new drugs and vaccines, healing dread diseases. They did not know exactly what risks were involved.

The experimentation centered on *Escherichia coli,* a bacterium that inhabits the human gut. Plentiful and accessible, it has been described as the most thoroughly understood of all organisms.

One question worried some scientists. Suppose their genetic modification of *E. coli* should transform this benign bacterium into a lethal one. Then suppose the new bacteria should escape the laboratory. Was it possible that they would unwittingly inflict a new disease on people? And might it be that people would have no immunities against it, of the sort they have built up against diseases that have been around for aeons? There were many sound scientific reasons to think this highly improbable. Nobody really expected the worst to happen. But if the chances were slight, the possible harm might be very great.

Some of the scientists at the forefront of the work deliberately decided to hold off the next steps. At one stage the questions of a student raised the warning. The scientists talked with colleagues. Some asked the National Academy of Sciences to appoint a committee to study the issues. The committee recommended an international conference and, in the meantime, issued a letter through *Science* (in the United States) and *Nature* (in England) calling on scientists to observe a moratorium on the research in question. So far as is known, the moratorium was fully observed from July of 1974 until the Asilomar, California, conference February 24–27, 1975. At the conference 150 scientists from Europe, North America, Japan, and Australia discussed the issues with great intensity.[7]

The pressures, conscious and unconscious, resisting any slowdown were intense. There was the honored scientific tradition of freedom of inquiry and the fear that public attention might lead to clumsy political interference. There was the excitement of discovery, sometimes heightened by competitive ambition. There was—a little further down the pike—the commercial possibility of huge profits. There was the desire for progress in preventing and healing human suffering. The remarkable thing is that, in the face of these pressures, scientists around the world complied with the moratorium and acquiesced in the findings of the conference, which specified safeguards and guidelines for further research. In the United States the National Institutes of Health issued a code for practice. Congress debated the issues, but stopped short of legislation. That means that the NIH code is enforceable only in institutions that get some federal funding. Other laboratories can disregard the code. But the prestige of the NIH and the formulators of the guidelines is so impressive that the rules have great influence throughout the world. As experience has increased, the guidelines have been somewhat relaxed.

This procedure did not end controversy. The rules and guidelines, whether in their original or their relaxed forms, are still criticized from two sides. Some distinguished scientists think the regulations are not strict enough—that the peril in an accident is so great that, even if accidents are not probable, more restraint should be observed. Other scientists of equal repute think that the regulations are too strict and therefore inhibit research that could be of human value.

Enforcement of the regulations is not automatic. They can be violated either carelessly or deliberately. In one case that drew wide public attention the National Institutes of Health in 1981 reprimanded

Dr. Martin Cline of the University of California at Los Angeles for conducting an experiment in violation of federal guidelines and the judgment of the university review committee. In an effort to treat severe disease he had inserted recombinant genes into human beings —apparently the first time this had actually been done. The experiments were done in Israel and Italy, but NIH funding was involved. Some scientists thought that the risk was negligible and the possible gain great. But the act was a violation of the regulations and processes of peer review, worked out at great pains by the scientific community and a government agency. History may vindicate the particular procedure employed by Dr. Cline. However, the public situation is that a society cannot permit individuals to be the sole judges of the risks that they inflict on the world.

Another worry comes with the extension of biological techniques from the laboratories of universities or research institutes to the large-scale processes of industrial production. One study group, working on this issue, came to this opinion:

We do not believe that survival and risk assessment experiments carried out on one strain of *E. coli* can accurately serve to predict the behaviour of the great variety of genetically modified organisms that can be expected to be generated in future applications of recombinant DNA technology. In addition the pressures of commercial exploitation may well undercut the application of guidelines carefully developed in the academic context.[8]

The case has become, in a short time, a classic example of ways of dealing with a contemporary issue of risk. For the first time in history scientists throughout the world observed a self-imposed moratorium on a specific kind of scientific research, because a few leaders among them persuaded the rest that issues of risk needed investigation. That was an epochal event.

Yet the case leaves its perplexities. How do citizens fit into such a process? Legislators, from the U.S. Congress to city councils, found themselves debating the regulations to govern research in laboratories. They were not themselves technically competent to measure and estimate the risks. Yet a democratic society can scarcely abdicate all authority on issues of social policy to a body of experts, especially when the experts are divided and when some of the experts have a personal investment in one side of the controversy. That problem, as well as other issues of public risk, will be with the world for a long time.

ATTEMPTS TO MEASURE RISK: AN EXAMPLE FROM ENERGY

Statistics have something to do with ethics. Not everything, by any means, but something.[9]

Drunken driving, I have already mentioned, is risky. The risk is widely enough recognized that public law prohibits it. On any given occasion, however, a drunken driver may negotiate a trip without accident, while a sober driver may smash life and property. The success of the drunken driver does not vindicate the action. Drunkenness at the wheel is far more dangerous than sobriety. There is a mass of statistical evidence to validate the point. The statistical averages are more important to legal and ethical judgments than exceptional cases.

I have argued that all life involves risk and that some risks are worth taking. Of the various ways of accomplishing a worthwhile purpose, the ways that jeopardize the fewest lives and values are the best. Some dangers to life and value can be measured. Others can be estimated with varying degrees of reliability. At this point statistical data enter into ethical responsibility.

Often the evidence disagrees with popular opinion and anxiety. A case in point is the production of energy. All methods of producing energy entail some risks—as does any radical reduction of available energy. Populations and governments want to minimize the risks and to avoid methods with exorbitant risks. Public discussions and conflicts have centered most of all on the risks of nuclear energy.

In Chapter 3 I made the case that there are no panaceas for the world's energy emergency. I reaffirm that judgment here. Also, I am not here arguing the economics of energy production—an important issue in itself. And I am not here discussing the strange political history of decisions about energy. I am now looking solely at the issue of risk and its ethical meaning. The weight of evidence is very different from the most publicized opinions.

The overwhelming evidence, based on the record of experience thus far, is that nuclear power production is safer to human life than some of the alternatives—especially than the chief alternative in U.S. energy policy, coal. The four major studies on this issue, although they disagree on many details, concur on this judgment.

One such study came from the Council on Scientific Affairs of the American Medical Association, published in 1978. It ranked the four chief methods of generating electricity in the following order from safest to least safe:

> Natural gas
> Nuclear energy
> Oil
> Coal

The analysis was based on experience in extraction of resources, transportation and processing, pollution, release of radioactivity, storage of wastes—all the processes subject to investigation. The findings were that, given power plants of equal capacity, the coal-fired plant causes 48-285 times as many deaths as the nuclear plant. The coal-related deaths are to miners (mining accidents and black lung), to workers throughout the cycle, and to the public (pollution).[10]

The report candidly acknowledged one major limitation. Since it was based on actual experience, it did not include any major nuclear accident, of the kind that is feared but has not happened.[11] As I write this chapter, it appears that there has not yet been a fatality immediately due to a nuclear accident in the civilian production of energy in the United States or anywhere in that part of the world with a free press. Three Mile Island, of course, was a major accident in terms of property damage, but not of human fatalities. There was one major accident in the Soviet Union, on which most of the facts have been concealed[12] (it was probably related to a military program). If, by the time you read this, there should be an accident causing twenty or one hundred or one thousand deaths, the AMA figures would become obsolete. There have been deaths in the whole process of production of nuclear energy, including those that can (with statistical probability) be traced to nuclear radioactivity; these, according to the AMA study, are far fewer than those connected with coal and petroleum.

A second study, by Resources for the Future,[13] tries to take the process of risk assessment one step further and to reckon in the statistical probability of the major accidents that have not yet happened. Obviously estimates of something that has not happened are different from estimates based on extensive experience. What possible methods are available? The study group began with the probabilities of risk estimated in the famous Rasmussen Report. Since this report has been criticized and is admittedly imprecise,[14] Resources for the Future multiplied its probabilities of risk by one hundred to get a safe margin of error. (Of course, one might ask: why one hundred, rather than ten or two hundred? The question is a good sign of the uncertainties in all reckoning of risks.) The report comes to high, median, and low estimates of the risks related to coal and nuclear energy. In each case the estimate is that coal is about five times as hazardous as nuclear energy.

A third study, by Herbert Inhaber, a scientific adviser to the Canadian Atomic Energy Control Board, found nuclear energy more risky than natural gas but safer than the other methods of producing electricity, including even photovoltaic methods and wind, when these are backed up by coal systems for times when the sun does not shine and the wind does not blow.[15] (Passive solar energy is virtually riskless, unless somebody carelessly gets sunburn. Production of electricity from solar energy involves the risks typical of industrial and mining processes, and these, on any massive scale, become great.[16])

Inhaber's findings are sharply attacked in a fourth study by John Holdren and the Energy and Resources Group at the University of California.[17] This report maintains that solar energy is far safer than nuclear, but even so, it finds coal more risky than nuclear energy.

Why, in the face of so much evidence, is nuclear energy so much more frightening to the public than the major alternatives? I suggest three reasons.

(1) The story of nuclear energy, starting with the atomic bomb and continuing through the years since, is one of high drama, while coal is commonplace and dull. Intellectuals and filmmakers don't pay much attention to coal. The four reports I have described above, although publicly available, are stiff reading and are not media events. If the accident at Three Mile Island had killed a hundred or a hundred and fifty people, the outcry would have been overwhelming—and rightly so. But the world scarcely notices the one hundred to one hundred and fifty annual deaths that are routine in U.S. coal mines

—or the four thousand annual deferred deaths of miners from black lung. Furthermore, there is the possibility of the big accident—the meltdown that for a time seemed imminent at Three Mile Island. That risk cannot be dismissed lightly. No assurance from experts, who have repeatedly shown their fallibility, will quiet that fear.

(2) Radioactivity has a special mystique. Ever since the Curies, who discovered radium, radioactivity has harmed unsuspecting people. It is invisible and insidious, imposing cancer and genetic defects long after exposure. Now, of course, it is measurable with instruments and more easily detectable than many other poisons; but most of us don't carry around dosimeters or Geiger counters and don't know when we are subject to risk. It is not surprising that rumor and conjecture outrun the evidence, but there *is* evidence that is helpful for responsible decisions.

Sometimes it is assumed that a little radioactivity—perhaps like a little wine—does no harm but that a lot is dangerous. So scientists have sought to define a threshold of danger. Now the dominant practice is to assume not a threshold but a linear progression of danger. That more cautious assumption, at least for the present, would seem to be the ethically responsible one.

One major problem is that, threshold or not, everybody is exposed to some radioactivity every day. The average person is subject to about 100 millirems per year, of which more than a quarter comes from chemicals within the human body and the rest from the atmosphere (cosmic rays) and from the ground and buildings.[18] Rosalyn Yalow, a Nobel laureate in medicine, says that in the Denver area the natural radiation is twice that in New York, but that the cancer death rate in Colorado is lower than that in New York. She further says that in parts of Brazil and India the natural radiation is ten times that in New York, with no known harmful effects.[19] Except in unusual cases these variations in natural radioactivity are greater than the variations due to human intervention.

But humanly produced radioactivity is also part of the picture. For most people the greatest part is medical X-rays. In some specific places fallout from nuclear weapons, including tests, has been very serious.

An interesting conversation on radioactivity took place at a hearing in April 1979 of the Energy Subcommittee of the Senate Governmental Affairs Committee. The meeting was in the Dirksen Senate Office Building, which has granite walls. The witness, Alvin Weinberg, had brought a Geiger counter to the meeting. Senator John Glenn asked him for its reading on the spot, and this interchange followed:

Weinberg: It's 400 counts per minute, which comes to 250 millirems per year, which is about two and a half times usual background.
Glenn (in surprise): We are getting more right here than they got downwind from Three Mile Island?
Weinberg: You sure are.[20]

Because of the radioactive substances (including uranium) in coal, some coal-burning power plants emit more radioactivity than nuclear plants of the same capacity. Richard Wilson, professor of physics at Harvard University, reckons that any of the following acts increase the chance of death from cancer by one part in a million: smoking 1.4 cigarettes, one X-ray in a good hospital, eating one hundred charcoal-broiled steaks or forty tablespoons of peanut butter, living one hundred fifty years within thirty miles of a nuclear power plant. As for risk of accidental death through all causes (not only from cancer), he calculates the one in a million increase from any of these: spending three hours in a coal mine, traveling one thousand miles by jet plane, living fifty years within five miles of a nuclear plant.[21]

I assume that nobody can measure risks with *that* precision, but some such effort is important to social decisions. Frightened warnings about dangers are not much use unless they include comparisons with other dangers in an inherently risky world. To minimize risks a society needs to know which are the greatest risks. As for statistics, even one death in a million is too many if that death is in my family. But I would rather have my family take statistically low rather than statistically high risks. A responsible ethic will think of society in the same way.

(3) One further danger connected with nuclear energy, which does not apply to coal and petroleum, is the relation to nuclear weapons. It should be evident from Chapter 8 that I take this danger very seriously.

Most of the nuclear weapons that the world fears are not, of course, by-products of peaceful nuclear energy. Nuclear weapons preceded commercial nuclear energy by more than a decade. Every nuclear weapon in the world—with possibly a very few exceptions—would be there if there had never been any electricity-generating nuclear plants. The future may be different from that past. Israel, bombing the Iraqi nuclear generator in Baghdad (1981), charged that the Iraqis were secretly planning to divert materials from the reactor into weapons. The horizontal proliferation of nuclear weapons may be facilitated by increasing use of nuclear energy throughout the world. The more dangerous vertical proliferation goes on unchanged. Until the great nations do something about vertical proliferation, their concern about horizontal proliferation is strangely unreal.

To sum up the bearing of statistical evidence on energy, I think that conventional opinion overestimates the peril of nuclear energy as compared with coal and some other alternatives. This opinion, I repeat, does not modify my conclusions in Chapter 3 that neither nuclear nor any other form of energy will spare us the necessity for major social changes to end the present extravagance of industrialized societies.

The measurement of risk is not itself a study in ethics; it is a scientific process. But it is part—one part—of the contribution that enters into ethical evaluation of options facing persons and societies.

CHOOSING RISKS

To choose among risks—to accept some and avoid others—is part of the human venture. In that venture, I have been saying, quantitative, statistical reasoning has a place, but if given too great a place, it becomes inadequate and misleading. It may dull ethical sensitivity by reducing to a quantitative base those values that cannot be quantified.

The quantifications involved in cost-benefit analysis are a case in point. In Chapter 9, I argued that such incalculable values as human dignity upset any strictly numerical analysis. That issue has its meaning for risk.

Fred Hapgood has explored the process of risk-benefit analysis, showing both its necessity and its tendency to distort values.[22] If a government agency with a budget, finite as all budgets are finite, sets out to reduce hazards to human life, it wants to know what procedures will accomplish the most for the dollars expended. It does not want to spend a million dollars to save two lives, if the same money spent differently would save two hundred lives. So risk-benefit analysts go to work. Hapgood reports that the National Highway Traffic Safety Administration came to the point of evaluating a human life at $287,175! As a specific technique even that procedure may have *some* usefulness in suggesting a guideline for expenditures: fund those projects that are cheaper and, for the time being at least, avoid those that are more expensive. But the absurdity of thinking confined to that groove becomes evident when I ask: is my life, is my wife's life, are my children's lives, are my best friends' lives each worth $287,175?

So in evaluating risks the quantitative assessment is only one question of import. Concentration on it alone excludes such questions as these:

For what purpose is the risk incurred? Is it for comfort, wealth, lust, the domination of other people, the vindication of pride? Is it for the kind of purpose that ennobles sacrifice or that degrades it?

What is at risk? Is it life, money, health, love, beauty, vanity, perpetuation of a way of life that incorporates some values and distorts others?

Is the risk voluntary? Or is it imposed upon people who would not, given the right of free decision, accept it?

How is the risk distributed? Do those who enjoy the benefits accept the risk, or do they inflict it on others? Are miners of coal and uranium put at special risk in order that other people, risk-free in that respect, may enjoy luxurious comforts?

Does the present generation indulge its desires at the risk of future generations? Since future generations (and infants) are the one group that inherently cannot form a pressure bloc to defend their interests, how are their interests made effective in social decisions?

Questions like these suggest that risk distribution deserves as big a place as wealth distribution in discussion about social justice. But it usually gets nowhere near so much attention. Ideally one might dream of a system where everyone accepted risks in direct ratio to the expected benefits. But any such ideal assumes an unreal individualism. All persons are part of a body social and a body politic. Children do, in painful fact, suffer for the sins of their fathers and mothers and grandparents and great grandparents. In the nexus of life we all inevitably, to some degree, bear one another's burdens. If the president of the United States makes mistakes, as any president will do, many people in the United States and around the world will suffer the consequences.

But there are ways of increasing the power of people to make personal decisions and to participate in social decisions so that they are not simply the risk-bearers for the decisions of others. And there are ways of spreading the cost of risk—for example, mining regulations that increase safety even though they reduce productivity, and thereby give stockholders and consumers some participation in the costs. And there are ways of compensating for risk, not only in terms of the market (which often assigns high pay to risky jobs) but also in terms of special health care for those most at risk.

Two more general issues belong in any effort to cope with risk. The first is that all sound planning must assume the inevitability of mistakes. People are fallible and technologies are imperfect. It is morally irresponsible to plan on the assumption that everything will function as planned. In trying to hit a target, as Hans Jonas puts it, the successful hit is *one* possibility, while there are *many* possibilities of misses.[23]

In a time when many experimental ventures are going on, even if in each one the odds favor success, there will be some failures. In Russian roulette (which, for all I know, Russians may call American roulette) the chances in any single case are that the hammer of the gun will fall on an empty chamber. But if many people try the game many times, a lot of casualties are sure. A society in this "age of hypotheticality" is in such a situation. The answer is not to avoid risks —an impossibility—but to choose risks wisely and to exercise more rigorous care than has been necessary in some more stable times.

The second general issue has to do with the relation of risk to the meaning of life—ultimately a religious issue even in the most secularized cultures. Contemporary discussions of risk tend, for good reasons, to emphasize survival, because in an age of diverse and confused values survival is one almost universally recognized value. Without it, most other values become meaningless.

But there is a deep fallacy in concentrating on an ethic of survival.[24] No individual will survive for long; so personal survival, as a goal, is surely self-defeating. The human race will not survive forever, but it has a long prospect; the very real perils before it, including even nuclear war, are not likely to wipe out every last person.

What matters in the choices before humanity is the perpetuating and renewing of some kind of meaningful community. Or, if any community can be said to have some kind of meaning for its participants, what matters and what is threatened now is a future embodying some of the values and hopes of contemporary societies. Individuals, who must die in any case, want to die with an expectation that the human community will go on, will have some continuity with the good in past and present, will reach toward some possibilities unrealized in past and present.

That expectation can be destroyed by excessive concentration on survival. Daniel Callahan, in a book well entitled *The Tyranny of Survival,* writes:

The potential tyranny of survival as a value is that it is capable, if not treated sanely, of wiping out all other values. Survival can become an obsession and a disease, provoking a destructive singlemindedness that will stop at nothing.[25]

The most obvious case is nuclear war. A too frenzied drive for the weaponry designed to ensure survival probably threatens the physical survival of the nation. It certainly threatens the survival of a community that evokes loyalty and concern. Writing about the war in Vietnam, which was far less than a nuclear war, the political "realist" Hans Morgenthau says:

What will it avail us to save our face in a war without end if we cannot save our souls, if we cannot save ourselves as a nation worthy to be saved? And what kind of face would it be we would be saving at the price of our souls and our purpose as a nation?[26]

As essential as physical survival is the preservation of a kind of social life worthy of survival. That is why I have argued in Chapter 8 that, in a world where risk is inevitable, it is better to take some risks for peace than to take all the risks of war. In the case of decisions about war, as in all the forced options of this book, there is a place for calculation of odds and reasoned efforts to maximize values and minimize losses. But finally decision rests on commitments about human good—the commitments that make life authentically human.

12. Science, Faith, and Ideology in Policy Decisions

Last of all in the argument of this book I come to the question of method. Confronting forced options, the world is making fateful decisions. *How* do persons, communities, and nations decide? What reasons can they find for their decisions? Are there methods that can bring clarity into the blundering and stumbling that we all do?

The matter of method is more fundamental—I do not say more urgent—than any of the specific problem areas I have discussed. I assume that many of the opinions I have stated will need refinement, correction, refutation. But *how* do my critics and how do I validate or correct opinions? What use of evidence, what criteria of judgment become important?

It would have been neater to start by enunciating a method, then to apply that method to the problems one by one. But that is not the way the world works. What happens is that persons and communities are deciding all the time, in the complex and messy ways that I described in Chapter I. Or, equally often, they realize in retrospect that at some past time they unwittingly made a decision that affects life now.

But sometimes, in deciding, they may stop to reflect, "How do we make this decision?" They may consciously look for a method. Or, after facing the consequences of a past decision, they may wonder, "How did we decide? How could we have done better?" Such questions may lead to refinement of method and a greater wisdom about the next decision.

There are parallels here with "scientific method." Some of us in high school were taught, in the first week of a course, that there was a scientific method that we would apply throughout the course. Actually scientific methods developed through centuries of groping, of successes and failures, or revising old methods and trying new ones. As physicist Harold Schilling wrote: "Many inexperienced graduate students have been genuinely puzzled and disturbed by what seemed to them to be the unmethodical and 'unscientific' procedures of active, experienced investigators in a research laboratory. They were unable to discern in what was going on around them any 'system' even remotely suggestive of the 'scientific method,' with its alleged necessarily sequential 'steps,' about which they had heard so much in high school or college." Schilling goes on to say that science "demands rigorous thought and renounces sloppy or wishful thinking."[1]

Society, which is not a controlled experiment in a laboratory, does not lend itself to the precision appropriate to physics. It cannot aspire to the kind of quantification, repeatability, and verifiability appropriate in the physics laboratory. But those who would participate responsibly in its decisions can strive for "rigorous thought" and can renounce at least the worst of "sloppy or wishful thinking."

I intend here to describe some processes that normally go on in the making of policy decisions, not to prescribe some new method. But in the description I hope for some clarification and illumination of the processes.

INFORMATION AND SCIENCE; PURPOSE AND FAITH

Every policy decision, whether made consciously or unconsciously, depends upon the *information* available to the deciding agents and upon their *purposes*. That statement may seem too obvious to bother writing down. Yet the failure to take it seriously and to analyze both sides of it brings much of the confusion in contemporary societies.

A useful starting point is a common saying attributed to many people, perhaps most often to Karl Barth. The Christian, so the saying goes, meets the world with the Bible in one hand, the daily newspaper in the other. Both hands are essential; neither alone is adequate. The Bible represents a faith, a loyalty, a commitment coming out of a heritage, but it does not tell contemporary believers what to do in all the situations they face. The newspaper represents what is happening in the world today. It does not probe the meaning of all that happens or provide the purposes that will direct readers in responding to events.

The statement can be generalized. All people and communities meet the world with some awareness of their own interests, purposes, and values. Such is the case with atheists and believers, bourgeoisie and proletariat, tribalists and nationalists and internationalists. In the past it was often argued that values and purposes could be derived from some universal reason or some "nature" of the cosmos, but today's pluralistic world makes that venture difficult. Values are rooted in some sense of the meaning of life, some hope for a better world, some venture of commitment, some trust in a reality both personal and wider than personal. The classical name for this response is *faith,* whether it be the faith of religious traditions or some more inchoate faith that pervades most of life. That faith has much to do with the way people appropriate experiences, recognize purposes, and make decisions.

But faith of itself does not give persons or communities their information about what is going on in the world. In the industrialized world the newspaper helps. In the rest of the world most people do not get their information from newspapers, but everywhere people have some methods (more or less adequate, just as newspapers are more or less adequate) for gaining the information they need: firsthand experience, conversations, wall posters, transistor radios, public speeches, and so on. People and communities, as they make decisions, respond to information. They may find the information encouraging or discouraging. They may welcome it, rage in anger over it, bless or curse the gods because of it, make money out of it, or reluctantly acquiesce in it. Those responses will depend largely on their interests, their values, their faith. But purposeful action wants to be informed action.

In the contemporary world science provides much of the information that is important for policy decisions. It has not always been so. When Isaiah of Jerusalem addressed the king and when Socrates talked with his friends in the agora of Athens, they paid little attention to science. Today their intellectual and spiritual descendants must pay great attention to scientific knowledge about armaments, nutrition, biology, economic processes, and a lot else. But science does not prescribe the social uses of science. It can invent methods of birth control, of increasing food supplies, of changing genetic patterns of life, of destroying cities, and much more. People and societies decide what to do with these accomplishments.

I am tempted to revise an aphorism of Immanuel Kant. For major policy decisions of societies in our time, *faith without science is silent; science without faith is aimless.*

A DISTINCTION AND A RELATION

To recognize the difference between information and commitments is essential for decisions about policy. Perhaps the *second* most important factor in clarity of decision making is to see that difference. The *most* important factor, then, is to see the relation between the two.

Logical positivism, following a cue offered by David Hume long before, sought to divide all discourse into two kinds:

(1) statements of knowledge that are true or false because they are either tautologies (e.g., 2 + 2 = 4) or empirically testable (e.g., there are more people in China than in the United States);

(2) pseudo-statements that are meaningless (neither true nor false) and are merely emotive expressions (e.g., ice cream is good and murder is bad).

That way of thinking was entirely too simple to last long, but it made a preliminary contribution. In an ethical perplexity there is some help in sorting out the contentions that are informational and those that are valuational.

Throughout this book, for example, many of the arguments hinge on information. There are facts or estimates on supplies of petroleum and coal, on the extent of starvation and hunger, on rates of population growth, on achievements in genetics, on armaments and war. If the information is wrong, it needs correction; and the correction will revise or refute the argument. In such a case agents of decision need accurate information. Wishful thinking, self-deception, and error stand in the way of sound decisions.

Hence it is important to get at the facts. Not all facts are available and not all facts are relevant, but facts are utterly essential for decisions. I emphasize facts because of a strong tendency in our time, which I share in part, to insist that there are no bare facts separate from interpretation and meaning. This tendency, pushed to its limits, says that people never argue about facts but only about perceptions of facts, and that perceptions are inalienably subjective. I agree that facts are always intertwined with meaning. Nevertheless, there are facts. To define *fact* with philosophical precision might require a whole book, but examples of facts are easy to find. Starvation is a fact.

The rate of consumption of petroleum in the world is a fact. The destructive power of nuclear weapons is a fact, and no interpretation revokes the fact.

Gustavo Gutierrez writes: "There is nothing more certain than a fact."[2] And Gunnar Myrdal coins the sentence: "Facts kick."[3] I quote these two writers because of their agreement about the importance of facts in the midst of their major differences in outlook on the world. Gutierrez is a Latin American, Roman Catholic theologian of liberation, much influenced by Marx. Myrdal is a Swedish social scientist, invincibly liberal in intellectual heritage. Both are social reformers; both recognize how human purposes and social situations influence perception and interpretation of information. Yet both insist on the reality and importance of facts.

On some of the major ethical and social decisions of our time, the great religious and moral traditions are silent, because the salient facts —or the knowledge of the facts—are new. Neither Moses nor Lao-tse, neither the Buddha nor the Christ has advised us: "Thous shalt—or shalt not—rearrange DNA." Neither Plato nor Epictetus, neither Spinoza nor Kant has counseled us: "Do—or don't—produce energy with breeder reactors." One reason for the ineffectiveness of religious communities and professional philosophers on policy issues today is that their efforts to relate moral insights to facts are often—not always —inadequate.

One ecumenical Christian study group addressed this issue forcefully:

We do not regard the Bible as the answer-book to our ethical questions. The Bible and Christian tradition are silent on many decisions that Christians must make today, e.g., about the ethical evaluation of specific discoveries in genetics.

Far from renouncing the biblical tradition, the group went on to say:

We do not think that the Bible is made obsolete by new sciences and technologies. We do not live in an age so "enlightened" that we have no need for biblical guidance. In fact, our rising ecological sensitivities have frequently made the Bible more rather than less relevant to our decisions and to the attitudes that underlie those decisions.[4]

But why does a religious tradition, "silent on many decisions," become "more relevant" in the face of new knowledge? Because information, including the scientific information that is overwhelmingly important for our times, does not tell persons or societies how to respond to the information.

Consider the information about the steadily diminishing reserves of petroleum and the rising worldwide demand for liquid fuels. That information leads to a set of factual questions. How great are the reserves? How much petroleum is recoverable by present methods or innovative techniques? What are the costs of recovery? At what point does the extraction of petroleum consume more energy than it gains? What are the usable alternatives to petroleum? These questions find no answers in the religious and ethical traditions. The questions are scientific and technical. Answers are controversial—and one recurrent human perplexity is that momentous policy decisions often depend upon uncertain knowledge and estimates. But there is no help in appealing from scientific uncertainty to religious or moral conviction on such questions.

But the technical questions quickly lead to a quite different set of questions. What are my rights and the rights of my society to the world's petroleum as compared with the rights of other people? I can buy more petroleum than most of the people of India, and my nation can buy far more than the nation of India. Is that an adequate basis for distribution? What is the meaning of our patterns of consumption, of our exercise of power, of our definition of personal and national security? What are we willing to do in order to maintain a predominance of wealth and power, and what are we willing to do in order to change the existing situation? The physical sciences will not answer these questions. They drive us to the most basic issues of ethics and of faith.

On any controversial questions of social policy there is some help in sorting out two kinds of arguments: those about information and those about commitments. Usually the two are intertwined in discussion. But there is hopeless confusion in answering complex questions about facts with declarations of moral fervor or in answering questions about the meaning of life and commitment with appeals for another project in empirical research.

Another way to get at the same point is to ask of any controversial declaration: what would lead you (or me) to change your (or my) mind? On many of the declarations in this book I am ready to change my mind if better evidence refutes the evidence I have reported. Among many examples are the opinions I have stated on the effects of the Green Revolution or the relative safety of coal-burning and nuclear power plants. What I want here is the best factual evidence. On some other declarations I doubt that any new evidence will change my commitments. Among the examples are a concern for human rights around the world and a belief that ethical responsibility includes care of the earth as well as human advantage. I do not always live up to the best I believe on these subjects, but I do not expect a new laboratory experiment or a new statistical report to change my beliefs.

On some judgments intelligence requires an open mind, ready to change opinions in the light of new evidence. On other judgments loyalty requires commitment in the face of challenges. Both intellectual clarity and ethical integrity require a distinction between the two situations.

All this has to do with what I call the *second* most important factor in the understanding of decision making: recognition of the distinction between information and commitments. But already I have begun to encroach on the *most* important factor: appreciation of the relation between the two.

Information and commitments sometimes enrich each other. Commitment is one of the motivating factors that produce information. Commitment to human health has led to discoveries of information about healing. Commitment to relieve human hunger has led to discoveries about the science and technologies of food production. Or, to take a more disturbing example, commitment to national interests has led to vast scientific-technological research about weapons production. And, contrariwise, some areas of ignorance remain unexplored because there has been little commitment to enter them.

For the most part, inquirers find only the information they are looking for. Honest inquiry will acknowledge information that upsets the inquirer's wishes or prejudices. And sometimes information, even unsought, confronts and disturbs us. That is why Myrdal can say, "Facts kick." But people and societies have a remarkable ability to find, amid the world's confusion of information and misinformation, the fragments of knowledge or error that sustain their own interests. To get true information and to build a policy upon it, therefore, requires both an intellectual-scientific skill and a self-searching of motivations and commitments.

An ecumenical consultation prior to the one I quoted a few paragraphs back stated the situation in relation to decisions about genetics. Its particular language is addressed to churches, but the import of the language is universal:

Churchmen cannot expect precedents from the past to provide answers to questions never asked in the past. On the other hand, new scientific advances do not determine what are worthy human goals. Ethical decisions in uncharted areas require that scientific capabilities be understood and used by persons and communities sensitive to their own deepest convictions about human nature and destiny. There is no sound ethical judgment in these matters independent of scientific knowledge, but science does not itself prescribe the good.[5]

THE ROLE OF IDEOLOGY

Policy decisions, I have been saying, take place at the point of interaction between commitments and information, which often means the interaction between faith and science. The arena of interaction is culture. For many decisions, the arena is that aspect of culture called politics. Social policies are worked out in the political process. And even many personal decisions are colored by political settings, national and international.

Therefore an understanding of policy decisions requires attention not only to commitments and information, but also to a third concept: ideology.

The word *ideology* has many meanings, of which two are important here. In one meaning, enunciated by Karl Marx[6] and elaborated by Karl Mannheim[7] and others, it is a false consciousness. It is the *distortion of reality* due to the efforts of persons or social groups to protect a privileged position. That distorted perception victimizes other persons or social groups. But its errors eventually harm the perpetrators. Seeing the world falsely, they cannot act wisely even for their own interests. That is why Marx could say that the bourgeoisie are their own grave diggers.[8] They do not volunteer for that job, and they do not intend it, but their false perceptions lead them to do things, intended for their advantage, that actually defeat their real interests.

Ideology in that sense—call it Ideology A—is by definition intellectually erroneous and ethically wrong. The only thing to do with it is to try to purge it from thought, feeling, and decision making. The effort is not easy.

In a second meaning, which has gradually become the more common meaning, ideology is *a set of conceptions or a picture of society and the world that helps to guide action*. Ideology in this sense—call it Ideology B—is necessary for functioning in the world. Every person and every group has an Ideology B. It helps them project expectations and choose ways of acting to attain their purposes.

There is no sense in trying to get rid of Ideology B. It is an asset to purposive action. And it is ineradicable, though not unchangeable.

An ideology (whether A or B) is neither sheer information nor sheer purpose, although it incorporates both. It incorporates a lot else, from experience and common sense. It is an amalgam—powerful though often imprecise—of information, ideas, purposes, and emotional tones.

In the modern world ideology usually includes some political awareness of human rights, of individual freedom and community responsibility, of the role of government, of the participation of people, of the kinds of power that accomplish different aims, of the relation of utopian hopes and realism. It includes economic ideas about production and consumption, about the importance of work, about unemployment, about money, inflation, industrialization, and commerce. It includes a sense of identity—with race, sex, social class, nation. It includes ideas or feelings about the role of coercion and violence in society and history.

Usually ideology takes shape in slogans, not necessarily consistent. The slogans are sources of comfort and are often weapons. Some familiar ideological slogans in twentieth-century ideologies are: "one person, one vote," "racial equality," "sexual equality," "free enterprise," "the greatest good of the greatest number," "majority rule," "minority rights," "self-determination," "class warfare," "classless society," "from each according to his ability, to each according to his need," "small is beautiful," "economies of scale," "government of the people, by the people, and for the people."

All people and groups have some Ideology B. It may be true to say that the more they ignore or deny ideology, the more powerful it is. They cannot question or doubt the ideology they do not acknowledge. An ideology includes information. But it is not primarily a collection of information. It is the framework into which people fit information or the skeleton around which they assemble information. Ideology determines what information, among the infinite possibilities, will grab attention. Ideology raises some things to visibility—the things that are important to human purposes in a given time and place. It filters out other things—the things that might distract from important concerns.

Ideology depends in large part on social location. Observers in a valley, on a mountain top, and in an airplane see the landscape differently. Similarly different social locations permit differing perceptions of society and the universe. Today the world is more aware than in most past ages that poor people, racial minorities, and women experience the world differently from the groups whose perceptions have usually dominated world history. The particularity of a social situation limits possibilities of seeing and understanding the world; hence every particularity needs completion by other particularities. But particularity is also an opportunity for insight; hence the many particularities have their contribution to a more comprehensive understanding of things. The most dangerous groups and ideologies are those that, failing to recognize their particularity, claim to be universal. This is a characteristic failure of powerful groups and of intellectuals.

Differing ideologies and the differing social situations that underly them are the reason why, when people look at the world, some see immediately the population problem and others see social inequalities. Some see triumphal technologies and others see exhaustion of resources. Some see the threat of an enemy nation's weapons and others see the threat to world security of the contest for more destructive weapons. If some proudly claim to see all of these, they see with accents and priorities guided by ideology.

I have distinguished between Ideology A, which I would like to purge, and Ideology B, which I endorse. But the relation between A and B is a subtle, complex, and perennial problem.

The reason is that all knowledge is purposeful. It is the knowledge of human beings who are inalienably purposeful. Their purposes guide their search for knowledge, lead them to seek some facts and neglect others, move them to notice and remember some things while ignoring or forgetting others. Without selectivity the world would be an overwhelming confusion. But selectivity is risky. It can lead to sharpened perception and creative action. And it can lead to purposeful ignorance, distortion of information, and destruction. And in the human situation, although I want Ideology B and do not want Ideology A, I rarely find Ideology B without some infection from Ideology A.

So it is important, so far as possible, to bring ideology into awareness and to criticize it. There are possibilities for correction of ideology by both science and faith. But that is not easy.

First, the correction of science. Everybody past infancy has had some experience of correcting erroneous opinions with more scientifically accurate knowledge. But nobody can know and take account of everything. Everything is too much. There is too much in any instant of experience for anybody to take account of it all. The important thing is to concentrate on the relevant. But ideology largely determines what any person or society considers relevant. It is hard to correct ideology by science when ideology determines the focus of scientific attention.

Second, the correction of faith. Any religiously serious person recognizes a responsibility to bring ideology under the judgment of faith. But that is hard to do when faith is already infused with ideology. There are important occasions when persons or communities of faith, by a serious searching of their scriptures or an experience of prayer, correct their ideologies by their faith. More frequent, perhaps, are those occasions when scripture or prayer simply reinforce existing ideology.

It is frequently charged in arguments on social issues that certain persons or groups are "too ideological." That criticism may be valid, if it means that ideology makes the contestant impervious to facts and values that are evident to others. So concerned people may call for less ideological and more empirical thinking. In the era of the Kennedy presidency the United States heard many pleas, from political and intellectual leaders, for an "end of ideology."[9] Real progress is possible in confronting ideological dogmatism with accurate information and with articulated values. Some of that has happened in regard to human rights in this century. But it is not desirable or possible that there be an "end" to Ideology B—to conceptions of the world that guide action. And Ideology A—the distortion of reality by the interests of partisan groups—remains a constant temptation.

PARTICIPATION IN DECISION MAKING

In some ways scientific technologies enhance the opportunities for the public, or the many publics in pluralistic societies, to participate in social decisions. Universal suffrage gives the opportunity to vote with ballots. Rising affluence increases the opportunity to vote with money in the market. And communication systems flood the populace with information. A person of ordinary education in a city or on a farm in an industrialized country can know far more about what is going on in China, South Africa, or Cuba than George Washington and the most learned intellectuals of his time could know. New communications systems mean that, in an increasing number of cities, people in their homes can watch a TV debate on public issues, then immediately record their responses, which are tabulated and broadcast back to the homes.

The flaw in this cheerful outlook is that nobody can manage the overload of information that characterizes our time. The well-publicized "knowledge explosion," it is sometimes said, brings with it an "ignorance explosion." Year by year more knowledge, known to the human race, is unknown to each person within the human race, even though much of that knowledge bears on the well-being of people. The best educated people are the most aware of their ignorance. In academia it becomes almost a matter of pride to insert into conversations the ritual phrase, "That lies outside the area of my competence."

The result is that nobody is expert on very much, and everybody relies on experts for important personal and social decisions. We, the people, look for authorities, and we ask: do they really know, and are they trustworthy? And we ask on questions that are truly important to us. Women want to know, is the contraceptive pill really safe, or does it contribute to heart disease or cancer? Parents want to know, are our prospective children at risk for genetic disease? Urban dwellers want to know, how hazardous is the nuclear or coal-powered generating plant that makes the electricity for our homes? The list of questions is almost infinite. And the only answer to many of them is pathetic trust in the experts who claim to know. The contribution of scientists to the process of decision-making thus becomes utterly important. Yet no elite—scientific, political, or religious—can become the ethical arbitrators for modern industrial society. Guidance can come only as specialists interact with concerned people from many walks of life. The body politic has a right to challenge the experts, who if they are humanly responsible will not disdain to enter into the public conversation.

A few examples will show both the importance and the insufficiency of specialized expert opinion on public policy. The first is from economics. The whole society has a stake in the functioning of the economy. Most people do not know how, and do not want, to participate directly in the intricate details of national fiscal and monetary policy; and a direct poll of people, following a TV debate, might be the worst way of settling, say, the Federal Reserve rediscount note. But neither do people simply want to trust some "experts" in Washington or New York or Houston. Economist John Kenneth Galbraith observes that "what is called sound economics is very often what mirrors the needs of the respectably affluent."[10] So citizens would like experts (1) who are truly expert and (2) who share the interests and values of the nonexpert citizens.

A second example comes from Daniel D. McCracken, a computer specialist, in his short but incisive book, *Public Policy and the Expert*.[11] McCracken investigated the U.S. Senate hearings of 1969 on proposals for an elaborate system of antiballistic missiles (ABM). A large number of computer experts, including some of the most eminent in the country, came to the conclusion that—quite apart from all the other political and ethical issues centering in the ABM—the computer technology involved in the guidance systems simply was not reliable. The Defense Department produced experts who testified that the technology was adequate. Senator J. William Fulbright pointed out in the hearings that all the scientific witnesses for the ABM were employees of the Pentagon or of corporations which had contracts with the Pentagon. Without impugning their honesty, he thought it important to get testimony of independent experts. (To use the categories of this chapter, he was asking for witnesses from different social situations and different ideologies.) The reply, from Assistant Secretary of Defense David Packard was that scientists "are objective about such matters." (He was asserting the irrelevance of social situation and ideology.)

The most disturbing thought coming out of the process was the speculation that perhaps only those working on the system could know enough to evaluate it, and they would inevitably have the ideological biases of people committed to a project. If that is the real situation, it represents a near bankruptcy of the system of representative government.

Anybody with democratic instincts is disturbed by the dependence of the public on experts with highly specialized knowledge that other people are not able to understand or evaluate. The whole situation is offensively elitist. It is no comfort to read a scholarly estimate of our predicament:

The common man has never been less in control of his life and livelihood than he is today. Whether confronted by the threat of atomic annihilation or something as trivial as a balky home appliance, almost all of us must place our trust in the hands of the relevant specialists. . . . As our common pool of scientific knowledge increases, the ignorance and powerlessness of each individual increases correspondingly.[12]

The writers of that statement go on to look at many examples of public policy—the supersonic transport, the antiballistic missile, herbicides and insecticides, cyclamates, and others—that hinged on scientific testimony. They conclude that scientists were used less to advise than to legitimate decisions made on political-economic grounds, and that too often scientists are hired by government and industry to give the information and opinions that their employers want.

There is some help in recognizing that the world cannot set up a privileged caste of experts for the simple reason that *everybody is inexpert* on most technical issues and *everybody is expert* on some. The best nuclear physicist may depend utterly on the expertise of the surgeon, and the surgeon depends on the expertise of the auto mechanic. Technological societies cannot endure total, rigid hierarchies; they require a kind of democracy of interdependence. And in the interdependence each person is expert at some point. The ancient saying is that I know better than anybody else where my shoe pinches.

That doesn't mean that I can make a shoe; it means that my knowledge of the shoe is superior to the shoemaker's in some respects.

When a public relies on experts, as often it must, that public wants to know two things about the experts: are they technically competent, and what are their values and ideologies? I, for one, want to know of a physician or lawyer or any other specialist: do you really know your stuff, *and* are you on my side? If you are not on my side, your very competence may hurt me.

Especially when experts give conflicting testimony, most of us ask the two questions. And, because technical competence is hard to judge, we are likely to rely on those experts whose values and ideologies are closest to our own. That is not *entirely* a mistake. Since ideology has so much influences on perception and understanding, it is often the clue to differences of opinion, even on highly technical subjects. But the ideological test is not enough. Sometimes we need to pay attention to those with different ideologies. They may have discovered something useful for us to know. And there is usually some information that is important, no matter what our ideology.

The technological situation puts a special moral responsibility on scientists with expert knowledge. They have no right—and most of them make no claim—to be arbiters of social good. But they know some things that the public needs to know. As Linus Pauling, in conversational language, said to Horace Freeland Judson:

I have contended that scientists—first they have a responsibility because of their understanding of science, and of those problems of society in which science is involved closely, to help their fellow citizens to understand, by explaining to them what their own understanding of those problems is. And I have contended that they have the duty also to express their own opinions —if they have opinions.[13]

The rest of us, in listening to scientists, will try to distinguish between those points on which they have a scientific authority which we had better respect and those on which their opinions are neither more nor less valid than our own. For the reasons I have already discussed, it is not always easy to make that distinction. Andrei Sakharov, the courageous Russian physicist writing from his enforced isolation in Gorky, puts it well:

My view of the situation of scientists in the contemporary world has convinced me that they have special professional and social responsibilities. It is often difficult to separate one from the other—the communication of information, the popularization of scientific knowledge, and the publication of endorsements or warnings are examples of activities with both professional and social aspects.[14]

If public policy must rely on expert scientific opinion, as increasingly is the case, that does not mean that scientists become authorities delivering unquestioned knowledge and opinions. There are ways of drawing them into the give and take of the public forum.

Take, as an example, a current argument, highly important for national and international policies. It is an argument where scientific opinion is critical; yet anybody who is interested can contribute to the argument. It is the argument about available land that might be put into food production.

Frances Lappé and Joseph Collins, in a book that helped me in Chapter 4, maintain that "only about 44% of the world's potentially arable land is actually cultivated."[15] But Georg Borgstrom, in another book that I have relied on, says that "the plowing of new land has already gone too far."[16] Here are widely divergent opinions on a matter of information that is highly important for an answer to the world's hunger. Furthermore, they come from people who agree in their concern about hunger and in their criticism of predatory economic systems. What can a concerned public make of the disagreement?

To accent the problem, notice the statement of Peter Oram, Deputy Director of the International Food Policy Research Institute: "So many people say there is plenty more arable land available, but when you check estimates against each other, you find discrepancies of a billion and a half acres—fully the present area of the world's arable cropland!"[17] How can a U.N. staff member, a U.S. Senator, an ordinary citizen think responsibly in the face of such conflicting expert opinions?

Those of us who are inexpert on geography and food production are not left helpless. We can at least ask the experts some questions. Where is the uncultivated land? How much of it is wasted by absentee landowners, and how much of it is in forests and wilderness? What will be the consequences for climate and rainfall of transforming more and more forests into croplands? What dry lands can be irrigated? Is the water available, and how much coal, petroleum, or nuclear energy will be needed to run the pumps? What about soil erosion and dust-lands? What can we learn from Khrushchev's experiments in plowing up virgin prairies for croplands in Russia and from the Chinese deci-sion, after severe floods, to restore some forests and grasslands that had been turned into grainlands? How far should flower gardens and recreational areas be turned into food production? Is it good that the earth include some wilderness and some domains for wild animals, or should everything be subordinated to human utility? Those questions show how inextricably related are matters of fact, values, social sys-tems, and ideologies.

I claim no competence to answer all these questions. What I claim is that a public need not abdicate authority to experts in facing them. At a minimum publics must choose which experts to believe. If de-mocracy is to survive in a technological era, it must devise methods for the interaction of people of different expert skills and opinions, different ideologies, and different social situations.[18] We have the be-ginning of such methods in the interrogation of experts by congression-al committees. Other interactions go on in panel discussions at meet-ings of the American Association for the Advancement of Science, in forums in universities and churches, in various seminars and study groups. Possibly some new social inventions will do for this problem what the invention of parliamentary democracy did for the resolving of differing political opinions. The task will not be easy. I hope it is not impossible.

RETROSPECT AND PROSPECT

Human life in its million or two million years on earth has been a hazardous adventure all the way. It has been a story of hope and despair, of creation and destruction, of exaltation and defeat.

For a brief time in the eighteenth through the twentieth centuries —scarcely an instant in the whole of human history—there flourished the confidence that science, technology, and education would break the traditional cycles of the rise and fall of civilizations. I have noted examples of that confidence in Dewey (Chapter 2) and Gibbon (Chap-ter 8). Now the world lacks that confidence. It has great expectations and equally great fears of the consequences of its scientific triumphs.

Likewise, some forms of traditional confidence in religion are gone. Given the resurgence of fundamentalisms in Christianity and Islam, with their considerable political influence, and given the eruption of cults in recent times, nobody can say for sure that religious enthusiasm has waned. But those who value rationality and faith cannot look to religion for two solaces that it has often provided to some people. (1) No *deus ex machina* will rescue the human race from its follies. There is no divine guarantee that civilization will not blow itself to pieces in a burst of fire and radioactivity, that hungry populations will not learn to terrorize rich and indifferent nations, that strains on energy supplies and water will not impoverish affluent societies. (2) No past revelation of ethical codes will provide answers to new questions that never occurred to people in past centuries. I do not mean that our proud but anxious civilization is capable of revoking the ethical inheritance of the past. The love of God and neighbor arouse about as much response, whether fervent or skeptical, in our age as when those commands were enunciated in the Hebrew scriptures and repeated as the heart of ethics in the New Testament. But the meaning of these commands for many an issue in a technological age remains to be revealed or discovered.

So a faith for this age must be a venturing faith. I have suggested some of its accents, as I see their importance, in Chapter 10. I said there that such a faith will not be primarily a faith in religion but a faith that enables religious communities to join in the divine judging and healing acts that they discern in history. In this chapter I have added the idea that faith, whether dimly formed or carefully articulated, is part of every policy decision, since such decisions depend upon commitments as well as information.

The world's people in this generation are custodians of a precious earth. And they are custodians of a flawed but precious human heritage. They can respond with gratitude and responsibility in a time when these gifts are at risk.

Maybe the future is brightest to those who do not strive too frantically to control that future. Graceful and gracious living, in any deep sense, are responses to grace—to a gift that we do not create and do not control. But grace evokes responsibility—a resolve to act so as to preserve and enhance the gift.

As for the content of a faith that offers some hope for the future,

I have made a few suggestions in Chapter 10. Many of its formulations —whether in doctrine, song, visual arts, or works of mercy—will be new. But some old accents, I believe, will endure. One of its big tasks will be negation: the dethronement of idols, whether idols of nation, of military strength, of wealth, or of security through technical achievement. Its affirmations will include some of the perennial affirmations of tradition—affirmations verbalized in such old words as reverence, thanksgiving, grace, love, justice, freedom, responsibility. Both the negations and the affirmations will find their meaning not solely in that sphere of life called religion but, as always in profound faith, in all the loving and striving and living and dying of human existence. There the options before the human race are momentous. And they are forced.

Reconsiderations

It is almost a decade since I first wrote this book. I can now assume wide acceptance of some of the arguments that I earlier struggled to make. The press ceaselessly calls attention to issues of population, resources, environmental degradation, and homelessness in the face of wealth. But the world is still reluctant to meet painful forced options, and destructive activities have a powerful momentum. So I must fight harder than ever to make some of my arguments. And, on a few issues, I have revised my opinions in the light of events.

A TUMULTUOUS DECADE

Has history ever seen a decade that brought such radical change—so unpredicted, so global in impact, so momentous to so many societies and people—as the decade just past? Probably not.

Since 1982 we have watched the end of the Cold War and the collapse of communism in Eastern Europe. President Mikhail Gorbachev withdrew troops from Afghanistan, introduced *glasnost* ("openness") and *perestroika* ("restructuring"), twisted backwards and forwards, and repulsed the attempted coup of 1991. The Berlin wall came tumbling down. East European nations overthrew communist dictatorships. Nobody knows what political configurations will follow the Soviet Union over the next century, but the once fearsome Leninist-Stalinist imperialism and its mystique have surely been broken.

China, the world's most populous country, saw first an apparent end of Maoism with increased freedom and a move toward a mixed economy; then came the student protests of 1989, followed by suppression and tightened dictatorship. India, the second most populous country, suffered internal conflicts and two major assassinations, of Indira Gandhi in 1984 and Rajiv Gandhi in 1991.

In a startling realignment of major powers, the Soviet Union and China, for whatever arcane reasons, joined the United States in endorsing a war against Iraq, a country that the anti-Iranian United States had been supporting in Iraq's previous war with Iran. But the Middle East remained an area of turmoil, with unpredictable portents. South Africa saw political changes beyond any predictions, but nobody knew when a genuinely interracial democracy might come.

Throughout the world, old problems of drug traffic, crime, and terrorism exploded with new magnitude. Industrial-technological catastrophes erupted on a gigantic scale: an explosion in a chemical factory in Bhopal, India, killing thousands of people; a diaster in a nuclear plant in Chernobyl, USSR; the *Exxon Valdez* oil spill in Alaska; and many others. There were also natural disasters, though often compounded by political factors: earthquakes, volcanic eruptions, floods, hurricanes, and famines. AIDS, first identified in 1981, became a worldwide concern.

Amid spectacular changes, powerful human processes continued. People went on reproducing. Every person consumed food and other resources—or quickly died. Most clamored to consume more. Some people struggled for freedom; others accepted new restraints for the sake of security. The worldwide gap between rich and poor persisted—and increased.

In such a world nobody understands all that is going on. We human beings, at best, perceive and comprehend only a small part of all that impinges on us. Jesus once told his critics: "You know how to interpret the appearance of the sky, but you cannot interpret the signs of the times [Matt. 16:3b]." Despite some awkward errors, we do fairly well in anticipating changing seasons and weather. But in recent years the United States and its leaders understood little of what effect U.S. policies were having in Southeast Asia, Latin America, the Middle East, or even in American cities.

There are two main reasons why it is hard to "interpret the signs of the times." The first is that out of the almost infinite data

available, we can take in—or "process," in the going vocabulary—only some fragments. We select evidence—and all evidence
is selectively chosen—to prove that the economy is booming or
precarious, that freedom is increasing or withering, that new
weapons protect or endanger national security.

The sure thing about the future is that it will bring surprises.
But some things now happening are portents of things to come.
Which events, then, offer revealing clues? How do we discern the
difference between a trend and a blip? If in the late fall the
weather turns warmer, that is not a trend. Even if warmth persists
for a week, we understand it as a blip in autumn's turn toward
winter. If the stock market jumps today, we wonder whether the
rise is a blip or a trend. Months later we can look back and know.
When we learn of an industrial accident, a Soviet-American
irritation, or a famine, we do not know immediately whether the
perils of life are increasing.

The second reason, even more disconcerting, is that knowledge
and ignorance are usually purposive. Desires and fears skew the
evidence and our interpretation of it. We readily spot the "rationalizations" of others as they spin faulty arguments that meet their
needs; we overlook our own. Even the most factual argument
usually has emotional components, and many seemingly factual
arguments involve deep loyalties and prejudices.

So what reasons have I to think that my arguments are more
valid than the arguments of my critics? One thing I can do is
listen to those who disagree and examine their evidence. Another
is to try the difficult task of examining the ideologies (in the
double sense of Chapter 12) of all of us in public argument and
try to correct for distortions.

In doing this I know no infallible rules, but I find two guidelines
helpful. The first is to remind myself, day in and day out, that my
society is part of a far vaster world. In examining the forced
options facing humanity, I need to guard against the American
provincialism that ignores the majority of the world.

The second guideline is to pay extra attention to groups who
do not control the world's politics and communications—the
poor, the racially oppressed, societies without big weapons,
women (in American society a majority, often treated as a minor-

ity). These groups often see realities that the powerful and privileged miss or repress. And the realities they see are important for justice and for the public interests of all of us.

FOUR GENERALIZATIONS

In this bewildering world, I venture to make four generalizations impressed upon me by events since the first edition of this book.

1. The past decade refuted both the most dismal and the most euphoric predictions of "experts." That is no guarantee for the next decade or next century, but it is an obvious fact.

Prophets of doom were often mistaken. On page 167, I pointed to C.P. Snow's "certainty" in 1960 that some atomic bombs would go off within ten years. Similarly, the respected Stockholm International Peace Research Institute (SIPRI) predicted in 1971 that by 1985 about thirty-five countries would have a nuclear capability and nuclear war would become "inevitable."[1] Those predictions were simply wrong. The concern behind them was right. The world may be a little safer because Snow and SIPRI sounded alarms. This human race may still annihilate itself. But nuclear war is not inevitable.

The prophets of euphoria were equally mistaken. The ebullient Herman Kahn in 1972 reckoned that, if we got through a "1985 technological crisis," we would enter a new postindustrial, post-economic society. "Presumably there will be so much money around that people will not feel hard pressed to make a living." Buckminster Fuller, the naive and erratic genius, thought that by the present time, technology would eliminate scarcity, and nations and classes would disappear.[2]

Such wild expectations may discredit prediction. They do not discredit foresight. Although nobody can predict earthquakes with precision, planning for the contingency of earthquakes saved many lives in Japan in 1983 and California in 1989. The anticipation of catastrophe can sometimes fend off disaster—an important insight for a world facing forced options.

2. The past decade has brought new kinds of affluence, even for rather ordinary people, and also new austerities. Many a

college student in a dormitory room has computer power unavailable to vast corporations a generation ago. Homes of average citizens are becoming centers of communication that millionaires could not enjoy a few years back. People with bank accounts—most people in some societies, but not most people in the world—have access to cash at all hours of all days. Affluence, when it does not require extravagant energy and materials, may have a bright future. Microchips and fiber optics open immense possibilities, and nobody can reckon the limits of human ingenuity.

But new austerities are painful. Wherever rising population meets limited resources, people suffer. Wherever pollution strains the natural cleansing devices of local or planetary ecosystems, people must accept new disciplines or dangers. The affluent North American society meets new austerities in the shortage of "affordable housing" (a phrase that has entered the language recently), in parking space, in the increasing costs of waste disposal, in conflicts for water rights (the Colorado River is an example), and in bitter fights over city and state budgets. Less affluent societies face far more desperate pains.

Given the power conflicts of this world, one "solution" is to assign the affluence to privileged groups and the austerities to the rest. That answer, frequent throughout history, has always been an ethical atrocity. In the interconnected contemporary world, it is a more dangerous answer than ever before.

Yet this answer is frequent. In March 1989 the Ways and Means Commitee of the House of Representatives released a report of more than a thousand pages showing that between 1973 and 1987 the average household income of the poorest fifth of Americans dropped by 11.8 percent while the richest fifth gained 24.1 percent—using figures corrected for inflation. The report prompted political controversy about causes of the change but little controversy about the accuracy of the data.[3] Later annual editions of the report, sometimes called the Green Book, showed continuation of the same trends. Meanwhile, the prosperity of some came at a cost to the next generation, which must repair a deteriorating national infrastructure that economist Robert Heilbroner calls "an unmitigated disaster."[4]

On a world scale the disparities were even worse. The World

Bank in 1990 called attention to the "staggering" problem of poverty, with a fifth of the world's population living on incomes of less than $370 a year. It foresaw improvements by the end of the century—the World Bank has almost a professional obligation to believe in improvement—but expected a worsening of poverty in sub-Saharan Africa. It found the causes and remedies to be more complex than most polemicists (of the Left or Right) acknowledge, but it pointed to facts that are irrefutable.[5]

3. There has been a moderation and multiplication of conflict. A decade ago the most world-threatening conflict was between the Soviet bloc and the North Atlantic bloc. The "Third World"—or the "Two-Thirds World," since it included a majority of the world's people—was often victimized by the major conflict but sometimes wangled small advantages by playing off the "superpowers" against each other. If the end of the Cold War came like an impossible dream, it did not bring world peace. Ethnic and religious conflicts—in the Middle East, India, Sri Lanka, Africa, Yugoslavia, the Soviet Union, Cyprus, and Ireland—made the emerging world even less stable than the old bipolar world. Historian Arthur Schlesinger Jr. wrote: "Ethnic and racial conflict—far more than ideological conflict—is the explosive problem of our times."[6] Or, using the definitions of my Chapter 12, racial, ethnic, and religious identities have become dominant ideologies of our world.

4. Ecology and liberation are converging interests. The original edition of this book described a conflict between two ethical concerns: social justice and ecology. The poor often saw ecological issues as a hobby of the comfortable and a distraction from the pain of the poor. Ecologists saw the poor's struggle against oppression as self-defeating if it ignored the wider natural context of humanity. I tried to make the case that these two interests need not conflict but actually should reinforce each other.

Now the two interests are converging. Agencies of the United Nations are accenting environmental issues as they affect the international economy. A new term, eco-justice, has entered the vocabulary. Religious communities are exploring their traditions, recovering old insights about the relationship of God, humanity, and nature.

Two innovative books, among many others, are symbols of the convergence. One is *The Liberation of Life: From the Cell to the Community* by Charles Birch, an Australian biologist, and John Cobb, an American theologian. These two have joined in proposing "an ecological model" of biology and the human community, integrating the theme of justice (liberation) and responsibiity toward nature. The other book is the work of the Uruguayan theologian Juan Luis Segundo, *An Evolutionary Approach to Jesus of Nazareth*. As a "liberation theologian," he argues that politics and ecology are "two complementary dimensions that must be taken into account if we are to make existing society and human interrelationships more humane."[7] The work of ethical and theological reconstruction is well under way.

FROM "LIMITS" TO "SUSTAINABLE DEVELOPMENT"

The original edition of this book gave attention to the theme of "living with limits," the main substance of Chapters 3 through 6. Starting with the axiom that infinite physical growth is impossible in a finite system, I examined the empirical situation in relation to food, population, energy, and material resources, including water and breathable atmosphere. The phrase, "limits to growth," the title of the first report to the Club of Rome, had leapt into prominence and brought strenuous controversies.

During the past decade the international conversation on this subject has changed its vocabulary. There is less talk about limits, more about sustainable systems. There are good reasons for the shift.

The language of "limits" often provokes frustration and despair (pages 114-15.) Nobody wanted to stop *all* economic development *everywhere*. As early as 1974 a conference of scientists and theologians, convened by the World Council of Churches (WCC) in Bucharest, called for a "sustainable and just society." In 1976 the WCC endorsed a "just, participatory and sustainable society" (page 54). The shift in language took hold in international discussions, whether secular or religious. Later the WCC adopted the theme of "justice, peace and the integrity of creation," perhaps because "the integrity of creation" has a biblical resonance not evident in "sustainable society." The disadvantage is that the new language tends to distance the churches from the wider interfaith and secular conversations.

Following the report of the Brandt Commission in 1980 (discussed on pages 124–25, 152 in this book), the United Nations gave increasing attention to the issues. The secretary-general asked Gro Harlem Brundtland, then prime minister of Sweden, to chair a World Commission on Environment and Development. She and the vice-chair, Mansour Khalid of the Sudan, appointed the members, with the double understanding that a majority come from "the developing world" and that all serve as individuals rather than as representatives of governments. In 1987 the commission presented its report, *Our Common Future* (commonly called the Brundtland Report), to the General Assembly. Its central theme was "sustainable development."[8]

"Sustainable development" stirs a response among many who resist talk of limits. It suggests opportunity rather than barriers. In practical meaning the terms may not differ greatly. The authors of *Limits to Growth* argued against any freezing of the world situation. They saw the possibility of tripling the average income of the world and increasing "indefinitely" many kinds of human activity (pages 113, 116 in this book). And they urged major redistribution to help the poor (pages 114–15). From the other side the advocates of sustainable development recognized the problem of limits. One of their chapter titles was "Industry: Producing More with Less."

Actually the two themes are complementary. Without the jolting collision with limits, the world would not address the issue of sustainability. Without the hope of sustainable development, the news of limits freezes people in fear.

FOOD AND POPULATION

In the past decade the world's food production has increased, but population has increased faster, with the result that today there is less food per person than when I first wrote this book. The increase in food was largely the product of the Green Revolution with all its benefits and hazards (pages 63–66). But the world's per capita production of grains peaked in 1984 and has declined since then. The situation is far worse in Africa, where production peaked in 1967 and then dropped by 28 percent in the interval until 1990.[9]

The statistics point to intense suffering. Famine in sub-Saharan Africa had taken about 2 million lives by mid-1985, and nobody has counted the deaths since then. Three quarters of the dead were children under five. The survivors are often maimed for life by brain damage, eye ailments, and weakened bodily structure.

If we examine a worst case, Ethiopia, we find extremely complex causes. Desertification, due partly to nature (drought) and partly to human acts (deforestation and soil depletion), accelerated. Civil war interfered with agriculture. An inept government spent 46 percent of the gross national product on military purposes and suppressed early news of the famine because of its tenth-anniversary celebration. The same government gave priority at docks to the unloading of weapons instead of food. Inadequate delivery systems—airports, roads, vehicles, and fuel—left food rotting while people starved. The United States was slow to respond because Ethiopia had a communist government. Population growth was close to the highest in the world. Well-intended relief programs of past years had sometimes undermined the local agricultural economy. Ethiopia exported livestock and other foods—partly because exports were to the advantage of some Ethiopians, partly because even a starving society needs foreign exchange. The terms of international trade, including rises in oil price, wrought havoc. Multinational corporations directed economic activity to purposes undesirable for the people of Ethiopia. Foreign experts sometimes gave bad advice.[10]

So intricate a complex of causes refutes all simple one-shot answers to hunger. It also offers easy rationalizations for those who want an excuse to do nothing. Actually the American public, once it saw the horrendous pictures on television screens, responded generously. But a few years later the press reported "disaster fatigue" as a consequence of worldwide catastrophes. Furthermore, any long-term response to hunger requires the yoking of good will with technical skills and changes in the world's arrangements of power. I reaffirm my four-pronged approach to the issues (pages 75–82) with an even deeper awareness of their complex interrelationships.

As a last sad note on hunger, I add that the Physician Task Force on Hunger in America, after a year-long investigation, affirmed in 1985: "Hunger is a problem of epidemic proportions across the nation." Even in a time of economic recovery, said the task force, "hunger is getting worse, not better."[11] Then economic recession and retrenchment of government programs intensified the suffering. This nation, which does not know how to handle its agricultural surpluses, knows even less how to build a society where hungry people can obtain food.

On the world scene hunger is related to population growth. I reaffirm my argument against both the population monomaniacs, who assume that population growth is the one major cause of hunger, and the population innocents, who think it is inconsequential. In the first years after the original edition of this book, population growth moderated slightly and seemed to show signs of moderating more. But then in the late 1980s it resumed its acceleration. So my table on page 88 remains about right.[12]

On pages 93–94, I described the beginnings of a shift in worldwide ideological argument about population. That shift has accelerated. At the United Nations World Population Conference (Bucharest, 1974) the industrialized countries lectured the Less Developed Countries on the perils of the population explosion. The poorer countries snapped back, accusing the rich countries of plundering the world's wealth. Some also argued that socialism could cope with expanding populations as capitalism could not. By the time of the second World Population Conference (Mexico City, 1984), most of the world agreed on the need to moderate population growth. China had reduced its birth rate by 46 percent in a decade, and socialist Cuba had the lowest birth rate in the Western hemisphere. Ironically, the United States delegation, appointed by President Reagan, insisted that population was no problem for market economies.

One influence on American policy was a book by Julian Simon with the beguiling theme, "The ultimate resource is people."[13] Simon alternates between two positions: (1) There is no problem of population, because more people mean more minds and imaginations to solve problems. (2) The demographic transition (see page 100) will bring a rational and voluntary leveling of population. The two arguments clash, and both fit strangely the pain of China, India, Africa, and Mexico.

Simon maintains that resources, including energy, are for all practical purposes infinite—an argument that Garrett Hardin, among others, finds scientifically "appalling."[14] The argument rests on selective short-term data—Simon regards 1920–1980 as "a very long span of history"—and takes no account of the curve of exponential growth, which can turn quickly from a benign to a disastrous effect.

ENERGY AND POLLUTION

Energy is an example of the confusion of blips and trends. Blips career wildly from crisis to glut to crisis. One trend remains constant. "Humankind expends in one year an amount of fossil fuel that it took nature roughly a million years to produce."[15] That trend cannot go on forever. The world is moving toward the end of the era of fossil fuels.

Nobody can write the timetable, because nobody knows how fast consumption will rise or what unknown reserves will be discovered. I earlier offered a "rough estimate" of "serious permanent shortages" of petroleum in the 1980s and the virtual exhaustion of petroleum as a fuel in the early twenty-first century (page 35). If we look at the United States alone, the serious permanent shortage is not obvious. We can spend the money to buy petroleum—at the cost of a rising national debt and war. In some countries the permanent shortage is painfully evident.

Edward Renshaw estimates that, at present rates of consumption, global reserves will last forty-seven to eighty-eight years, but that if all societies consumed at the rate of the United States, the time would be shortened to eight to fifteen years.[16] That estimate presents some perplexing social and ethical dilemmas.

To complicate the issue, 70 percent of those reserves are in the area of the Persian Gulf, the occasion for a major war in 1991. Another complication is that the Soviet Union is presently the world's largest producer of oil and is second only to Saudi Arabia as an exporter of oil. But it is expected that the Soviet Union will become an importer of oil early in the twenty-first century, which will put new pressures on international markets. (Recall that the United States was the world's leading exporter of oil in 1945 and is now the leading importer.) Thus geographical and political factors interact with global ecology.

A few signs brighten this picture. In the United States, between 1973 and 1985, the gross national product rose 40 percent, while energy consumption stayed constant.[17] I have criticized GNP as a measure of social welfare (pages 125–126), but the figures are impressive evidence of possibilities of conservation of energy. The causes were a combination of education, government regulation, and market efficiency. (I said on page 40 that the market does some things, but not all things, well.) In 1986, as petroleum prices dropped, the United States resumed its increase in energy consumption.

The story of Project Independence is symptomatic. In 1973, President Nixon announced plans to make the United States self-sufficient in energy by 1980 (page 46). In the next few years oil imports almost doubled. With occasional blips, they have remained at the higher level—about half of our consumption. But few people noticed. The Reagan administration in October 1983 had formally abandoned the goal of energy self-sufficiency.

The nation lacks the self-discipline to face its energy problems. According to some reckonings, the cost of gasoline in the United States dropped, prior to the Gulf War of 1990–91, to the lowest price (in real dollars) ever. In most European countries the price, including tax, is double or triple that in the United States. The low American tax is virtually a subsidy, bcause it does not cover the economic externalities of auto-induced smog, global warming, military protection of national interests in the Middle East, or interest on that part of the national debt incurred by extravagant imports.

Consideration of energy leads inevitably to issues of pollution—a catchall word for the many activities that harm the ecosystem including human life. Energy consumption is not the sole cause of pollution, but it is a major cause. The first edition of this book underestimated the seriousness of the problems.

Scientists affirm that the past two centuries have brought faster changes in the earth's atmosphere than at any time in past human history. Most of these changes are the result of human activities—the burning of fossil fuels and other vegetation, various industrial and agricultural practices, and deforestation.[18] The effects are not precisely measurable and are even less predictable; again, it is a case of recognizing blips and trends. But the eminent climatologist Stephen Schneider, one of the more moderate specialists, reckons: "The developed world might have to invest hundreds of billions of dollars every year for many decades, both at home and in financial and technical assistance to developing nations, to achieve a stabilized and sustainable world."[19]

The "greenhouse effect" (pages 208–209) is becoming more ominous. The second World Climate Conference in 1990 received a report from an international group of scientists, affirming that the risks are greater and more imminent than earlier studies had estimated. The conference asked for cutbacks in production of carbon dioxide. The United States representatives blocked still stronger recommendations.

The original edition of this book mentioned acid rain (page 109) and the depletion of ozone in the upper atmosphere (pages 10, 12, 209), but I did not even bother to include them in the index—an egregious omission I am correcting in this edition. Ozone is paradoxical. Automobile emissions increase it at ground level, where it is toxic; other industrial processes reduce it in the upper atmosphere, where it is a protective shield against harmful radiation. The ominous "hole" in the protective cover of ozone led to an unprecedented treaty of 1987, in which fifty-seven nations agreed to reduce by half their emissions of chlorofluorocarbons by the end of the century. As evidence of the peril mounted, ninety-three nations agreed in 1990 on more radical steps to ban the most dangerous chemicals. The United States, after dragging its feet, agreed to contribute to an international fund to support the program.

One scientific judgment illuminates the nature of the problem: "Even if chlorofluorocarbon emissions stopped today, chemical reactions causing the destruction of stratospheric ozone would continue for at least a century," as a result of past emissions into the atmosphere.[20] A deep trait in human nature, exaggerated by our culture and economy, makes people reluctant to accept a sure inconvenience now to avoid a probable disaster at a later time. By the same logic an individual might refuse to pay now for life insurance that would help dependents at some unknown future date.

Knowledge of the dangers in burning hydrocarbons has, in a curious twist of history, led to reconsiderations of nuclear power as a cleaner and safer source of energy. I earlier argued that nuclear energy at best would not "spare us the necessity for major social changes to end the present extravagance of industrialized societies [page 219]." But I presented evidence that it is safer than coal, perhaps even than oil (pages 214–19).

I was writing after the serious but scarcely lethal accident at Three Mile Island in 1979 (see pages 216–18) but before the major disaster at Chernobyl in 1986, actually the second Soviet catastrophe.[21] Later Spencer Weart, taking Chernobyl into account, came to similar conclusions.[22] But the United States and most of the world stopped building nuclear reactors. Now, with the first generation of nuclear reactors nearing the end of the forty-year period for which they were designed and licensed, the United States must decide (1) to abandon nuclear energy, (2) to relicense old plants, or (3) to build a new generation of safer reactors. The National Academy of Sciences in 1991 urged the development of a new generation of reactors, with standardized designs and fail-safe features that greatly reduce risks. But the public, disillusioned by past "scientific" assurances, has not been persuaded.

Solar energy remains the ideal favorite, even though its development has lagged far behind the expectations of its advocates. Its use for space heating and water heating is increasing. The great hope is for a breakthrough on electricity. The Worldwatch Institute reports, "Over the past two decades, the cost of photovoltaic electricity has fallen from $30 a kilowatt-hour to just 30c."[23] That already makes this method economically desirable in some areas of the world, but the price is still about ten times what most Americans pay for their electricity—not counting the externalities of environmental damage of other methods. In the case of fossil fuels those costs include the incalculable damage to climate for years to come. In the case of nuclear energy, they include the great costs of waste disposal and decommissioning of worn-out reactors.

If the United States were to get serious about energy efficiency, as we showed signs of doing in the years 1973–1985, and if we were to develop the solar option, we could reduce the burning of hydrocarbons and do without nuclear energy, which now provides about 21 percent of our electricity. France, which gets about 75 percent of its electricity from nuclear generators, and Japan could not make the change so easily.

The answer must evolve over the coming years with frequent adaptation to new developments. The best I can do is warn against a profligate way of life and point out a forced option that is now hidden in a murky mess of concealment and evasion.

NUCLEAR WEAPONS AND WAR

Of all the issues in this book, the nuclear arms race has seen the most unexpected changes in the past decade. As Wiesner and York foresaw (pages 153–54 above), the reason was not a technical solution but a changed political climate.

The last fling at a "technical fix" was President Reagan's proposal for a Strategic Defense Initiative (SDI), often called Star Wars. The stated objective was to create an impenetrable barrier against nuclear attack—a benign shift from the cruel threat of deterrence to an innocent defense. But soon news broke of a new Advanced Strategic Missiles program, designed to develop weapons that would outmaneuver any Star Wars defense that the Soviet Union might develop. Then came further news of plans to integrate offensive weapons with the projected antimissile defenses.[24] Next came evidence that the system would be immensely costly and would be designed primarily to protect our weapons rather than our people. By this time the innocence of SDI looked more and more like a massive hoax.

Meanwhile, the United States and the Soviet Union saw more and more clearly that a nuclear war could not serve any national interest. A nuclear attack would invite nuclear deterrence, and both sides would suffer far more than they could possibly gain. Furthermore, even without incurring the deterrent, a massive nuclear attack would risk a "nuclear winter" that could irreparably damage the attacker.[25] That recognition, combined with the political changes in Eastern Europe, led to a relaxation of the arms race. Finally, after long negotiations, Presidents Bush and Gorbachev signed an agreement in 1991 for an actual reduction—not simply a limitation, as in past pacts—of nuclear weapons.[26]

A decade ago any forecast of the present relaxation of East-West tensions would have seemed too good to be true. Now that it has happened, it has its obvious problems. The old bipolar world, with all its perils, had a kind of stability and predictability. The present world is more chaotic, more volatile. The Persian Gulf War brought suffering and death that continued long after the war itself; and the long-term ecological damage of flaming oil fields in Kuwait cannot be measured. The proliferation of nuclear weapons continues, though not as fast as predicted. There are still five nations with nuclear arsenals: the United States, the Soviet Union, Britain, France, and China. At least four other nations apparently have a nuclear capacity: India, Pakistan, Israel, and South Africa. The world wonders nervously how close Iraq is to joining this group. More nations could join at almost any time. A sane awareness of consequences might restrain even the most angry nation from using nuclear weapons; but sanity is a weak restraint against the ethnic, religious, and ideological furies of our world.

The Non-Proliferation Treaty (NPT) is a crude but somewhat effective attempt to stop the spread of weapons (see pages 150–151).It is hard to find an ethical justification for its double morality, distinguishing between nuclear-armed nations and the other nations that are pledged not to acquire these weapons. Even so, new nations continue to sign the NPT or agree to its terms: Brazil, Argentina, France, and South Africa, in recent years. If the United States and the Soviet Union were to engage in radical reduction of nuclear weapons, more nations might be content to forego this dubious asset.

In this context I reaffirm the proposals on pages 162–68, with a few modifications to fit the changed situation. By this time, many military strategists think that the United States and the Soviet Union could mutually cut their arsenals in half. Hans Bethe, Kurt Gottfried, and Robert McNamara propose that these two nations shift from a strategy of maximum deterrence (the MAD doctrine, described on pages 156–60) to a strategy of "minimum deterrence," a capacity for deterrence that no rational adversary would want to absorb.[27] They reckon that one twentieth of the present arsenals would be sufficient. Such a program would lead to a very different world, a world in which still better possibilities might emerge. Like the earlier proposals of Weisskopf and Kennan (page 166), this more recent one is probably beyond the imagination of present-day national leaders. But, again like the earlier proposals, it can only enlighten the present discussions.

BIOETHICS

Biological science continues its spectacular advances that rival those in nuclear physics and microchips. New discoveries affect human life and require decisions. Bioethics has become a growth industry.

Here, as in Chapter 8, I am selecting genetics as the chief example. Almost monthly, new experiments enlarge frontiers of possibility. Researchers have transplanted genes into mice and calves, altering the animals and their descendants. With mingled eagerness and caution, they are undertaking human gene therapy (see page 139).

The first stage is the transplanting of genes into the human body to remedy ailments in the somatic cells without altering the germ cells (the inheritance that persons transmit to their children). For example, laboratory experiments point toward a possible cure for cystic fibrosis. In 1990 the Food and Drug Administration authorized genetic therapy for one type of cancer, and soon actual treatment of patients began.

Far more awesome is the alteration of human germ plasm—an undertaking not yet attempted but often conjectured. Press reports talk of "designer genes" and "made-to-order babies." A report issued by the Congressional Office of Technology Assessment (December 1984) said that such treatment would require much more public evaluation before its initiation. Controversies about modification of the human gene line are already stormy.

Jeremy Rifkin, author of *Algeny*,[28] in June 1983 released a resolution signed by a few scientists and many religious leaders (including several Roman Catholic bishops and the chief officers of many Protestant denominations) affirming that "efforts to engineer specific genetic traits into the germline of the human species should not be attempted." Both the World Council of Churches and the National Council of Churches had earlier issued study documents deliberately avoiding such a position.[29] So had the President's Commission for the Study of Ethical Problems in Medicine and Biomedical and Behavioral Research.[30] Some signers of Rifkin's statement later withdrew or qualified their endorsement.

Rifkin reasoned that persons today have no right to alter the genetic constitution of future generations. After participating in the study processes of both the World Council and the National Council of Churches, I disagree. Any alteration of the human genetic inheritance requires extraordinary caution, but I would not a priori forbid actions that might eliminate some terrible hereditary diseases. The danger is that scientists, in their enthusiasm for the experiment, may jeopardize human values; or that, in their desire to heal, they may do unintended harm. Those dangers are indeed serious. But the time may come when, as with all forced options, the failure to act is itself an act—in this case an act perpetuating human pain and disability.

Nobody knows what may come of genetic engineering. The genome project, planned as a fifteen-year, $3 billion investigation, aims to locate the 3 billion base pairs in the 50,000 to 100,000 genes that govern human heredity. It could lead to elimination of dread diseases or to redirection of human heredity in portentous ways.

Besides genetics, many other issues of bioethics raise new public debates day by day. Organ transplants are on the increase. Is it legitimate to conceive a child *for the purpose* of donating an organ to a sibling? Artificial insemination by donor becomes more frequent, rarely for genetic purposes (page 135) but often as a remedy for infertility. Is this a desirable practice for single parents and lesbian couples? Women who want children but cannot bear them sign contracts with "surrogate mothers." Should these contracts be legally enforceable? Injection of growth hormone remedies the pituitary deficiency in dwarfs. Should the treatment be available to short persons who want to grow taller? Fetal surgery becomes possible. What are the "rights" of the fetus as patient, particularly if they conflict with the rights of the mother? Death can be deferred far beyond any possibilities of the past. Does a person have a right to refuse to receive death-delaying treatments or to commit suicide? There is an increase of selecting the gender of children by prenatal diagnosis and abortion. Is this practice ethical? New medical treatments become extremely expensive. Who should pay the costs?

While specialists debate these issues, some instances of them strike without warning into the lives of ordinary people. The whole society becomes an intermittent but persistent seminar on some of the most perplexing ethical issues that human beings can face.

EXPLORATORY ETHICS

The burden of this book—and for me its delight—has been the investigation of decisions for which there are few direct historical precedents. In Chapter 12, I put forward a few ideas about ways of deciding responsibly. They require relating firmness of commitment and changing historical situations.

This generation lives in a time when we cannot simply repeat old patterns of behavior. New realities and new possibilities call for imaginative responses. Yet, to repeat a point, no stack of information, though it reach to the moon, does away with the need to evaluate that information, incorporate it in human worlds of meaning, and direct it toward purposes. No mountain of facts adds up to a commitment.

So I have emphasized the interaction of values with data, of loyalties with evidence, of historical faith with new information. Along the way I have expressed some ethical judgments, but I have not offered the grand plan for society to work through its time of troubles. Such plans interest me. I am grateful for the

Brundtland Report, already mentioned. I welcome the collaboration of economist Herman Daly and theologian John Cobb in their provocative book, *For the Common Good*.[31] Such efforts enlarge vision and sharpen insight by expanding the context of our normal efforts to solve problems.

History, however, will not follow any plan. It is a maelstrom of conflicts and harmonies, of necessity and contingency, of purpose and accident. Religious faith discerns in its mysteries some signs of divine grace and judgment, but the doings of God are largely hidden.

The next generation or two or three will, like our own, face forced options, whether knowingly or not. Their successes and failures will come through experiments, insights, blunders, acts of courage, gleams of imagination, moments of serendipity.

Times of perplexity intensify yearnings for certainty. One answer to new questions is repetition of old dogmas, evident in revived fundamentalist strains in many religions. Strangely, the the very scriptures that attack false authority (that is, idolatry) sometimes become idols.

The most famous (though not the most scholarly) biblical exegete of recent times said in a news conference on February 21, 1985: "I've found that the Bible contains an answer to just about everything and every problem that confronts us, and I wonder sometimes why we won't recognize that one Book could solve a lot of problems for us." What can that possibly mean? Did President Reagan, discovering that the White House is a "bully pulpit," indulge in extravagant pulpit rhetoric? Was he saying that the Bible should be the main datum of the Federal Reserve Board, the Council of Economic Advisers, the Pentagon, the diplomatic corps? How many times has that president or any president found in the Bible the direct solution to problems of state?

To ask such questions is not to disdain traditional faith. *Homo sapiens* is the species guided by memory and expectation. Tradition and expectation combine to give persons and societies their identity and imagination. The biblical story and some other stories, not understood as collections of oracles but internalized as memory and anticipation, can contribute to awareness of history, sensitivity to human need, enlivening of hope.

In ancient times a people was instructed in the name of God to harvest their fields so as to leave some food for the poor. That is not the method for getting food to the hungry in Ethiopia or in American urban slums. Concern for the poor today must be exploratory, even as it must incorporate perennial human sensitivity. A creative ethic usually comes from people who live out of, yet continuously renew and revise, a tradition.

An ethic for today and tomorrow must combine heritage and expectation, courage and caution, fidelity and innovation. It must relate commitment to tough-minded factuality, imagination to hard evidence, vision to reality. So it may come to pass that our heirs will find their lives blighted because we, by deciding badly or failing to decide, have destroyed their brightest possibilities. And they may find that we, in generosity and foresight, have offered them opportunities beyond those we enjoy. What they can do with their forced options depends, more than I like, on what we do with ours.

Notes

Chapter 1. Social Decisions

1. William James, "The Will to Believe," in *Essays on Faith and Morals* (New York: Longmans, Green, 1947), p. 34. (The essay was first published in 1898.)
2. Jean-Paul Sartre, "Existentialism Is a Humanism," trans. Walter Kaufmann, in *Existentialism from Dostoevsky to Sartre,* ed. Walter Kaufmann (New York: Meridian, 1956), p. 295.
3. *New York Times,* October 13, 1974, p. 34.
4. Herman J. Muller, "What Genetic Course Will Man Steer?" *Proceedings of the Third International Congress of Human Genetics,* ed. James F. Crow and James V. Neel (Baltimore, Md.: Johns Hopkins University Press, 1967), p. 521.
5. I agree with the Report of the Committee on Scientific Freedom and Responsibility of the American Association for the Advancement of Science, which rejects "the idea that we must pursue new technological possibilities, wherever they may lead." I shall quote this report in Chapter 9.
6. Jacques Ellul, *The Technological Society,* trans. John Wilkinson (New York: Random House, Vintage Books, 1964; first French edition, 1954), p. xxxi. In a quite different way Lewis Mumford, though worried by technological determinism, thinks it possible for human beings to escape "the myth of the machine" and "the technocratic prison" by an exercise of freedom. See *The Myth of the Machine: Technics and Human Development* (New York: Harcourt, Brace and World, 1967) and *The Myth of the Machine: The Pentagon of Power* (New York: Harcourt Brace Jovanovich, 1970). Victor Ferkiss, directly challenging Ellul, argues: "Man can buy his freedom from the effects of technology, but only at a price, sometimes at a price so high that he may be unwilling to pay it." *Technological Man: The Myth and the Reality* (New York: New American Library, Mentor Books, 1970; first published in 1969), p. 39. Cf. Victor Ferkiss, *The Future of Technological Civilization* (New York: Braziller, 1974). Langdon Winner has made a comprehensive and incisive study of the relation of technology to human decisions: *Autonomous Technology: Technics-out-of-Control as a Theme in Political Thought* (Cambridge, Mass.: MIT Press, 1977).
7. Wolf Häfele, "Hypotheticality and the New Challenges: The Pathfinder Role of Nuclear Energy," *Anticipation* (World Council of Churches), 20 (May 1975), p. 22. Reprinted from *Minerva,* July 1974.

Chapter 2. Some Scenarios and Preliminary Reflections

1. The figures are the projection of Mihajlo Mesarovic and Eduard Pestel, *Mankind at the Turning Point: The Second Report to the Club of Rome* (New York: Dutton and Reader's Digest Press, 1974), p. 132.
2. Oswald Spengler, *The Decline of the West,* trans. Charles Francis Atkinson (New York: Knopf, 1937; first German edition, 1918, 1922), vol. 2, p. 505.

3. Jerome B. Wiesner and Herbert F. York, "National Security and the Nuclear-Test Ban," *Scientific American* 211, no. 4 (October 1964), pp. 27–35. I discuss this essay further in Chapter 8.

4. Garrett Hardin, *Exploring New Ethics for Survival: The Voyage of the Spaceship Beagle* (New York: Viking, 1972), pp. 250–251. The first printing of the essay was in *Science* 162 (December 13, 1968), pp. 1243–1248, and it has been reprinted in many places.

5. Donella H. Meadows et al., *The Limits to Growth* (New York: Universe, 1972), p. 150.

6. *Estimation of Human and Financial Resources Devoted to R & D at the World and Regional Level,* UNESCO Publication CSR-S-7, 1979. The figures are for 1974.

7. John Dewey, "Progress," *International Journal of Ethics* 26 (1916), p. 314.

Chapter 3. The Worldwide Energy Emergency

1. Erik P. Eckholm, *Losing Ground: Environmental Stress and World Food Prospects* (New York: Norton, 1976), p. 101.

2. Jimmie Carter, text in *New York Times,* April 19, 1977.

3. Robert Stobaugh and Daniel Yergin, eds., *Energy Future: Report of the Energy Project at the Harvard Business School* (New York: Random House, 1979), pp. 18, 42.

4. Shem Arungu-Olende, "An Interpretation of the Global Energy Problem," in *Faith and Science in an Unjust World: Report of the World Council of Churches' Conference on Faith, Science and the Future,* vol. 1, ed. Roger L. Shinn (Geneva: World Council of Churches, 1980), p. 235. The recent slowdown in this trend, caused by high prices and worldwide economic recession, has caused great suffering in some societies.

5. Gerald Foley with Charlotte Nassim, *The Energy Question* (Harmondsworth, Middlesex, England: Penguin Books, 1976), p. 88.

6. In past history, says Gunnar Myrdal, "full democracy with universal suffrage" has followed "prior attainment of a fairly high level of living and a high degree of equality of opportunity." While Myrdal endorses contemporary efforts to attain democracy in poor countries, he recognizes the difficulties. *Beyond the Welfare State: Economic Planning and its International Implications* (New Haven, Conn.: Yale University Press, 1960), p. 125.

7. Charles E. Lindblom, *Politics and Markets: The World's Political-Economic Systems* (New York: Basic Books, 1977).

8. Foley, *The Energy Question,* p. 61.

9. Stobaugh and Yergin, *Energy Future,* p. 232.

10. Daniel Patrick Moynihan, as quoted in Wallace Irwin, Jr., *Great Decisions 1980* (New York: Foreign Policy Association, 1980), p. 91.

11. Robert D. Hershey, Jr., "Sawhill Synthetic Fuel Chief," *New York Times,* September 11, 1980, p. D1.

12. Ibid., p. D6.

13. Foley, *The Energy Question,* p. 122.

14. Lester Brown, *Food or Fuel: New Competition for the World's Cropland,* Worldwatch Paper 35 (Washington, D.C.: Worldwatch Institute, 1980).

15. Stobaugh and Yergin, *Energy Future,* p. 211.

16. Committee on Nuclear and Alternative Energy Systems of the National Academy of Sciences, *Energy in Transition, 1985–2010* (San Francisco: Freeman, 1980).

17. Amory B. Lovins, *Soft Energy Paths: Toward a Durable Peace* (Cambridge, Mass.:

Ballinger, 1977). Detailed analysis and debate on Lovins's proposals are found in the two volumes of *Alternative Long-Range Energy Strategies:* Joint Hearing before the Select Committee on Small Business and the Committee on Interior and Insular Affairs, United States Senate, Ninety-Fourth Congress (Washington, D.C.: U.S. Government Printing Office, 1977).

18. Gus Speth, Letter to the Editor, *New York Times,* February 26, 1980, p. A14.
19. Nicholas Panagakos, "Science Highlights of 1974," *Information Please Almanac,* 1975 (New York: Simon & Schuster, 1974), p. 430.
20. See Stobaugh and Yergin, *Energy Future;* Sam H. Schurr et al., *Energy in America's Future: the Choices Before Us* (Baltimore: Johns Hopkins University Press, 1979); Hans H. Landsberg et al., *Energy: The Next Twenty Years* (Cambridge, Mass.: Ballinger, 1979).
21. *Anticipation* (World Council of Churches) 24 (November 1977), pp. 15, 17.
22. E. F. Schumacher, *Small Is Beautiful: Economics as if People Mattered* (New York: Harper & Row, 1973).
23. William K. Stevens, "Texas Leading 10 Major States in Gasoline Use," *New York Times,* May 28, 1979, p. A1.
24. Foley, *The Energy Question,* p. 97.

Chapter 4. Food for a Hungry World

1. Maurice Williams, "Toward a World Without Hunger," Report by the Executive Director to the World Food Council, March 23, 1979, pars. 28, 29.
2. Richard M. Nixon, message to Congress. The text is in the *New York Times,* July 19, 1969.
3. Ivan L. Bennett, Jr., "People and Food," in *This Little Planet,* ed. Michael Hamilton (New York: Scribners, 1970), p. 104.
4. Special Supplement to *UNA Quarterly,* The Newsletter of the United Nations Association of the USA, 2, no. 4 (Winter 1979/80): 1.
5. Georg Borgstrom, *Too Many: An Ecological Overview of Earth's Limitations,* rev. ed. (New York: Collier, 1971), pp. 322–323.
6. Bennett, "People and Food," p. 82.
7. Raymond F. Hopkins and Donald J. Puchala, "Perspectives on the International Relations of Food," in *The Global Political Economy of Food,* ed. Raymond F. Hopkins and Donald J. Puchala (Madison: University of Wisconsin Press, 1978), p. 24.
8. See Joseph Gremillion, ed., *Food/Energy and the Major Faiths* (Maryknoll, N.Y.: Orbis, 1978).
9. Kenneth E. Boulding, *The Meaning of the 20th Century* (New York: Harper & Row, 1964), p. 7.
10. Carol and John Steinhart, *The Fires of Culture: Energy Yesterday and Tomorrow* (North Scituate, Mass.: Duxbury Press, 1974), p. 38.
11. Norman Borlaug, "The Fight against Hunger," in *Finite Resources and the Human Future,* ed. Ian G. Barbour (Minneapolis, Minn.: Augsburg, 1976), p. 67.
12. Frances Moore Lappé and Joseph Collins, *Food First: Beyond the Myth of Scarcity* (Boston: Houghton Mifflin, 1977), p. 145.
13. Steinhart, *The Fires of Culture,* pp. 38, 56–57.
14. Gerald Leach, *Energy and Food Production* (London: International Institute for Environment and Development, 1975), p. 2.
15. Steinhart, *The Fires of Culture,* p. 56.
16. Borlaug, "The Fight against Hunger," p. 83.

17. Ibid., p. 84.

18. Lester Brown, *By Bread Alone* (New York: Praeger, 1974), p. 141.

19. Ibid., p. 143.

20. Williams, "Toward a World Without Hunger," par. 10.

21. Ibid., par. 92.

22. William and Paul Paddock, *Famine 1975! America's Decision: Who Will Survive?* (Boston: Little, Brown, 1967).

23. Ibid., p. 212.

24. Paul Ehrlich, *The Population Bomb* (New York: Ballantine, 1968), pp. 159, 161.

25. Paul R. and Anne H. Ehrlich, *Population, Resources, Environment: Issues in Human Ecology* (San Francisco: Freeman, 1970).

26. Paddock, *Famine 1975*, pp. 227, 228.

27. Dick Clark, "Food and Development," in *Finite Resources and the Human Future*, p. 97.

28. Garrett Hardin, "Lifeboat Ethics: The Case Against Helping the Poor," *Psychology Today*, September 1974, pp. 38ff.

29. Garrett Hardin, "Lifeboat Ethics: Food and Population," in *Finite Resources and the Human Future*, p. 41.

30. For a wide range of appraisals see George L. Lucas, Jr., and Thomas W. Ogletree, eds., *Lifeboat Ethics: The Moral Dilemmas of World Hunger* (New York: Harper & Row, 1976).

31. My interchanges with Garrett Hardin are recorded, in abridged form, in *Finite Resources and the Human Future*, pp. 32–64. The printed record does not include his advocacy of increased security measures, made in response to my warning about the danger to the world of destructive acts by desperate nations.

32. Lappé and Collins, *Food First*, p. 7.

33. *New York Times*, September 9, 1979, p. 6.

34. Paddock, *Famine 1975*, p. 96.

35. Hardin, "Lifeboat Ethics: Food and Population," p. 44.

36. Williams, "Toward a World Without Hunger," pars. 9, 60.

37. "Current World Food Situation," a document prepared by the Food and Agriculture Organization of the United Nations in consultation with the Secretariat of the World Food Council, April 15, 1979, p. 9.

38. Williams, "Toward a World Without Hunger," pars. 5, 143.

39. Warren Boroson and Nick Eberstadt, "The International Food Policy Research Institute," *RF Illustrated* (Rockefeller Foundation), September 1979, p. 13. Cf. Borgstrom, *Too Many*, p. 302.

40. Paul and Arthur Simon, *The Politics of World Hunger* (New York: Harper & Row, 1973), p. 19.

41. Ibid., p. 21. *The New York Times* in two editorials (December 29, 1980 and February 1, 1971) compared two surveys by medical teams in 1969 and 1979. The second found that the malnutrition, so obvious in the first survey, had "substantially disappeared," due in large part to a federal antihunger campaign funded at nearly $15 billion per year. The budget cuts initiated by President Reagan in 1981 threatened the achievement.

42. Williams, "Toward a World Without Hunger," par. 123.

43. *New York Times*, November 11, 1978, p. 1.

44. Brown, *By Bread Alone*, p. 61.

45. Ibid., p. 70.

46. This is a specific example of an agreement between Garrett Hardin and the team of Lappé and Collins, despite vast ideological distance.

47. Borlaug, "The Fight against Hunger," p. 68.

48. Gunnar Myrdal, *The Challenge of World Poverty* (New York: Random House, Vintage Books, 1970), p. 279.

49. Brown, *By Bread Alone,* p. 250.

50. Lappé and Collins, *Food First,* pp. 368–369.

51. Maurice Williams, "Hunger and Malnutrition, and Greater Equity in Distribution of Food," Report by the Executive Director to the World Food Council, April 9, 1979, par. 7.

Chapter 5. Population and Its Paradoxes

1. Maurice Williams, "Toward a World without Hunger," Report by the Executive Director to the World Food Council, March 23, 1979, par. 145.

2. "Current World Food Situation," Food and Agriculture Organization of the United Nations, April 1978, Tables 1, 2, and 3.

3. Senator Ernest Gruening, in *Population Crisis,* Part I, 1966, Hearing before the Subcommittee on Foreign Aid Expenditures of the Committee on Government Operations, United States Senate, on S. 1676 (Washington, D.C.: U.S. Government Printing Office, 1966), p. 11.

4. John Nuveen, "The Facts of Life," in *Family Planning in an Exploding Population,* ed. John A. O'Brien (New York: Hawthorne, 1968), p. 35.

5. Harrison Brown, *The Challenge of Man's Future* (London: Secker & Warburg, 1954), p. 8.

6. Erik P. Eckholm, *Losing Ground: Environmental Stress and World Food Prospects* (New York: Norton, 1976), pp. 101–103.

7. Brown, *The Challenge of Man's Future,* p. 69.

8. Fox Butterfield reports this opinion from a Chinese physician. See "China's Legislators, Long a Docile Group, Are Starting to Ask Some Tough Questions," *New York Times,* September 10, 1980, p. A3.

9. Jonathon Kandell, "Argentina, Hoping to Double Her Population This Century, Is Taking Action to Restrict Birth Control," *New York Times,* March 17, 1974, p. 4.

10. Craig R. Whitney, "Ethnic Russian Proportion in Soviet Falls to 52.4%," *New York Times,* February 10, 1980, p. 4. Theodore Shabad, "Moslems in Soviet Show Big Increase," *New York Times,* February 28, 1980, p. A9.

11. Nathan Hare, "Black Ecology," *The Black Scholar* (April 1970), p. 7.

12. *Population Profile* (Population Reference Bureau, Inc.), July 1969, p. 4.

13. Frank W. Notestein, Dudley Kirk, and Sheldon Segal, "The Problem of Population Control," in *The Population Dilemma,* ed. Philip M. Hauser (Englewood Cliffs, N.J.: Prentice-Hall, 1963), p. 132.

14. Charles Westoff, Director of the Office of Population Research at Princeton University, so reported to the annual meeting of the Population Society of America in 1978. Jane E. Brody, "New Study Shows Decline in Fertility of Catholic Women," *New York Times,* April 18, 1978, p. 27.

15. *Population Profile,* July 1969, p. 5. The study was made by the U.N. Latin American Demographic Center (CELADE) and Cornell University.

16. André E. Hellegers, M.D., "Factors and Correctives in Population Expansion," *SAIS Review* (School of Advanced International Studies of the Johns Hopkins University) 13, no. 3 (Spring 1969), p. 24.

17. Nick Eberstadt, "Program in Context: Population," *RF Illustrated* (Rockefeller Foundation) 2, no. 2 (March 1975), p. 10.

18. The most thoughtful study of the ethical issues of abortion that I have found is

Daniel Callahan, *Abortion: Law, Choice, and Morality* (New York: Macmillan, 1970).

19. Paul and Arthur Simon, *The Politics of World Hunger* (New York: Harper & Row, 1973), p. 56.

20. The phrase is from Garrett Hardin's famous essay, "The Tragedy of the Commons," originally published in *Science* 162 (December 13, 1968) pp. 1243–1248. It has been reprinted in many places, including Hardin's book, *Exploring New Ethics for Survival: The Voyage of the Spaceship Beagle* (New York: Viking, 1972).

21. Robert C. Cook, in *Population Crisis*, Part I, 1965, p. 565.

22. Philip M. Hauser, in *Population Crisis*, Part 2, 1967–1968, p. 492.

23. Roger Revelle, "Can Man Domesticate Himself?," in *Population Crisis*, Part 5–B, 1966, pp. 1532–1539. (Reprinted from the Bulletin of the Atomic Scientists XXII, no. 2, February 1966).

24. Data are from "1970 World Population Data Sheet" (Washington, D.C.: Population Reference Bureau, Inc., 1970).

25. Eberstadt, "Program in Context: Population," p. 10.

26. Georg Borgstrom, *The Hungry Planet: The Modern World at the Edge of Famine* 2d rev. ed. (New York: Collier, 1972), pp. 1–2.

27. Eberstadt, "Program in Context: Population," p. 10.

28. My sources are the public press, personal interviews with China watchers in Hong Kong, and reports from visitors to China. Especially useful is the Draper Fund Report No. 8 (March 1980) on "Birth Planning in China." A more skeptical estimate from Nick Eberstadt appears in the *New York Review of Books*, April 5, 19, and May 3, 1979.

29. Reported as a directive in the form of an open letter, UPI dispatch, in *New York Times*, September 27, 1980, p. 3.

30. Claude Levi-Strauss, interview in *New York Times*, January 21, 1972.

31. "Report of an Ecumenical Conference on the Scientific, Technological and Social Revolutions in an Asian Perspective," *Anticipation* (World Council of Churches) 14 (August 1973), p. 35.

Chapter 6. Living with Limits

1. See J. Donald Hughes, *Ecology in Ancient Civilizations* (Albuquerque: University of New Mexico Press, 1975). René Dubos, *A God Within* (New York: Scribners, 1972), pp. 153–156.

2. Georg Borgstrom, *Too Many: An Ecological Overview of Earth's Limitations*, rev. ed. (New York: Collier, 1971), pp. 85, 155.

3. William K. Stevens, "Back to Basics: Mining Water Deep Below Heart of Texas," *New York Times*, July 27, 1980, sec. 4 (The Week in Review), p. 22.

4. Kathleen Wiegner, "The Water Crisis: It's Almost Here," *Forbes*, August 20, 1979, p. 57.

5. Kenneth E. Boulding, *The Meaning of the 20th Century* (New York: Harper & Row, 1964), pp. 7–8.

6. William Pollard, "God and His Creation," in *This Little Planet*, ed. Michael Hamilton (New York: Scribners, 1970), p. 60.

7. Mihajlo Mesarovic and Eduard Pestel, *Mankind at the Turning Point* (New York: Dutton and Reader's Digest Press, 1974), pp. 23, 84.

8. Harrison Brown, *The Human Future Revisited: The World Predicament and Possible Solutions* (New York: Norton, 1978), p. 55; cf. pp. 213–214. Cf. Robert Heilbroner, *An Inquiry into the Human Prospect, Updated and Reconsidered for the 1980s* (New York: Norton, 1980), pp. 168–171.

9. Ivan L. Bennett, Jr., "People and Food," in *This Little Planet*, p. 117.
10. M. Rupert Cutler, Assistant Secretary of Agriculture for Natural Resources and Environment, "The Peril of Vanishing Farmlands," *New York Times*, July 1, 1980, p. A19 (Op-ed).
11. Harrison Brown, *The Challenge of Man's Future* (London: Secker & Warburg, 1954), chap. 7 and Bibliography.
12. Borgstrom, *Too Many;* also *The Hungry Planet: The Modern World at the Edge of Famine*, 2d rev. ed. (New York: Collier, 1972).
13. Kenneth E. Boulding, "The Wisdom of Man and the Wisdom of God," in *Human Values on the Spaceship Earth* (New York: National Council of Churches, 1966). Cf. Boulding, "The Economics of the Coming Spaceship Earth," in *Environmental Quality in a Growing Economy*, ed. Henry Jarrett (Baltimore: Johns Hopkins University Press, 1966).
14. E. J. Mishan, *The Costs of Economic Growth* (New York: Praeger, 1967).
15. Garrett Hardin, "The Tragedy of the Commons," *Science* 162 (December 13, 1968) pp. 1243–48.
16. See among others the following, listed chronologically: Paul R. and Anne H. Ehrlich, *Population, Resources, Environment* (San Francisco: Freeman, 1970). Jay W. Forrester, *World Dynamics* (Cambridge, Mass.: Wright-Allen, 1971). Richard A. Falk, *This Endangered Planet* (New York: Random House, 1971). Herman E. Daly, ed., *Toward A Steady-State Economy* (San Francisco: Freeman, 1973). John Harte and Robert H. Socolow, eds., *Patient Earth* (New York: Holt, Rinehart and Winston, 1971). Garrett Hardin, *Exploring New Ethics for Survival: The Voyage of the Spaceship Beagle* (New York: Viking, 1972). E. F. Schumacher, *Small Is Beautiful: Economics as if People Mattered* (New York: Harper & Row, 1973). Robert L. Heilbroner, *An Inquiry into the Human Prospect* (New York: Norton, 1974). Paul R. and Anne H. Ehrlich, *The End of Affluence* (New York: Ballantine, 1974). Robert Stivers, *The Sustainable Society* (Philadelphia: Westminster, 1976). Rufus Miles, *Awakening from the American Dream: The Social and Political Limits to Growth* (New York: Universe, 1976). Dennis Pirages, ed., *The Sustainable Society* (New York: Praeger, 1977). William Ophuls, *Ecology and the Politics of Scarcity* (San Francisco: Freeman, 1977). Herman E. Daly, *Steady-State Economics* (San Francisco, Freeman, 1977). E. J. Mishan, *The Economic Growth Debate* (London: Allen & Unwin, 1977). Fred Hirsch, *Social Limits to Growth* (London: Routledge & Kegan Paul, 1977). Harrison Brown, *The Human Future Revisited* (New York: Norton, 1978). Hazel Henderson, *Creating Alternative Futures* (New York: Berkley, 1978). Lester R. Brown, *The Twenty-Ninth Day* (New York: Norton, 1978). To these should be added the many publications of the Worldwatch Institute of Washington, D.C., established by Lester Brown in 1975; and *Anticipation* (World Council of Churches, Geneva, Switzerland), especially valuable for maintaining an international conversation.
17. Edward Goldsmith et al., eds., *A Blueprint for Survival*, first published as *Ecologist* 2 (January 1972), then as a book by Houghton Mifflin, Boston, also 1972.
18. Ibid., par. 110.
19. Ibid., par. 161.
20. Donella H. Meadows, Dennis L. Meadows, Jørgen Randers, William W. Behrens, III, *The Limits to Growth* (New York: Universe, 1972).
21. Meadows et al., *The Limits to Growth*, p. 23.
22. Ibid., p. 24.
23. Ibid., p. 150.
24. Ibid., p. 158.

25. Ibid., pp. 165–166.

26. See, for example: John Maddox, *The Doomsday Syndrome* (London: Macmillan, 1972). Peter Passell and Leonard Ross, *Retreat from Riches* (New York: Viking, 1973). H.S.D. Cole et al., eds., *Thinking about the Future: A Critique of the Limits to Growth* (London: Chatto & Windus, 1973); the American edition is entitled *Models of Doom* (New York: Universe, 1973). *Daedalus:* Journal of the American Academy of Arts and Sciences 102 (Fall 1973), issue entitled "The No-Growth Society." Mancur Olson and Hans Landsberg, eds., *The No-Growth Society* (New York: Norton, 1973). Andrew Weintraub et al., *The Economic Growth Controversy* (New York: International Arts & Sciences Press, 1973). Alfred Sauvy, *Zero Growth?* (New York: Praeger, 1976; original French edition, 1973). Wilfred Beckerman, *In Defense of Economic Growth* (London: Jonathon Cape, 1974). Willem L. Oltmans, ed., *On Growth* (New York: Putnam, vol. 1, 1974; vol. 2, 1975). Herman Kahn, William Brown, and Leon Martel, *The Next 200 Years* (New York: Morrow, 1976). Lester C. Thurow, *The Zero-Sum Society* (New York: Basic Books, 1980).

27. Donella Meadows, "Limits to Growth Revisited," and "Panel on Resources and Growth," in *Finite Resources and the Human Future*, ed. Ian G. Barbour (Minneapolis, Minn.: Augsburg, 1976), esp. p. 136.

28. See Robert Stivers, *The Sustainable Society*, esp. pp. 156–158.

29. See Ian Barbour, *Technology, Environment and Human Values* (New York: Praeger, 1981), Chap. 12.

30. Meadows et al., *The Limits to Growth*, p. 175.

31. See W. W. Rostow, *The Stages of Economic Growth* (London and New York: Cambridge University Press, 1960; 2d. 1971), esp. Chap. 2, 3, 4.

32. John Kenneth Galbraith, *Economics and the Public Purpose* (New York: New American Library, 1975; orig. ed. Houghton Mifflin, 1973), pp. 96, 98.

33. E. F. Schumacher, *Small is Beautiful*, esp. pp. 167–169.

34. Peter S. Albin, *Progress without Poverty: Socially Responsible Economic Growth* (New York: Basic Books, 1978).

35. Meadows et al., *The Limits to Growth*, p. 22.

36. Ibid., p. 20.

37. Mihajlo Mesarovic and Eduard Pestel, *Mankind at the Turning Point* (New York: Dutton and Reader's Digest Press, 1974).

38. Interview with Henry Ford II by Agis Salpukis, *New York Times*, February 17, 1975, p. 33.

39. Ernest Petric, "Some Remarks on Marxism and Limits to Growth," in *Faith and Science in an Unjust World: Report of the World Council of Churches' Conference on Faith, Science and the Future*, vol. 1, ed. Roger L. Shinn (Geneva: World Council of Churches, 1980), p. 197.

40. Denis Goulet "Needed: A Cultural Revolution in the U.S.," *The Christian Century* 91 (September 4–11, 1974), p. 816.

41. See Fox Butterfield, "Chinese Ecology Upset by Food Drive," *New York Times*, April 7, 1980, p. A12.

42. Günter Grass, interviewed by Gwen Kinkead, *The New Republic* 179, nos. 26 & 27 (December 23 & 30, 1978), p. 27.

43. Meadows et al., *The Limits to Growth*. "There is no question that many of these deaths [from malnutrition] are due to the world's social limitations rather than its physical ones" (p. 52). ". . . present patterns of population and capital growth are actually increasing the gap between the rich and the poor on a worldwide basis, and the ultimate result of a continued attempt to grow according to the present pattern will be a disastrous collapse" (p. 178).

44. "Response to Sussex," in *Models of Doom,* pp. 236–237.

45. See note 1 above. Also Arnold J. Toynbee, *A Study of History,* vols. 4–6 (London: Oxford University Press, 1939), esp. discussions of internal and external proletariats, *passim.*

46. Robert Lekachman, *New York Times,* November 1, 1979, p. D1.

47. *Newsweek,* November 19, 1979.

48. Mesarovic and Pestel, *Mankind at the Turning Point.* Jan Tinbergen, co-ordinator, *Reshaping the International Order* (London: Hutchinson, 1977).

49. Wassily Leontief, Anne P. Carter, and Peter A. Petri, *The Future of the World Economy: A United Nations Study* (New York: Oxford University Press, 1977), pp. 10–11.

50. Geoffrey Barraclough, "The Struggle for the Third World," *New York Review of Books,* November 9, 1978, p. 58. Cf. Robert Heilbroner's analysis of Leontief's report in *An Inquiry into the Human Prospect, Updated and Reconsidered for the 1980s* (New York: Norton, 1980), pp. 168–171.

51. Willy Brandt et al., *North-South: A Program for Survival* (Cambridge, Mass.: MIT Press, 1980), p. 12.

52. *Global 2000,* 3 vols., (Washington, D.C.: U.S. Government Printing Office, 1980).

53. *World Development Report, 1980* (Washington, D.C.: The World Bank, 1980).

Chapter 7. New Frontiers in Genetics

1. Albert Rosenfeld, *The Second Genesis: The Coming Control of Life,* with a New Introduction (New York: Random House, Vintage Books, 1975). Horace Freeland Judson, *The Eighth Day of Creation: The Makers of the Revolution in Biology* (New York: Simon & Schuster, 1979).

2. See, for example, the four-volume *Encyclopedia of Bioethics,* Warren T. Reich, editor-in-chief (New York: Free Press, 1978). Two major centers of bioethical study in the United States are: Kennedy Institute of Ethics at Georgetown University, Washington, D.C.; and Institute of Society, Ethics and the Life Sciences, Hastings-on-Hudson, N.Y.

3. The spectrum in the United States ranges from the enthusiasm for new biological technologies of Joseph Fletcher to the grave caution of Paul Ramsey. See Fletcher, *The Ethics of Genetic Control: Ending Reproductive Roulette* (Garden City, N.Y.: Doubleday, Anchor Press, 1974); Ramsey, *Fabricated Man: The Ethics of Genetic Control* (New Haven, Conn.: Yale University Press, 1970).

4. James D. Watson has told the story of his participation in *The Double Helix: A Personal Account of the Discovery of the Structure of DNA* (New York: Atheneum, 1968). The small book has already become a classic for the comparison of abstract "scientific method" and the actual activities of scientists engaged in discovery.

5. Herman J. Muller, "What Genetic Course Will Man Steer?" in *Proceedings of the Third International Congress of Human Genetics,* ed. James F. Crow and James V. Neel (Baltimore: Johns Hopkins University Press, 1967), p. 521.

6. Marshall Nirenberg, "Will Society Be Prepared?" *Science* 157 (August 11, 1967), p. 633.

7. Reports of the first experimental prenatal diagnosis of hemophilia appeared in the *New England Journal of Medicine,* April 26, 1979, so clinical diagnosis may be on the way to feasibility.

8. See Chapter 5 and note 18.

9. Marc Lappé, "How Much Do We Want to Know about the Unborn?" *Hastings Center Report* 3 (February 1973), p. 8.

10. See the discussion of the issue in *Hastings Center Report* 10 (February 1980), pp. 15ff.

11. *Human Life and the New Genetics*, ed. Roger L. Shinn (New York: National Council of Churches, 1980), p. 45.

12. Boyce Rensberger, *New York Times*, August 18, 1971.

13. Muller published his proposals in various books and articles. I am using primarily his final version. See note 5 above.

14. The phrase comes from Robert K. Graham, organizer of the bank. Harold M. Schmeck, Jr., "Nobel Winner Says He Gave Sperm for Women to Bear Gifted Babies," *New York Times*, March 1, 1980, p. 6.

15. See Robert G. Edwards, "Judging the Social Values of Scientific Advances," in *Genetics and the Quality of Life*, ed. Charles Birch and Paul Abrecht (Elmsford, N.Y.: Pergamon, 1975).

16. Report from London, *New York Times*, June 8, 1973.

17. Theodosius Dobzhansky, "Changing Man," *Science* 155 (January 27, 1967), p. 413.

18. J. B. S. Haldane, "Biological Possibilities in the Next Ten Thousand Years," in *Man and His Future*, ed. Gordon Wolstenholme (Boston: Little, Brown, 1963), p. 345.

19. Arthur M. Okun, *Equality and Efficiency: The Big Tradeoff* (Washington, D.C.: The Brookings Institution, 1975), p. 85.

20. Interview with William B. Shockley by Syl Jones, *Playboy* 27, no. 8 (August 1980), p. 74.

21. *Faith and Science in an Unjust World: Report of the World Council of Churches' Conference on Faith, Science and the Future*, vol. 2, *Reports and Recommendations*, ed. Paul Abrecht (Geneva: World Council of Churches, 1980), pp. 49, 52.

22. Hudson Hoagland, "Some Biological Considerations in Ethics," in Harvey Cox et al., *Technology and Culture in Perspective*, an occasional paper published by the Church Society for College Work, Cambridge, Mass., 1967, p. 15. Hoagland attributes the data to Francis Crick.

23. Judson, *The Eighth Day of Creation*, pp. 173, 185. Lewis Thomas in *The Lives of a Cell* (New York: Viking, 1974) writes with scientific understanding and poetic insight about the marvels of the cell.

24. Jacques Monod, *Chance and Necessity* (New York: Random House, Vintage Books, 1972), p. 164.

25. Herman J. Muller, "Genetic Progress by Voluntarily Conducted Germinal Choice," in *Man and His Future*, p. 255.

26. See "Gene Therapy," *Encyclopedia of Bioethics*, vol. 2, including my entry on "Ethical Issues," pp. 521–527.

27. Dobzhansky, "Changing Man," pp. 411–413.

28. Robert S. Morison, "Comments on Genetic Evolution," in *Evolution and Man's Progress*, ed. Hudson Hoagland and Ralph W. Burhoe (New York: Columbia University Press, 1962), p. 41.

29. William Shakespeare, *Hamlet*, II, ii.

30. See, for example, Bernard Häring, *Ethics of Manipulation: Issues in Medicine, Behavior Control and Genetics* (New York: Seabury, 1975).

31. Julian Huxley, "The Future of Man—Evolutionary Aspects," in *Man and His Future*, p. 12.

32. Judith Hall, "The Concerns of Doctors and Patients," in *Ethical Issues in Human*

Genetics, ed. Bruce Hilton and Maureen Harris (New York: Plenum, 1973), p. 31.

33. Margaret Mead, *Male and Female: A Study of the Sexes in a Changing World* (New York: New American Library, 1955; first published in 1949), p. 19.

34. Alexander Capron, "Genetic Therapy: A Lawyer's Response," in *The New Genetics and the Future of Man,* ed. Michael Hamilton (Grand Rapids, Mich.: Eerdmans, 1972), p. 137.

35. Catherine Roberts, *The Scientific Conscience* (New York: Braziller, 1967), p. 24.

36. Herman Muller, "What Genetic Course Will Man Steer?" p. 537.

37. U.S. Supreme Court, *Diamond* v. *Chakrabarty,* Majority Opinion, June 16, 1980.

38. See Cary Fowler, "Plant Patenting," *The CoEvolution Quarterly* (Winter 79/80): 34ff. Also, Lawrence D. Hills, "Seeds of Destruction," *The Guardian* (Manchester, England), June 22, 1980, p. 5.

39. See Ann Crittenden, "Plan to Widen Plant Patents Stirs Conflicts," *New York Times,* June 6, 1980, p. A1.

40. "Genetics Gold Rush," cover story, *The Economist* (London) 279, No. 7189 (June 13–19, 1981), pp. 81–86.

41. Marc Lappé, *Genetic Politics: The Limits of Biological Control* (New York: Simon & Schuster, 1979), p. 215.

Chapter 8. The New Dimensions of War

1. I said some things in my book, *Wars and Rumors of Wars* (Nashville, Tenn.: Abingdon, 1972). That book combines personal memoirs with some social and ethical thinking about war. In that book I wrote my heart out and came to conclusions so disturbing that I have written rather little on the subject since then, although I have participated in modest ways in political and religious efforts for peace. While I still reaffirm that book and keep a few echoes of it here, I am trying to nudge my thinking forward a few steps.

2. Edward Gibbon, *The Decline and Fall of the Roman Empire,* end of chap. XXXVIII (New York: Modern Library, n.d.), vol. II, pp. 95, 96. Many years ago Arnold Toynbee used this quotation in a public lecture and in his generous way guided me, a student, to it in Gibbon's text.

3. Jerome B. Wiesner and Herbert F. York, "National Security and the Nuclear-Test Ban," *Scientific American,* 211, no. 4 (October 1964), p. 28.

4. Philip Morrison, "The Nature of Strategic Nuclear Weapons," in *Faith and Science in an Unjust World: Report of the World Council of Churches' Conference on Faith, Science and the Future,* vol. 1, ed. Roger L. Shinn (Geneva: World Council of Churches, 1980). The figures both for Vietnam and for the total U.S. arsenal are on p. 311.

5. United Nations General Assembly, *Comprehensive Study on Nuclear Weapons,* prepared by a Group of Experts and submitted to the 35th session of the General Assembly, September 12, 1980, p. 151.

6. Congress of the United States, Office of Technology Assessment, *The Effects of Nuclear War* (Washington, D.C.: U.S. Government Printing Office, 1980), p. 3.

7. U.N. *Comprehensive Study on Nuclear Weapons,* p. 151.

8. Harrison Brown, *The Challenge of Man's Future* (London: Secker & Warburg, 1954), p. 224. Kenneth Boulding makes the same point in *The Meaning of the 20th Century* (New York: Harper & Row, 1964) p. 76. Victor Weisskopf says the same thing in "A Soviet Inquiry," *Worldview* 24, no. 8 (August 1981), p. 7.

9. Harrison Brown, *The Human Future Revisited: The World Predicament and Possible Solutions* (New York: Norton, 1978), p. 59.

10. Ruth Leger Sivard, *World Military and Social Expenditures, 1979* (Leesburg, Va.: World Priorities, 1979), p. 5.
11. Ibid., p. 16.
12. *North-South: A Program for Survival.* Report of the Independent Commission on International Development Issues under the chairmanship of Willy Brandt (Cambridge, Mass.: MIT Press, 1980), p. 14.
13. *Faith and Science in an Unjust World,* vol. 2, ed. by Paul Abrecht, p. 169.
14. Wiesner and York, "National Security and the Nuclear-Test Ban," p. 27.
15. Ibid.
16. Ibid., p. 35.
17. Ibid.
18. William Temple, *Christianity and Social Order* (New York: Seabury, 1977; first published in 1942), p. 82.
19. Dwight D. Eisenhower, address to joint session of Brazilian Congress, text in *New York Times,* February 25, 1960, p. 8.
20. Lyndon B. Johnson, address to National Legislative Conference of the Building and Construction Trades Department of the A.F.L.-C.I.O., reported in *New York Times,* March 25, 1964, p. 4.
21. See, for example, the report of Khrushchev's address to the East German Communist Party Congress, *Time,* January 25, 1963. Leonid Brezhnev in his Report to the 26th Congress of the Soviet Communist Party in 1981 said that even a "limited" nuclear war in Europe would mean "certain destruction of European civilization." Although he said this in the context of a self-serving argument, there is no reason to think he does not believe it. See Leonid I. Brezhnev, *Report of the Central Committee of the Communist Party of the Soviet Union to the 26th Congress of the CPSU* (New York: International Publishers, 1981), p. 19.
22. Gene Preston, "Coffin Confronts the Cadets," *The Christian Century* 98 (July 12–22, 1981), p. 730.
23. Oppenheimer's figure of speech is used by Philip Morrison, "The Nature of Strategic Nuclear Weapons," pp. 314–315.
24. Brown, *The Human Future Revisited,* p. 182.
25. U.N. *Comprehensive Study on Nuclear Weapons,* p. 157.
26. Hans J. Morgenthau, *Truth and Power* (New York: Praeger, 1970), pp. 154–155.
27. John C. Bennett, "Countering the Theory of Limited Nuclear War," *The Christian Century* 98 (January 7–14, 1981), p. 10–13. The quotation is from p. 11.
28. Andrei D. Sakharov, "A Letter from Exile," *New York Times Magazine,* June 8, 1980, pp. 31ff.
29. Roger L. Shinn, "Military Technology and Human Hopes," *Christianity and Crisis* 23 (February 4, 1963), pp. 1–2.
30. Gordon W. Allport, *The Nature of Prejudice,* 25th Anniversary Edition (Reading, Mass.: Addison-Wesley, 1980), p. 444.
31. Herbert Butterfield, *Christianity, Diplomacy and War* (London: Epworth, 1953), p. 43.
32. Rollo May, *Love and Will* (New York: Norton, 1969), pp. 14, 30.
33. William Epstein, "Will the Russians Play 'American Roulette'?" *Saturday Review/World* 1, no. 21 (June 29, 1974), pp. 7, 42–43. The quotation is from p. 43.
34. Victor F. Weisskopf, "A Soviet Inquiry," *Worldview* 24, no. 8 (August 1981), pp. 7–8.
35. George F. Kennan, "A Modest Proposal," *New York Review of Books,* July 16, 1981, pp. 14–16. The quotation is from p. 16. I consider the concrete proposals of Weis-

skopf and Kennan to be far more helpful than Jonathon Schell's earnest but vague yearning to "reinvent" a politics without national sovereignty. See Schell, *The Fate of the Earth* (New York: Alfred A. Knopf, 1982).

36. C.P. Snow, "The Moral Un-Neutrality of Science," *Science* 133 (January 27, 1961), pp. 256–259. The quotation is from p. 259.

37. George F. Kennan, "Foreign Policy and Christian Conscience," *The Atlantic Monthly* 203, no. 5 (May 1959), pp. 44–49. The quotation is from p. 49.

Chapter 9. The Freedom and Accountability of Science

1. *Scientific Freedom and Responsibility: A Report of the AAAS Committee on Scientific Freedom and Responsibility,* prepared for the Committee by John T. Edsall (Washington, D.C.: American Association for the Advancement of Science, 1975), p. 1. Cf. the rich interchange of opinions in *Daedalus* (Journal of the American Academy of Arts and Sciences) 107, no. 2 (Spring 1978), "Limits of Scientific Inquiry."

2. Horace Freeland Judson, *The Eighth Day of Creation: The Makers of the Revolution in Biology* (New York: Simon & Schuster, 1979), p. 95.

3. James B. Conant, *On Understanding Science* (New York: New American Library of World Literature, Mentor Books, 1951; first published in 1947), p. 110. For a clash between two different opinions of the nature of science see the lecture by Australian astronomer Robert Hanbury Brown, "The Nature of Science," and the response by Brazilian political philosopher, Rubem Alves, "On the Eating Habits of Science," In *Faith and Science in an Unjust World: Report of the World Council of Churches' Conference on Faith, Science and the Future,* vol. 1, ed. by Roger L. Shinn (Geneva: World Council of Churches, 1980).

4. *Scientific Freedom and Responsibility,* p. 6. Cf. Robert S. Morison: "Science can no longer be content to present itself as an activity independent of the rest of society, governed by its own rules and directed by the inner dynamics of its own processes." "Science and Social Attitudes," *Science* 165 (July 11, 1969), p. 156.

5. Einstein's letter appears in *Einstein on Peace,* ed. Otto Nathan and Heinz Norden (New York: Avenal, n.d.; originally published in 1968), pp. 294–296. Much of the rest of the book details Einstein's resistance to most of the consequences of the process he initiated.

6. Garrett Hardin, *Exploring New Ethics for Survival: The Voyage of the Spaceship Beagle* (New York: Viking, 1972), p. 141.

7. Report of a Working Group on Ethical and Social Issues in Genetic Engineering and the Ownership of Life Forms, Vogelenzang, Netherlands, June 15–18, 1981. Organized by the Working Committee on Church and Society, World Council of Churches. Pt. II, B, 2, b, vi.

8. *Scientific Freedom and Responsibility,* p. 26.

9. Herman Kahn, interviewed by G. R. Urban, University Programs of Radio Free Europe, printed as "Herman Kahn Thinks about the Thinkable," *New York Times Magazine,* June 20, 1971, pp. 12ff. The quotations are from p. 24.

10. The events have been reported often, most completely in James H. Jones, *Bad Blood* (New York: Free Press, 1981).

11. Catherine Roberts, *The Scientific Conscience* (New York: Braziller, 1967), pp. 10, 13.

12. See Federal Register 46, No. 16 (Jan. 26, 1981), pp. 8365–8391, "Final Regulations Amending Basic HHS Policy for the Protection of Human Research Subjects."

Chapter 10. Faith and Doctrine Reconsidered

1. Lynn White, Jr., "The Historical Roots of our Ecologic Crisis," *Science* 155 (March 10, 1967), pp. 1203–1207. The quotations are all from p. 1205.

2. Arnold Toynbee, "The Religious Background of the Present Environmental Crisis," in *Ecology and Religion in History*, ed. David and Eileen Spring (New York: Harper & Row, 1974), pp. 137–149. The quotations are from pp. 142–143, 145, 147. Toynbee's essay originally appeared in the *International Journal of Environmental Studies* 3 (1972), pp. 141–146. (The book edited by the Springs includes also White's essay.)

3. See, for example, Alfred North Whitehead, *Science in the Modern World* (New York: Macmillan, 1925), p. 18. The emergence of science in the modern world came out of "the medieval insistence on the rationality of God, conceived as with the personal energy of Jehovah and with the rationality of a Greek philosopher."

4. Arend van Leeuwen, *Christianity in World History* (New York: Scribners, 1965; first Dutch edition, 1964), pp. 419–420.

5. Harvey Cox, *The Secular City* (New York: Macmillan, 1965), p. 82.

6. Joseph Sittler, "Called to Unity," *Ecumenical Review* 14, no. 2 (January 1962), pp. 175–187. Sittler went on to develop this theme in his book, *Essays on Nature and Grace* (Philadelphia: Fortress, 1972).

7. See, for example: Frederick Elder, *Crisis in Eden* (Nashville, Tenn.: Abingdon, 1970). H. Paul Santmire, *Brother Earth* (New York: Nelson, 1970). John B. Cobb, *Is it Too Late? A Theology of Ecology* (Beverly Hills, Cal.: Bruce, 1972). Paulos Gregorios, *The Human Presence: An Orthodox View of Nature* (Geneva: World Council of Churches, 1978). For qualified reaffirmations of "dominion" see: Richard Neuhaus, *In Defense of People* (New York: Macmillan, 1971). Thomas Sieger Derr, *Ecology and Human Liberation: A Theological Critique of the Use and Abuse of our Birthright* (Geneva: World Council of Churches, 1973).

8. Scholars, of course, usually assign Genesis 1 to the Priestly source and Genesis 2:4ff. to the Jahwist source. However, the issue here is the historical and cultural impact of the Bible, and that operated for centuries before modern source-criticism.

9. Georg Borgstrom, *Too Many: An Ecological Overview of Earth's Limitations*, rev. ed. (New York: Collier, 1971), p. 367. Borgstrom, it should be noted, refers to the "misinterpreted" mandate. He is himself capable of echoing both biblical fervor and biblical rhetoric in his own ethics.

10. John Calvin, *Commentaries on the First Book of Moses called Genesis* (Grand Rapids, Mich.: Eerdmans, 1948), vol. 1, p. 125.

11. Gerhard Liedke, "Solidarity in Conflict," in *Faith and Science in an Unjust World: Report of the World Council of Churches' Conference on Faith, Science and the Future*, vol. 1, ed. Roger L. Shinn (Geneva: World Council of Churches, 1980), pp. 73–79. The quotations are from pp. 75–77. Cf. Klaus Koch, "The Old Testament View of Nature," *Anticipation* (World Council of Churches) 25 (January 1979), pp. 47–52.

12. Sittler, *Essays on Nature and Grace*, pp. 24, 25, 37.

13. I cannot here go into the many sources. However, I would call attention to the argument of Jacques Ellul that the sources of technological society are not mainly Christian but are in fact largely anti-Christian. Ellul made his argument prior to White's famous essay, and White apparently was not aware of Ellul's case. Both are so provocative in their uses of history that a direct confrontation between them

would be illuminating. See Ellul, *The Technological Society* (New York: Random House, Vintage Books, 1964; first French edition, 1954), pp. 32–38.

14. Paul Goodman, "Can Technology be Humane?" *New York Review of Books,* November 20, 1969, p. 33.

15. Toynbee, "Religious Background," p. 148.

16. René Dubos, *A God Within* (New York: Scribners, 1972), p. 161.

17. For this concept in Max Weber, see (among other references) "Science as a Vocation," in *From Max Weber: Essays in Sociology,* ed. H. H. Gerth and C. Wright Mills (New York: Oxford University Press, 1958), esp. pp. 139, 155.

18. White, "Historical Roots," pp. 1206, 1207.

19. There is a sizable literature in response to White. White's reply to his critics appears under the title, "Continuing the Conversation," in *Western Man and Environmental Ethics,* ed. Ian G. Barbour (Reading, Mass.: Addison-Wesley, 1973), pp. 55–64. A short but discerning response to White is in Langdon Winner, *Autonomous Technology: Technics-out-of-Control as a Theme in Political Thought* (Cambridge, Mass.: MIT Press, 1977).

20. Dubos, *A God Within,* pp. 167, 168.

21. Ibid., p. 174.

22. Barry Commoner, *The Closing Circle* (New York: Knopf, 1972), p. 41.

23. P.B. Medawar, *The Future of Man* (London: Methuen, 1960), p. 100.

24. Georg Borgstrom, *The Hungry Planet: The Modern World at the Edge of Famine,* 2d rev. ed. (New York: Collier, 1972), p. 530.

25. Robert L. Heilbroner, *An Inquiry into the Human Prospect, Updated and Reconsidered for the 1980s* (New York: Norton, 1980), pp. 172–173.

26. Robert L. Heilbroner, *An Inquiry into the Human Prospect,* 2d ed. (New York: Norton, 1975), p. 161. The reference to China is more explicit in the second edition (pp. 161, 167) than in the first edition (1974) or third edition (1980). The 1980 edition mentions China, but not in any detail.

27. Heilbroner, *Human Prospect,* 3d ed. (1980), p. 164.

28. Percy Bysshe Shelley, *Prometheus Unbound,* final lines.

29. Heilbroner, *Human Prospect,* 3d ed. (1980), p. 164.

30. Ibid., p. 166.

31. Margaret Mead, recorded conversation in *To Love or to Perish: The Technological Crisis and the Churches,* ed. J. Edward Carothers, Margaret Mead, Daniel D. McCracken, and Roger L. Shinn (New York: Friendship Press, 1972), p. 125.

32. Saul Alinsky, interview by Stephen Rose, *Christian Century* 88 (May 19, 1971), p. 625.

33. Louis Harris, "Poll: U.S. Consumption Morally Wrong," *New York Post,* December 1, 1975, p. 15.

34. "Faith, Science and the Future—the African Context," (Geneva: World Council of Churches, 1981), part 4A.

Chapter 11. Living with Risk

1. Harrison Brown, *The Human Future Revisited: The World Predicament and Possible Solutions* (New York: Norton, 1978), p. 217.

2. UPI dispatch, reporting on a study by Dr. James F. Fries of Stanford University Medical Center in the *New England Journal of Medicine. New York Times,* July 18, 1980, p. A6.

3. Nick Eberstadt, "Myths of the Food Crisis," *New York Review of Books,* February

19, 1976, p. 34. Eberstadt goes on to report that in some areas of Sahelian Africa life expectancy is under thirty.

4. The interview is reported by Peter J. Schuyten, "Technology: Scientific Gains and the Risks," *New York Times,* May 22, 1980, p. D2.

5. Saint Augustine, *The City of God,* trans. Marcus Dod (many editions), I, 30.

6. Thomas Sheridan, "Computer Control and Human Alienation," in *Faith and Science in an Unjust World: Report of the World Council of Churches' Conference on Faith, Science and the Future* vol. 1, ed. Roger L. Shinn (Geneva: World Council of Churches, 1980), p. 299.

7. The events prior to, during, and after the conference are reported in detail, with quotations from many of the people involved, in Nicholas Wade, *The Ultimate Experiment: Man-Made Evolution,* 2d. ed. (New York: Walker, 1979).

8. Report of a Working Group on Ethical and Social Issues in Genetic Engineering and the Ownership of Life Forms, convened by the World Council of Churches, The Netherlands, June 15–18, 1981.

9. See Warren Weaver, "Statistical Morality," and Roger L. Shinn, "Statistics: Important But Not Enough," *Christianity and Crisis* 20 (January 23, 1961), pp. 210–215. Also, Warren Weaver, "For Statistical Morality," 21 (February 20, 1961), p. 18.

10. "Health Evaluation of Energy-Generating Sources," *Journal of the American Medical Association* 240, no. 20 (November 10, 1978), pp. 2193–2195.

11. I agree with the Swedish studies that indicate that major accidents, not disposal of wastes, are the most problematic issue. See Bo Lindell, "Ethical and Social Issues in Risk Management," in *Faith and Science in an Unjust World,* vol. 1, pp. 105–115. Waste disposal is important and expensive, but there are feasible methods.

12. See Zhores A. Medvedev, *Nuclear Disaster in the Urals* (New York: Norton, 1979). Medvedev's analysis of the evidence has been challenged by several American scientists in *Science* 206 (October 19, 1979), pp. 326–327. and 206 (October 26, 1979), pp. 423–425.

13. Sam H. Schurr, Project Director, *Energy in America's Future: The Choices Before Us* (Baltimore: Johns Hopkins University Press, 1979), chap. 12.

14. The Nuclear Regulatory Commission in 1975 issued the 18-volume Reactor Safety Study produced under the direction of Norman C. Rasmussen and initiated by the Atomic Energy Commission (a predecessor to the Nuclear Regulatory Commission). In January 1979 the NRC withdrew its endorsement of the study, saying that the bounds of error were greater—not necessarily worse or better—than the study indicated. Rasmussen concurred, saying that the element of uncertainty was larger than the study assumed.

15. Herbert Inhaber, "Risk with Energy from Conventional and Nonconventional Sources," *Science* 203 (February 23, 1979), pp. 718–723.

16. For a grim if unconventional opinion on the risks of large-scale solar energy, see Donald C. Winston, "There Goes the Sun," *Newsweek,* December 3, 1979, p. 35.

17. See Tom Turner, "The Inhaber Imbroglio," *Not Man Apart* (published by Friends of the Earth) 9, no. 10 (September 1979), pp. 19ff. Also "Renewable Risks," Soft Energy Notes VIII, 2 (December 1979), pp. 86–88.

18. The figures are from the Report of the Committee on Biological Effects of Ionizing Radiations, 1979. A summary chart of the data is in the *New York Times,* July 2, 1979, p. D6.

19. Rosalyn Yalow, "Fear of Radiation," *New York Times,* January 31, 1979, p. 22 (Op-ed).

20. "A Problem Seen 500 Years Ago Still Defies Scientific Resolution," *New York Times*, July 1, 1979, p. 28.

21. Richard Wilson, "A Rational Approach to Reducing Cancer Risk," *New York Times*, July 9, 1978, sec. 4 (The Week in Review), p. 17.

22. Fred Hapgood, "Risk-Benefit Analysis: Putting a Price on Life," *The Atlantic Monthly*, January 1979, pp. 33–38.

23. Hans Jonas, "Responsibility Today: The Ethics of an Endangered Future," *Social Research* 43 (Spring 1976), pp. 77–97.

24. One of my earliest essays in the subject area of this book was, to my annoyance, retitled by an editor, "Survival Ethics." *Christianity and Crisis* 32 (March 20, 1972), pp. 56–60.

25. Daniel Callahan, *The Tyranny of Survival* (New York: Macmillan, 1973), p. 93.

26. Hans J. Morgenthau, "Mr. Nixon's Gamble," *The New Republic*, 162 (May 23, 1970), p. 17.

Chapter 12. Science, Faith, and Ideology in Policy Decisions

1. Harold K. Schilling, *Science and Religion: An Interpretation of Two Communities* (New York: Scribners, 1962), pp. 36–37, 39. The whole chapter, with its citations from several other scientists, is useful on this issue.

2. Gustavo Gutierrez, *A Theology of Liberation* (Maryknoll, N.Y.: Orbis, 1973), p. 274.

3. Gunnar Myrdal, *Objectivity in Social Research* (New York: Pantheon, 1969), p. 40.

4. "Towards a New Christian Social Ethic and New Social Policies for the Churches," Report of Section 10 at the World Council of Churches' Conference on Faith, Science and the Future, in *Faith and Science in an Unjust World*, vol. 2, ed. by Paul Abrecht (Geneva: World Council of Churches, 1980), p. 153.

5. Charles Birch and Paul Abrecht, eds., *Genetics and the Quality of Life* (Elmsford, N.Y.: Pergamon, 1975), p. 203. The book came out of a consultation called by the World Council of Churches in Zurich, June 1973.

6. The major sources in Marx are, chronologically: *The German Ideology, The Poverty of Philosophy, The Communist Manifesto,* and *Preface to A Critique of Political Economy*.

7. Karl Mannheim, *Ideology and Utopia* (New York: Harcourt, Brace, 1936).

8. Karl Marx and Friedrich Engels, *The Communist Manifesto* (many editions), end of Part I.

9. See Daniel Bell, *The End of Ideology: On the Exhaustion of Political Ideas in the Fifties,* rev. ed. (New York: Free Press, 1962). Cf. *The End of Ideology Debate,* ed. Chaim I. Waxman (New York: Funk and Wagnalls, 1968).

10. John Kenneth Galbraith, *Money: Whence it Came, Where it Went* (New York: Bantam, 1976; first published, 1975), p. 105.

11. Daniel D. McCracken, *Public Policy and the Expert: Ethical Problems of the Witness* (New York: Council on Religion and International Affairs, 1971), esp. pp. 44–47.

12. Joel Primack and Frank von Hippel, *Advice and Dissent: Scientists in the Political Arena* (New York: Basic Books, 1974), p. ix.

13. Linus Pauling, interviewed by Horace Freeland Judson, *The Eighth Day of Creation: The Makers of the Revolution in Biology* (New York: Simon & Schuster, 1979), p. 74.

14. Andrei Sakharov, "The Responsibility of Scientists," *New York Review of Books*, June 25, 1981, p. 12.

Reconsiderations

1. Marek Thee, ed., *Armaments and Disarmament in the Nuclear Age: A Handbook of the Stockholm International Peace Research Institute* (Atlantic Highlands, N.J.: Humanities Press, 1976), pp. 65, 68.
2. Herman Kahn and B. Bruce-Briggs, *Things to Come* (New York: Macmillan, 1972), pp. 216, 225. Barry Farrell, interview with Buckminster Fuller, *Life*, February 26, 1971, pp. 46ff.
3. See reports in *New York Times* by Martin Tolchin, March 23, 1989, p. A1; James Lardner, April 19, 1989, p. A27; and Peter Passell, July 16, 1989, p. 1; and in *New Republic* by Robert B. Reich, May 1, 1989, pp. 23ff.
4. Robert Heilbroner, "Seize the Day," *New York Review of Books*, February 15, 1990, pp. 30–31.
5. *World Development Report* (Washington, D.C.: The World Bank, 1990).
6. Arthur Schlesinger Jr., "The Cult of Ethnicity, Good and Bad," *Time*, July 8, 1991, p. 21.
7. Charles Birch and John B. Cobb Jr., *The Liberation of Life* (London and New York: Cambridge University Press, 1981). Juan Luis Segundo, *An Evolutionary Approach to Jesus of Nazareth*, tr. John Drury (Maryknoll, N.Y.: Orbis, 1988), p. 15.
8. World Commission on Environment and Development, *Our Common Future* (Oxford and New York: Oxford University Press, 1987).
9. Lester Brown, "The New World Order," in Lester Brown et al., *State of the World 1991* (New York: W. W. Norton, 1991), p. 13.
10. Much of this information comes from a year-long seminar on the Ethiopian famine at Columbia University, involving specialists (including Africans) of many disciplines. For two summary reports on the famine see *Newsweek*, November 26, 1984, pp. 50–58 and June 3, 1985, pp. 28–38.
11. *New York Times*, February 27, 1985, p. A12.
12. See *1991 World Population Data Sheet* (Washington, D.C.: Population Reference Bureau, 1991). Brown et al., State of the World 1991, p. 16.
13. Julian Simon, *The Ultimate Resource* (Princeton, N.J.: Princeton University Press, 1981).
14. Garrett Hardin, "Dr. Pangloss Meets Cassandra," *New Republic*, October 28, 1981, pp. 31–34.
15. John H. Gibbons, Peter D. Blair, and Holly L. Gwin, "Strategies for Energy Use," *Scientific American*, September 1989, p. 136.
16. Edward Renshaw, a researcher at the State University of New York at Albany, reported in *New York Times*, August 12, 1990, Sec. 4, p. 3.
17. Gibbons, Blair, and Gwin, "Strategies," p. 136.
18. Thomas E. Gradel and Paul J. Crutzen, "The Changing Atmosphere," *Scientific American*, September 1989, pp. 58–68.
19. Stephen H. Schneider, "The Changing Climate," *Scientific American*, September 1989, p. 79.
20. Gradel and Crutzen, "The Changing Atmosphere," p. 64.
21. The first in 1957 (see p. 215) was long denied by government officials but was acknowledged in 1989. *New York Times*, June 18, 1989, p. 9.
22. Spencer Weart, *Nuclear Fear: A History of Images* (Cambridge, Mass.: Harvard University Press, 1988), pp. 331–39.
23. Christopher Flavin and Nicholas Lenssen, "Designing a Sustainable Energy System," in Brown et al., *State of the World 1991*, p. 28.

24. *New York Times*, February 11, 1985, p. A1, A19. *New York Times*, May 28, 1985, p. A8. An embarrassed Pentagon hastened to deny part but not all of the latter report. *New York Times*, June 1, 1985, p. 29.

25. In late 1983 a team of scientists known as TTAPS (the initials of their names) issued a statement that a nuclear war could so pollute the atmosphere with radiation and dust as to blot out the sun and induce a long planetary winter that could "destroy the current civilization in at least the Northern Hemisphere" and possibly lead to the extinction of human life. See R.P. Turco, O.B. Toon, T.P. Ackerman, J.B. Pollack, and Carl Sagan, "Nuclear Winter: Global Consequences of Multiple Nuclear Explosions." Also, Paul R. Ehrlich, Carl Sagan, et al., "Long-Term Biological Consequences of Nuclear War," *Science* 222 (23 December 1983), pp. 1283–92, 1293–1300. The quotation is from the latter article, p. 1299. A huge literature of controversy has arisen about the theory, with a dominant opinion that the TTAPS team may have exaggerated the danger, but that the problem is real and serious. My information comes from a five-day conference in November 1984 in Bellagio, Italy. Half the participants were scientists invited by the International Council of Scientific Unions (ICSU); half were religious leaders invited by the Inter-Faith Academy of Peace (Jerusalem) chaired by Theodore Hesburgh. The group came from many nations, including the five major nuclear powers, and from several religions. I have updated the findings of that conference with later information in the public press and in *Scope-Radpath*, a newsletter of ICSU.

26. At the time of this writing, the United States Senate has not yet ratified the treaty. The expectation is that the Senate, after some obligatory complaints, will do so.

27. Hans A. Bethe, Kurt Gottfried, and Robert S. McNamara, "The Nuclear Threat: A Proposal," *New York Review of Books*, June 27, 1991, pp. 48–50.

28. Jeremy Rifkin, *Algeny* (New York: Viking, 1983).

29. *Manipulating Life: Ethical Issues in Genetic Engineering* (Geneva: World Council of Churches, 1982). *Genetic Engineering: Social and Ethical Consequences: A Study Document of the National Council of Churches* (New York: Pilgrim Press, 1984).

30. President's Commission for the Study of Ethical Problems in Medicine and Biomedical and Behavioral Research, *Splicing Life* (Washington, D.C.: U.S. Government Printing Office, 1982).

31. Herman E. Daly and John B. Cobb Jr., *For the Common Good: Redirecting the Economy toward Community, the Environment, and a Sustainable Future* (Boston: Beacon Press, 1989).

Index

About the Author

ROGER L. SHINN is Reinhold Niebuhr Professor of Social Ethics Emeritus at Union Theological Seminary in New York. For twenty-two years he was Adjunct Professor of Religion and Society at Columbia University and was occasionally an Adjunct Professor at the New York University Graduate School of Business Administration and the Jewish Theological Seminary of America. Since retirement from Union, he has taught at the Pacific School of Religion, Princeton Theological Seminary, Vanderbilt University, and Drew University.

He is past president of the American Theological Society and the Society of Christian Ethics.

For many years Dr. Shinn was involved in the Working Committee on Church and Society of the World Council of Churches. He has traveled extensively in Asia, Africa, and Europe, studying issues of the relations between technology and social ethics. In the United States he chaired the National Council of Churches' Task Force on Human Life and the New Genetics.

He has lectured in many universities in the United States and overseas. He is author of a dozen books, some of which have been translated into Chinese, Japanese, Korean, Arabic, and Turkish. He is currently an Associate Editor of the *Bulletin of Science, Technology and Society;* a member of the Editorial Board of the *Journal of Religious Ethics;* and a Contributing Editor of *Christianity and Crisis.*